D0980105

The
Rise
and Fall
of
Childhood

C. John Sommerville

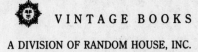

VINTAGE BOOKS

A DIVISION OF RANDOM HOUSE, INC.
NEW YORK

The Rise and Fall of Childhood

First Vintage Books Edition, August 1990

Copyright © 1982, 1990 by C. John Sommerville

All rights reserved under International and Pan-American Copyright Conventions. Published in the United States by Vintage Books, a division of Random House, Inc., New York, and simultaneously in Canada by Random House of Canada Limited, Toronto. Originally published, in different form, by Sage Publications, Inc. in 1982.

Grateful acknowledgment is made to *The American Scholar* for permission to reprint an excerpt from "The Case of Morality" by Leon Kass from *The American Scholar,* Volume 52, Number 2, Spring 1983. Copyright © 1983 by Leon Kass. Reprinted by permission of *The American Scholar.*

Library of Congress Cataloging-in-Publication Data
Sommerville, C. John (Charles John), 1938–
The rise and fall of childhood / C. John Sommerville.—1st
Vintage Books ed.
p. cm.
Reprint. Originally published: Beverly Hills, Calif. : Sage
Publications, c1982.
Includes bibliographical references.
ISBN 0-679-72829-5
1. Children—History. 2. Children and adults—History.
3. Children and adults. I. Title.
HQ767.87.S66 1990
305.23′09—dc20
89-40515
CIP

Book design by Chris Welch

Manufactured in the United States of America

10 9 8 7 6 5 4

*To
Susan,
mother and
teacher*

Acknowledgments

The author wishes to thank those who have read and commented on parts of this book: Carol Bullard, Corbin Carnell, David Chalmers, Sheila Dickison, Molly Harrower, Jane Laurent, George Rekers, and Todd Savitt. Also he is indebted to J. D. Ice, Mitchell Allen, and especially Peter Dimock, for helping to bring the project to completion.

Contents

Introduction

Historians have a way of noticing something just as it is about to disappear from their world and then trying to preserve it in our memory. This may explain why they have been so late in discovering children. Children used to be more plentiful than they are today. The median age in the United States, for example, is now around 32 years; in 1790 it was 16. We are an aging society, and as the birth rate falls to new lows and children are in danger of becoming a thing of the past, historians are taking more interest in them. The purpose of this book is to show the ways children have been important to adults throughout history and the reasons for the changes in their status. Thus it is a study as much of adult attitudes as of the actual lives of children. It is about that abstraction "childhood," which is made up of the expectations, hopes, and fears that societies have expressed about their youngest members.

Of course, these adult attitudes are a major part of the child's reality. And we will be interested in other features of the actual plight of children in the past as well. This aspect of our study will show the gap that often exists between what adults are doing and what they think they are doing, for the two are not always the same or even close. At some points we will try to uncover the effects of adult treatment on children, venturing into what is called psychohistory. But for the most part we will be creating a cultural history of childhood, out of the record of adult ideas and attitudes. In part, this is because we have so much more evidence of what parents have thought than of what they have actually done with their children. Also, it is the part of this story that has most relevance for us, as we reflect on our own approach to children and our self-deceptions.

Nowadays we are uneasy with a history that concentrates on cultural attitudes. We have a strong suspicion that economic realities, for instance, might be determining those attitudes. Or we may wonder if there are psychological factors—imprinted on us early in life—that we only rationalize in our treatment of children. Yet some of the earliest students of the history of childhood, looking for just such underlying causes, have shown that ideas often have a life of their own and develop through their own inner contradictions. For example, those who have been studying the fluctuations in population and birth rate expected to find that the abundance or scarcity of children would decide how welcome they were and how much attention they would get. But at times the opposite seems to have been true: Attitudes helped determine what efforts were made to limit family size even before modern contraceptives were available. Likewise, to say that attitudes toward children are related to economic considerations tells us little unless we know whether the families in a given society would rate a fourth child ahead of a radio in their scale of values, or would rate even a first child behind a second car. Although greater prosperity at times has led to higher birth rates, sometimes it has had the opposite effect. In certain "third world" countries traditional attitudes toward fertility continue to defy economic "imperatives." Likewise, those who investigate the different psychological styles of past ages sometimes hold philosophical or religious positions responsible for the particular forms of repression and training they find.

Attitudes toward family, toward children and child rearing, are among the hardest of all our ideas to change. After all, our deepest and most troubling memories come from our experiences of childhood and family life. But besides that fact, creating families—sitting down to a family dinner—may be the high point of our lives, just as we see it enshrined in advertising iconography. When we stop to think why we are even in the rat race, we usually recognize that the end of our earthly efforts is to create the human bonds that only some kind of family can foster. So we would expect ideas in this area to show a certain independence from other social factors.

This being the case, it makes sense to take up our subject in the broadest possible context, as part of the history of our entire civilization. Civilization is bigger than art or economics or religion or class relations or power. Historians have long been trying to sum up the whole thing and have produced an outline of the development of Western civilization that is already familiar. By putting our story into such a general context we can hope to make better sense of it than if we viewed it from only one angle. Some will feel that this book is too broad in time and geographical sweep. Others will think that the focus is too narrow, in ignoring other civilizations and preliterate cultures. A concentration on Western civilization will at least give the study relevance to our self-understanding, which is the goal of all historical investigation. And some breadth of view is necessary to show the amazing inventiveness of humanity through history.

Similarly, in dealing with youth as well as smaller children, we may seem to have taken on too much. But students of the history of childhood have found that however we may try to disguise the status of teenagers, in fact we treat them as children so long as they are economically dependent. The hardest aspect of this history has been to decide when the transition from childhood to adulthood was commenced or completed in any given society. Past ages were flexible in this regard, as we are, and it is usually a mistake to take the age breaks which they announced too literally. The fact that we read of a child being executed in eighteenth-century London does not necessarily mean that the execution of children was usual then, whatever the statute books said. The fact that we hear of an heiress being rushed into an early betrothal to secure her fortune does not mean that servant girls had to grow up that fast. Children were never exactly considered "little adults"; what has confused historians is that most societies have made the transition to adulthood an even longer process than it is today. There were many stages in gaining that status and its responsibilities, beginning very early but ending very late. Acknowledging this fact will make our story a little fuzzy but truer to life as children faced it.

Attitudes sometimes persist even though the treatment of children is changing under the impact of other factors. This may even be the case today. For the past 400 years children have enjoyed or endured increasing adult attention. That is largely because we have become more and more preoccupied with the future. Children will inherit the world we have created and carry on the changes we have begun. Or they will pass history's judgment on our world and resist its course. This fact has given them a certain power over us, as we worry or at least wonder about their judgment. We have become accustomed to looking to them for approval.

But something is happening that might change all this. After hundreds of years of economic expansion, the West now faces the possibility of long-term economic decline. The median income of husband-only-earner families in the United States has fallen (2 percent) in the last 20 years. Of course, all our economic and social and environmental problems are made worse by any rise in population and by the need to sacrifice for the welfare of our children and of future generations. So it is possible that we are at a turning point in the history of childhood, and that things are turning down.

When we were confident that our work was making their future brighter, it was easy to think of children as innocent and refreshing. But we have always known that they could also be messy, tiresome, and cruel. The temptation during any period of economic or psychological depression may be to start concentrating on these latter characteristics. Children are more obviously a liability nowadays. Can our determination to do the best for them stand up to the temptation of such a view? By contrast, does putting children on a pedestal, as was done in the nineteenth century at the height of the idolization of "childhood," really serve the best interests of children? Did the sentimentalization of childhood become another burden for children to bear? Were adults then simply trying to prove they were good-natured by their professions of approval? And now, as we become more frank about our feelings and admit that children are a chore as well as a joy, will we be able to do our duty to them? These are among the most pressing questions facing the world today. A look at the history of our civilization should help us think about them.

The
Rise
and Fall
of
Childhood

One

As
Other
Times
Might
See
Us

In looking back through history we are always too ready to assume that our present attitudes and habits are normal and to judge others on the basis of what seems to us self-evident. To ensure that this does not happen here, we shall begin by trying to see ourselves as our ancestors might see us, or as some future historian might look back on our times. What would others notice about our treatment of our children, and which of our attitudes would strike them as curious? If nothing else, this exercise should make us more sympathetic toward other ages. It should also alert us to some things to look for as we go back in time. A picture of American attitudes will not necessarily represent the industrialized West generally, but others do have a way of finding themselves in the same situation, even with our example before them.

Even a casual observer would notice that our attitudes toward children are contradictory. We do not seem to know exactly how we feel about children. This may be true of every period, but it is perhaps the most obvious thing about us. Our image of the child is still quite positive, if we can judge by advertisers' use of that image. Cheerful child models are used in ads promoting cameras, toilet paper, tires, junk food, and vacations (this is one of our more benign forms of child labor). Presumably the ad writers know what they are doing; they spend a lot of money finding out which images produce the most positive responses. Children have the still harder job of promoting peace (on the covers of United Nations publications) and generosity (on United Way posters). But by contrast, a chain of dance studios advertises that in their establishments "youth is not wasted on the young." Nothing could capture our ambivalence more perfectly. We like the idea of childhood but are not always crazy about the kids we know. We like it, that is, when we are imagining our own childhoods. So part of our apparent appreciation of youth is simply envy.

Historians will someday note that we read a lot about children. For all our belief in the irresistibility of social forces, we buy countless books on how to strengthen our families against the corrosive trends of our times. The all-time best-selling book in American history, after the Bible, is Benjamin Spock's *Baby and Child Care*—it sold 30 million copies in its first 30 years. That is more than twice as many copies as any novel or cookbook or dictionary has sold in this country. The effect of all this reading is harder to judge. Dr. Spock himself now admits that expert advice has undermined parents' self-confidence and made it harder for them to cope with their children. There is more knowledge of children than ever before, but it is largely confined to professionals. And the very fact that there are experts may be intimidating; we hate to think that there must be one best way to handle any situation as parents and that we don't know what it is. So as we get more and more advice we seem less and less sure of what we ought to do for our children. Even after getting the advice we may not really use it. One study has indicated that child-rearing books affect primarily what parents *say* they are doing with their children and have little relation to what they can be observed doing under the pressure of circumstances. As traditions of child rearing fade, parental authority seems both more hesitant and more arbitrary. Children are quick to notice this because parents are the most important thing in their world.

Despite our many expressions of concern for children, experts have indicated that the amount of interaction between parents and children has been declining for at least 20 years. There are unmistakable signs that children of all classes are neglected in American society. There was hopeful talk of a cure for this situation—"quality time"—but we have had the honesty to give this up as another euphemism for neglect. Indeed, we are becoming painfully honest; columnist Ann Landers recently found that 70 percent of the readers answering one of her polls reported that they would not have children if they could do it over again. She hoped this figure was to be explained by the rule that the unhappy are more likely to answer such surveys. But it could be that there is a general disenchantment with children. This may even be behind the recent surge in pet ownership. More homes contain pets (55 percent in 1983) than children, and the gap is widening. Animals may meet our need to nurture better than human children. We may distrust our children's love; animals' loyalty is more dependable. Animals don't rebel or play raucous music, and we can dominate them with a better conscience.

On the other hand, Americans are notorious for looking to their children for approval. How our children turn out and what they think of us has become the "final judgment" on our lives. As a nation we have always been oriented toward the future and to new frontiers. So long as this is true, we will imagine that the rising generation is rendering history's verdict on us. We may resent children simply because we expect a harsh judgment from them. Recently, however, we have begun to doubt our nation's and even the world's future. For several centuries industrialization has steadily increased economic opportunities and thereby brightened the future. But now we are told that industrialization is propelling us past the limits of our planet's resources. Our children now represent a time that may bring only bigger problems and not a better life. So we have lost some of our zest for change. We may begin to worry less about what the future and our children think of us. Worse than that, we may resent the fact that these little citizens to come are already compounding all our problems—energy, food, employment, pollution, crowding. Babies are the enemy. Not your baby or mine, of course. Individually they are all cute. But together they are a menace.

Americans are taking action to meet this threat. We are reaching new lows in the fertility rate—from 278 per 1000 women in the child-bearing years in 1800 to 130 in 1900, 80 in 1940, and 65 in 1980. That hovers around replacement level. Some other countries are actually below that level and have adopted pronatalist population policies. Pro-natalism strikes some of us as almost obscene. This is a far cry from most of history, when children were welcomed with much fanfare and less calculation of the inconvenience they cause. For mothers, children were what life was about. Nowadays we are shocked when unmarried teenagers insist on having their babies just to enjoy them. Our minds tell us that fertility outside very restricted limits is a bad thing. But why should our emotions be telling us the same thing? Traditionally, childbirth was greeted with public rejoicing; now pregnancy is often cause for chagrin or even shock. Other ages would express the same shock at the techniques we use to avoid fertility.

Thus, as we have tried to be guided by economic responsibility, there has been some cost to human feeling. Since child labor was restricted children have been a liability. In our accustomed fashion we have even managed to put a dollar figure on this burden: In 1980 terms a child would cost a middle-income family $85,000, not counting a mother's lost income. Such figures are useful in the increasing amount of litigation surrounding our children's lives.

Still, we express a concern for children's welfare in other ways. The problem of child abuse is being faced more openly now than in the past. We would like to think that increasing reports of abuse represent primarily a rising public conscience against this crime, but it is possible that abuse *is* becoming more widespread—better record keeping aside. Between 1960 and 1980 the U.S. murder rate doubled, assault tripled, robbery and rape quadrupled; there is no reason to think that violence against children did not follow suit. And if it is rising at anything like the reported rates, one could guess why. Addiction and unemployment have always caused abusive behavior toward the helpless. And nowadays the very fact that most children are planned may worsen the situation. More is expected of planned children. Parents often want children to meet some unfulfilled need in their own lives and psyches, and of course the children cannot. Abusive parents usually report that they did not receive the approval from their children that they had hoped for and that they had missed from their parents. As the birth rate goes down, the percentage of children born to such needy parents is probably rising. Since we can no longer blame Providence for bringing our babies along, we may be more likely to blame the children themselves for the inconveniences they cause. There is less tolerance for such trouble as children make now that they are not inevitable. So we should not be surprised to hear that 91 percent of the battered children reported in one city were planned. And in the greater privacy of our households these days there is a greater chance of battering going unnoticed by the community at large.

Of course, we had hoped that family planning would mean that each child would be better cared for and feel more approval. No doubt this hope has been realized in many cases. Some children are probably better cared for now than ever before in history. Better health care, better diet, a greater understanding of emotional needs, and families which can adjust to everyone's most pressing needs have made many children's lives happier. But we may have reached the point at which families are so small that we cannot consider managing the home a full-time job. The justification for fewer children was that we could spend more time with each one, but the figures show us moving the other way.

We have long accepted the notion that man's place is not in the home. One sample of American fathers spent an average of 37 seconds per day in verbal interaction with their newborn children. That might not have been as worrisome when the mothers of these infants could take up the slack. But in the United States 50 percent of all infants have mothers who work outside the home, and 65 percent of all preschoolers have mothers who do. Many such mothers are the family's sole support. Others think they have no choice, meaning that without a second income the family could slip into a lower social class. In 1950, 12 percent of preschool children had mothers who worked outside the home. Now there are probably that many "latchkey children" (an estimated 7 million), who baby-sit themselves with the help of TV and telephone. All this is at a time when psychologists are almost alarmist on the various kinds of damage that may result from the absence of parent-infant bonding in the first two years.

Marriage remains popular. A larger percentage of the American population marries now than at any time on record. The expectation of remarriage is high enough that it may even encourage some divorces. But the popularity of marriage and remarriage is not necessarily evidence of commitment to the institution of the family. Originally marriage was to create financial and social security for the children to be expected from the union. In Thomas Aquinas's classic expression of this point, "The certainty [or legitimacy] of one's children is the principal purpose of marriage"—a matter of assuming responsibilities. Nowadays marriage is thought of primarily as a way of legitimizing sexual relations between the partners, and the child's interest in the permanence of marriage is almost ignored. Because of the promises involved, marriage was traditionally one of the things society tried to hold sacred. Now marriage is viewed as a utilitarian arrangement, whose members can decide that it no longer meets their needs. And children are not members in that sense. The possibility of divorce does limit the damage that can be done by truly impossible situations. We are constantly reminded of this fact on talk shows and the like—showing a certain bad faith in the matter. Actually divorce often worsens the damage, as children become caught in continuing struggles over custody and support.

Ambivalence reaches the level of schizophrenia in our treatment of violence among the young. Parents do not encourage violence, but neither do they take up arms against the industries which encourage it. Parents hide their eyes from the books and comics, slasher films, videos and lyrics which form the texture of an adolescent culture. While all successful societies have inhibited instinct, ours encourages it. Or at least we profess ourselves powerless to interfere with it—with some frightening results. If there were a typical American child, by age 16 he or she would have witnessed 200,000 acts of violence on TV. Even when the children create some violence of their own, parents don't want to hear about it. One extensive study of crime in Illinois estimated that a third of all juveniles had committed a "serious" crime and that, except for the violent categories, these acts were as likely to be the work of the rich as the poor, girls as boys, children from intact homes as children from broken ones. Parents were unaware of four-fifths of these crimes, and they seemed unconcerned when they were informed of them—unless the child's occupational future was jeopardized. The same parents might be enraged by a bad report card.

By now parents are used to being made to feel guilty about reports such as this, as well as about their contribution to the population problem, the school tax burden, and declining test scores. They expect to be blamed by teachers and psychologists, if not by police. And they will be blamed by the children themselves. It is hardly a wonder, then, that they withdraw into what used to be called "permissiveness" but is really neglect.

All these guilt-raising tactics may not work as well in the future, however. As our culture has encouraged us to be more honest about our feelings and desires, it has broken the crust over a good deal of latent hostility toward the young. We vote down bond issues for schools and exclude children from apartment complexes and whole retirement communities. Experts are on hand to relieve our guilt. The founder of Kinder-Care, the day care franchise, believes that one of his accomplishments was "[taking] the guilt away from the working mother." For a while after 1976 there was a stream of movies in which children represented all kinds of evil, from prostitution and murder to demon possession. A low point was reached in the ad for *It's Alive*: "It was born three days ago. It has killed seven people. Its parents are human beings. Whatever it is . . . It's Alive." Even the Middle Ages did not project such fiendish hostility onto the little changelings in its folklore. It is something of a relief in the 1980s to have a rash of movies and sit-coms showing adults being cute as parents.

All this comes just a few years after our nation experienced a high birth rate (highest between 1947 and 1961). Perhaps we are seeing a reaction against a surfeit of family. Could it be that those who were reared in the postwar years really were spoiled, as we used to hear? Did a child-centered generation, raised in depression and war, produce a self-centered generation that resents children and parenthood?

The uncertainty of our attitudes toward children is eloquently expressed in our confusion over what to pass on to them in education. This would surely be a surprise to anyone visiting from the past. Children are going to school for an ever longer period, but we seem less and less sure of what they should be getting from it. True, things are changing so fast that we are not positive what will be important to them in 20 years' time. In the 1970s anthropologist Margaret Mead was frequently quoted to the effect that we should be learning from our children. They are already the inhabitants of a new world, the thinking went, while we are fossilized by outworn attitudes. It is adults, of course, who are changing the world, but those same adults cannot settle on the shape of the curriculum for their children.

Even our educational clichés have lost their meaning. We all approve of the notion of educating "the whole person." But the idea that schools should build character is denied or even ridiculed whenever steps to that end are marked out. We feel that there must be something almost illegal about teaching values—that doing so may violate the constitutional separation of church and state or undermine the individual's integrity. So the schools concentrate on intellectual skills, ignoring the fact that they cannot help but teach values so long as there are adult models in the classroom. Even when teachers simply ignore students' petty thefts from each other, the students are learning something about our institutions and standards. It may be that positive values are best taught when teachers are unaware that they are teaching them—when these values are treated as self-evident. But the novel point is that society should feel inhibited when it recognizes that its values are being promoted. Ours is the first society that has narrowed the scope of education to this extent, allowing the relativity of the issue ("But whose values are being taught?") to paralyze us.

Debate in this area can become heated. When certain values are taught under the guise of self-realization or sensitivity training—notions which bristle with ethical assumptions—parents protest. But those parents are not much help in identifying the standards that should be maintained. So teachers and parents are engaged, often unconsciously, in undermining each other's values. Parents may see no point in certain readings or discussions except the desecration of their ideals. Teachers may think of this as their duty—overcoming "cultural deprivation," meaning the values of the home. Yet they could not say what the goal of their enterprise is except to free the child from fixed ideas.

The same lack of comprehension is shown in our courts' suggestion that the teaching of comparative religion might satisfy parents who are concerned about an absence of religious training in the schools. Parents rightly sense that such instruction would be relativistic by its very nature, corroding the attachment to any particular tradition. Teachers would be bound to treat all religious traditions as of equal worth, or at least of equal interest, and this is precisely what the parents do not want. They want a particular faith encouraged. They suspect that a secularist and scientific faith is being insinuated by teachers who may think of it as self-evident. Moral education, too, is seen differently by parents than by teachers. The teachers only mean to bring students to recognize the variety of choices involved, whereas parents want them to get practice doing the right thing. Only the schools' athletic programs are allowed to proceed by the old-fashioned methods, and they are popular for that reason.

Given these disagreements and uncertainties, one might expect some discussion of shortening the educational process. But schools dominate more of children's time than ever before. We hear more and more proposals to operate the schools year-round and to begin their involvement with children at birth. The implication is that nothing is learned outside of school. But in fact less is being learned in school if we can judge from the downward drift of achievement scores. The public retaliates by insisting on literacy tests before graduation. The slights the two sides in this debate deliver reveal the frustration they feel at not being able to define their goals more convincingly. The present truce, in agreeing on the importance of literacy, shows the level to which we have sunk. For in the past literacy was only considered the precondition of education.

No other period in history has been so modest as to doubt that its values and cultural heritage are worthwhile enough to teach to its children. But the circle of knowledge we think our children "must know" has shrunk to almost literally nothing. Instead, we have taken to speaking of skills, and of the child's creativity. If our entertainment culture seems debased and unsatisfying, the hope is that our children will create something of greater worth. But it is as if we expect them to create out of nothing, like God, for the encouragement of creativity is, in the popular mind, opposed to instruction. There is little sense that creativity must grow out of tradition, even when it is critical of that tradition, and children are scarcely being given the materials on which their creativity could work.

One has to sympathize with our hard-pressed educators, however, for a visitor from the past would surely notice the status our society accords to those who work with children. It is an index of the status of those children. However much we may be drawn to an image of childhood, the status of teacher and parent in our society is low. The restless experimentation in educational technique may be largely our teachers' attempt to achieve the status of a technical elite. Technical expertise is, after all, what gains respect in our society. Mothers are encouraged to think of almost any job outside the home, though it may only be selling clothes or real estate, as more challenging than parenting. Fathers have long since lost sight of the fact that having and rearing children is the prototype of creativity. Artists, writers, and builders are only doing the next best thing. The person who designed a robot that could act and think as well as your four-year-old would deserve a Nobel Prize. But there is no public recognition for bringing up several truly human beings.

The way we imagine the future can tell us much about ourselves. If we can judge from recent science fiction, our plans for the future will have little place for children. Family issues are a major element in most novels but are almost absent from futuristic ones. This fact may be related to the increased longevity we expect. Up until now half of life or more has been spent being a child or rearing children. But if, for example, we were to double our life span, only a quarter of it would be so occupied. Caring for children has always been our main opportunity to be generous and altruistic. Writers seem to sense that longer life will involve our becoming more selfish. Nowhere is this more obvious than in their descriptions of the ruthless control the societies they imagine exercise over their birth rates. This fiction is describing something not entirely foreign to our expectations.

Still, the fact that we are taking a greater interest in childhood in the past may indicate some advance in realism about and sympathy toward the young. The efforts of historians to recover the history of the plight of children and of efforts in their behalf is evidence of this interest. Some historians have shown proudly that we are avoiding the mistakes of the past. Others intend their work as a warning, so that we do not fall behind earlier generations in our concern for children.

Two

The Dawn
of History,
and
Children
Already
a Problem

"Our earth is degenerate in these latter days.
Bribery and corruption are common. Children no longer obey
their parents. . . . The end of the world is evidently approach-
ing." Sound familiar? It is, in fact, the lament of a scribe in one
of the earliest inscriptions to be unearthed in Mesopotamia,
where Western civilization was born. Complaints began early
because life seemed precarious. The gains these early societies
had made and prized could all be swept away. Security and
progress depended on how hard the rising generation was will-

ing to work. And yet the very comforts civilization represented were making children soft. Parents realized that they could not assume that children would learn all they needed to know in a more complex world, or be willing to help now that life seemed easier.

"Go to school," wrote another scribe to his shiftless son in about 1800 B.C. "Stand before your teacher, recite your assignment, open your schoolbag, write your tablet, let the teacher's assistant write your new lesson for you. . . . Don't stand about in the public square. . . . Be humble and show fear before your superiors." What was the cause of this parental outburst? Nothing else but the universal resentment felt toward children who do not appreciate their parents' efforts to make their lives easier. "Never in all my life did I make you carry reeds. . . . I never said to you 'Go with my caravans.' I never sent you to work, to plow my field. . . . Others like you support their parents by working. If you spoke to your kin, and appreciated them, you would emulate them. They provide ten gur barley each—even the young ones provided their fathers with ten gur each. . . . But you, you're a man when it comes to perverseness, but compared with them you are not a man at all." To help him become a man, the scribe offers some advice in the form of proverbs. His final blessing expresses the hope that his son will be as successful and prominent as he is.

Family ambition has always been a major source of the attention given to children, of course, and it has been one of the burdens children have had to bear. The valuable scribal training that this father wanted for his son made childhood a grim experience for the young Sumerian. To escape manual labor, pupils were forced to study under teachers who were underpaid and mean, who caned students for being late and for sloppy work. School lasted all the daylight hours for years on end while students mastered the cuneiform script. Without an alphabet, they simply had to memorize long lists of words. Apparently they did not learn mathematical principles either, but memorized the solutions to the many problems they would face as accountants. For a change of pace they could memorize and copy the epics, hymns, myths, and essays of their culture. This, at least, kept their training from being too severely practical. The author of this tirade mentioned the knowledge of poetry as one of the advantages of being a scribe. For literature was considered to be the sum of all wisdom. In this sentiment he gave one of the few indications of a desire for his son's personal happiness.

We know almost nothing of what girls were doing at this early date, even among this higher, professional class. We can assume that they helped in the family's work as soon as they were able. But apparently they also played. In the absence of much evidence for such an early period, we are glad to find some toys that have survived—not just balls and tops, but dolls and rattles, boats and marbles, stick horses and even wheeled horses (in ancient Persia). From Greece (somewhat later) we find pictures of dog carts and hoops, as well as jacks (using knucklebones) and yo-yos. They are a welcome reminder that parents have long recognized children's right to enjoy themselves. We cannot always be sure that what looks like a toy was given to children, however. Some dolls were apparently used as idols. Rattles, too, often had a ritual use. The ancient Egyptians left model people, animals, and boats in the tombs of their kings to serve them in the afterlife. Whether they made some for children, too, we do not know. Even the jointed, painted clay dolls found in Greece and the animal marionettes from Egypt may have served as puppets for general amusement, and not only for children. All of this points up a common conclusion among those who study toys—that they usually begin as something adults use and are left to children only after their practical value has ended.

Egyptian civilization is nearly as old as Mesopotamian and has a reputation for phenomenal stability. This is more remarkable in a country as prosperous as Egypt than it would be in the primitive societies existing today, which have also probably changed little over thousands of years. For wealth has a tendency to bring restlessness and change. It would therefore be logical to assume that the socialization techniques Egyptians used with their children were among the reasons for their stability. Unfortunately, our knowledge of their everyday life is scanty. It often depends upon Greek historians, who were not always above exaggerating and who described a late period in Egypt's development.

The Greeks were impressed by the fact that Egyptians did not appear to practice infanticide, or at least were punished for doing away with unwanted children. They connected this with the fact that Egypt was a rich and fertile country and could afford a growing population. (On the other hand, we know of birth control advice from Egyptian texts of around 1500 B.C.) It also surprised them that the Egyptians did not swaddle their children. Greeks, like most peoples, took this wrapping or binding of infants for granted. Apparently, there are as many different justifications for the practice as there are societies which do it. Some societies claim that it gives the child a straighter frame, or that it keeps him warm. Others assumed that it was needed to keep the child from tearing at herself or frightening herself at the sight of her own limbs. Surely they all reduce to the fact that swaddling immobilizes the child. Parents can hang the bound infant up on a nail and go about their business, secure in the knowledge that he cannot crawl into the fireplace or fall down a well. The fact that at least some Egyptians did not wrap their children this way must indicate that they were not too busy to pay attention to them. A concern for the child's comfort can also be seen in Egyptian medical texts which prescribe opiates to get children over the rough periods. Anyone who has sat up with an infant too young to say what hurts will recognize a bond of sympathy with these ancient parents. The texts also mention doctoring children; thus, we may conclude that they did not consider children simply expendable.

An interest in children was not beneath Egyptian artists either. Boys and girls are often pictured, usually naked and sometimes as professional mourners or dancers. They were often shown with their parents, in hunting or party scenes, which indicate that they had a recognized place in the family's activities. We know that some children were held in awe by Egyptian society as having the gift of divining the future. But even rather ordinary families buried their children's toys with them, showing some respect for their desires and some hope for their continued existence.

Mesopotamia and Egypt were not the societies which gave Western civilization its distinctive character. The Greeks and Hebrews are more important to an understanding of our cultural heritage, and left far greater records of their attitudes toward children. One of the Greek states, Sparta, particularly impressed the others with the wisdom of its child-rearing principles. From Plato to Rousseau, accounts of Spartan practice have been cited as an example of the success of a hard line with children.

The rationale behind Spartan customs was military preparedness and unthinking obedience to the state. Boys were trained very deliberately to be soldiers and girls to be mothers of soldiers. By the sixth century B.C., when the Spartan system was in its classic form, Greek warfare was no longer a matter of individual combat, as in the epic days of Homer. It was carried on by formations of infantry. So the goal of Spartan training was to mold boys into parts of a military machine. Plutarch wrote that the Spartans had "neither the wish nor the ability to live for themselves; but like bees they were to make themselves always integral parts of the whole community, clustering together about their leader, almost beside themselves with enthusiasm and noble ambition to belong wholly to their country."

Many countries, then as now, have wished this for their people. But the cost was great. According to the accounts others left, the Spartan elders began to shape this personality from the child's earliest years. They inspected every free-born child at birth, deciding whether the child would be allowed to live. Those who failed this inspection were abandoned in the dung pit.

John Boswell's recent book, *The Kindness of Strangers,* warns us not to imagine the worst when we read about child abandonment in the past. Historians have assumed that abandonment or "exposure" was simply a cowardly form of infanticide. But it is clear that ancient authors who mentioned the practice expected many of these infants to survive—to be taken up and reared by couples who wanted children for one reason or another. Some evidence suggests that abandonment was a way of transferring children to where they were most wanted while preventing the later identification of these foundlings. The number of gods or dynastic founders of early legend said to have survived abandonment shows that the practice loomed large in the minds of these societies. As for abandonment of babies on garbage heaps, it is surmised that this was done because such sites were visited daily, though they were out of public view.

Sparta may have been one of the societies which looked upon exposure as an *alternative* to infanticide. For the first seven years, at any rate, those Spartan children who were chosen were put under the care of nurses, who began making Spartans of them. They taught the children to eat every kind of food without complaint, not to be afraid of the dark or of being alone, and not to cry. Again, the other Greeks remarked on the Spartans' failure to swaddle their infants. For they gave their babies the full use of their limbs in hopes that this would make them strong.

Spartan parents were not allowed to interfere in the child's training even at this early stage. The state did not want strong family bonds to develop, for the state itself was to be the focus of loyalties. So at seven the boys were sent to something like a boarding school or dormitory, to remain until age twenty. Their training in these years was mostly physical, exercising and exposing themselves to all kinds of weather. Meanwhile they barely learned to read. This did not mean they were without a literary culture, however, for they memorized the epics and histories of their people so they might remember examples of heroism while on campaign. Spartans were famous for their choral singing and sang the praises of past victories as they marched into battle. Likewise, their laws were not written down, so that all citizens would be forced to master the code of their nation. They were taught a mental toughness, too, by a process of hazing and ridicule which they learned to ignore. In short, everything was designed to produce boys who possessed an unquestioning loyalty and physical and mental stamina.

Plutarch tells the story of the Spartan boy who hid a stolen fox under his cloak when an elder came up to speak with him. Only when the boy fell down dead was it discovered that the fox had been tearing at his bowels underneath his cloak, for the lad had never flinched. It was the kind of story the Spartans themselves liked to tell. One sees the same attitude in the graduation exercise which accompanied the festival of Artemis Orthia. This was a kind of competition to see who could endure the most flogging. If one died without ever making a sound, he was honored as a hero of the state. No doubt the point of this test was to prove that graduates could bear torture if captured. But one cannot help thinking that the sadism of the proceedings must have been valued as entertainment. Parents cheered their sons on to endure greater tortures. It was one compensation for the pain and discipline the spectators themselves had experienced. For the Spartan child-rearing system produced adults who were mean as well as tough. One of the high points of their year was when the young men were sent to kill off troublesome serfs, as a sort of war game.

Whenever child-rearing techniques emphasize one thing they

neglect something else. Other Greeks noted that the Spartans grew up with certain character deficiencies. Their country had as little to do with foreigners as possible, but when they were sent abroad, perhaps as ambassadors, they were easily corrupted by foreign customs. It was said that they could not resist bribes and easily became dissipated. We would only have expected this. Their training had not fostered individual character. In fact it was designed to eliminate individualism, to teach obedience rather than initiative. Without the guidance of their community, Spartans became disoriented. To that extent their system failed.

But for hundreds of years their attention to children was a source of strength to the Spartan state. The absence of a defensive wall to protect Sparta was one of the wonders of the ancient world. Their security lay in the training of their citizens. Training the young was the job of every freeman in Sparta. Serfs did the agricultural work, and the children of the serfs were raised to replace their parents at the base of the Spartan economy. Meanwhile, free-born Spartans devoted themselves to molding the next generation.

It seems a well-thought-out program. The Greeks assumed it was the idea of a single legislator, the half-legendary Lycurgus. Those who have studied primitive puberty rites are struck by the similarity of Spartan customs to those widespread among preliterate peoples. The physical toughening, the training in concealment and survival, instruction in the dances and chants of their people, all resemble the initiation programs common in traditional societies. Usually, as societies become more civilized they allow education to become professionalized and leave the job of teaching to servants. For civilization offers many distractions which interfere with the tasks of child rearing. In the Spartans, we see a people emerging into the light of historical record who had not yet given up a community commitment to education.

Girls in Sparta underwent much the same training as boys. This, too, was a matter of surprise among other Greeks, who let girls grow up in a sedentary and secluded home atmosphere. Spartan girls did gymnastics with the boys and wore as few clothes as the boys did, which might be nothing at all. Their physical training—running, wrestling, throwing the discus and javelin—was supposed to make childbirth easier. As a consequence, Spartan girls had a greater sense of involvement in the national life than other Greek women. Of course, they were valued mostly as brood mares. But the boys were little more than cannon fodder, when it comes to that.

As mothers, Spartan women were encouraged to practice eugenics—that is, the breeding of the best possible children. If it did not seem likely that a married couple would have strong children, it was their duty to allow someone else to impregnate the wife. Other Greeks considered this practice as odd as we do, and it is not clear that it ever seemed natural or became common among the Spartans. But it may be that their egos were so bound up with the community that Spartan men would have felt little jealousy and their wives little repugnance.

Ancient Greeks sometimes made fun of the Spartans as barbarians or wild animals. But they also had a sneaking admiration for them. Sparta represented a simpler, better time, before men had grown soft, argumentative, and politically factious. Several writers, including Aristotle, described Spartan concern with eugenics and child care with approval. And Plato's *Republic*—his description of the perfect, changeless society—was modeled largely on Sparta. He improved on that model in one respect, he thought, by allowing free love. In this way, parentage would become so confused that a boy's natural respect for his father would necessarily extend to all his elders. Perhaps some Greeks did not think this respect was natural. Those who responded to Sophocles' *Oedipus Rex* may have sensed what Freud would describe in his classic discussion of the unconscious rivalry within the family. Perhaps Plato was actually trying to head off the antagonism behind the "Oedipus complex," or thought that Sparta had come close to doing so.

Later ages have also been inspired by descriptions of the Spartan program. Groups as different as the founding fathers of the American republic and the Nazi Party have admired the simplicity and public spirit of the Spartans. When individualism threatens public order and we sicken on our own sophistication, we find a new appreciation for the concern of this backward nation for its children. The fact that their program resulted in such a narrow and brittle personality is appalling. But certainly these virtually prehistoric people had nothing to learn from us about the possibilities of molding the child by a conscious and consistent plan.

Three

Athens
and
Jerusalem:
A Lifetime
of
Learning

The two great sources of the Western cultural tradition are the ancient Greeks, especially the Athenians, and the Hebrews. The reason they hold this position is that they lifted their eyes above the economic and political means of survival to reflect on the ends of human life. The two peoples represent very different views on many important questions. But in one respect they were similar: They both elevated education into a way of life. Childhood, therefore, was seen as a part of life and not simply a preparation for life, for the learning which began in childhood would never cease.

Having said this, it is necessary to point out that the Athenians paid almost no attention to the child's first seven years. It was education that began the process of making one human. Until boys were capable of formal education they were left to their mothers' exclusive care. The upper-class ideal was for children to live in separate apartments, away from the man's part of the house, while they were in that unformed stage. Of course Greeks could, and often did, show a good deal of sympathy for young people. Homer and many later authors like Euripides wrote touching and sentimental scenes of family affection. There is real pathos in the description of Hector's infant son, frightened by the nodding plumes on his father's helmet, as the doomed man leaves for battle. Defendants used to bring their weeping children to trial with them, in hopes of swaying the jurors. But when Greek artists pictured the *erotes* or cherubs who represented the link between the gods and humans, it did not occur to them to give such a responsible job to infants, as Renaissance artists were later to do. Rather, these figures were painted as pubescent youths, the age at which children began to become human.

There was little in the way of literary culture that small children could have learned from their mothers. For their mothers (and of course their sisters) had never been formally educated and lived in a wholly different world from the men. Even among the upper classes the woman's life was one of gossip and of working up wool into clothes, while men were occupied with affairs of state. Even the sons of the humbler classes were more likely to be literate than aristocratic women. They would also have been taught some trade, by their fathers or through apprenticeship. Solon, the great legislator of Athens, forced freemen to take their educational responsibilities seriously by declaring that if a son were not taught a trade he would not have to support his father in old age. The upper class did not need such utilitarian urging to see that their sons went to school. It would have been considered shameful to neglect the culture they would receive there.

In the Athens of the classical period (say 400 B.C.), the boys of the upper class were given over to a male servant called a *paidagogos* at age seven. The pedagogue (as the Romans would call him) became the child's constant companion until his late teens. He was not a tutor or teacher, but a companion. The job was not demanding; he took the boy to school each day, carrying his books and his lyre, and saw that he minded his manners. He then saw that his charge arrived home at night and was empowered to punish him if necessary. Thus, he could make a major contribution to the child's moral training.

The need for such a servant is something of a puzzle. They may have functioned partly to protect the boys from homosexual advances, in a society which preserved free-born children from these practices. But the use of pedagogues may simply show the low opinion the Greeks had of boys before they had been through the taming process. Plato, in *The Laws,* warned that children were the most stubborn of all wild beasts, because they were the most clever. It was as though these sneaky and insolent creatures could not be left alone for a minute. The status of their keepers, the pedagogues, was very low. They were usually slaves, and often old or otherwise unfit for anything else. Thus, the child's main adult companion was from the dregs of his society. To be bossed and perhaps beaten by such a person may have been part of what gave upper-class boys a lifelong distaste for childhood and for family life generally—a feature of Greek thought which we will consider later.

For these students, education was something quite separate from practical skills. It was not dictated by economic or military considerations, or even by any need to bolster a shaky social status. It was what the Romans would later call a "liberal education"—that is, the education of free men who would never need to earn a living by it. Liberal education was an end in itself. It was the beginning of self-knowledge and opened up the universe so that one could understand one's place in the world and the inner necessity of all things. After all, what does one find to do when one is already rich? The Athenians assumed that such a man would go in for speculation, among other things. Socrates thought that his fellow citizens' interest in philosophy was shallow. But they were undeniably curious about the nature of things and were always ready to sit in judgment on the latest theories. It was something they could give their whole lives to. In fact, they considered that the rest of society was organized as it was just so that they could devote themselves to this, the highest of all pursuits. The well-rounded life was the justification for human existence.

This was a new idea in human history, and it meant a new view of childhood. It implied that childhood would not be marked off from adulthood by the end of studies or by a "degree." Rather, adulthood was a continuation of the child's activities. Plato and Aristotle took this notion so seriously that they suggested that education should begin even before age seven, at home. Much could be learned through games, for instance. Just which games did not matter so long as the child got used to working within a set of rules. For this would be crucial to the citizens of a democracy. They also thought that more care should be taken in the stories nurses told to children. They feared that tales of bogeymen like Medusa, the Gorgon, and Cyclops, which were meant to scare children into behaving, might actually damage them mentally. Plato thought that even Homer and Hesiod, the most revered of the poets, ought to be expurgated for children because they portrayed the gods as absurd and even immoral. Whatever the value of these suggestions, we should note that the Greeks were the first to debate theories of education.

Nothing ever came of these ideas, however, because the state never took over the schools. They remained private enterprises. But the curriculum did become standardized. The free-born boy had three teachers: one for reading, writing, and arithmetic and for learning the poets by heart; one for athletics; and one for music, which consisted of playing the lyre and singing the lyric poets. Teachers were, again, poorly paid and little respected. But they were helped by a number of traditional techniques for making the learning process attractive. There were metrical alphabets and alphabetical riddles by which to teach the letters. There was a kind of dance-drama used to teach spelling in which the children postured in the shape of the letters. And from about 570 B.C. there were Aesop's prose fables (which may have been different from the tales which now bear that title).

From the very beginning, however, schoolchildren were introduced to adult culture. As soon as they could read they were given the Homeric epics and the works of the other poets and tragedians. In doing this, the Greeks believed they were teaching philosophy in disguise. For the poets were considered to have miraculously divined the innermost truths of the world. All wisdom was contained in their works, for those who could find the hidden meanings. Even those who did not see below the surface were absorbing these lessons subliminally, for the stories trained one's emotions as well as one's mind. To that end, children recited the poetry dramatically, as we might engage in psychodrama. They were thus building the character for a life of action. Of course, this was why Plato worried over the imitation of unworthy actions and destructive emotions, as described by Homer. He felt that Athens needed fewer heroes and more good citizens.

Music, too, was taught for its effect in harmonizing the soul. Proper harmony and rhythm were not irrational pleasures but had a moral purpose. They created a disgust for whatever is ugly and graceless. And they had a therapeutic value for the body and its humors. Each of the musical modes (the types of scales) was

identified with a particular emotion. Greeks worried that whoever wrote the music for a society could have as powerful an
effect as those who wrote its laws, for musicians could influence
even the psyche. Athletic training was related to music and was
often accompanied by music. Like music, it was for the purpose
of achieving a balanced and harmonious character. Athletics
were not just for soldiering but helped to make the body the
servant of the mind. Athletic specialization was positively
frowned upon because it might deform the body.

What the boys began at school they continued as men at the
gymnasiums, which combined the functions of social club, lec-
ture hall, and gym. Only then did the efforts of childhood reach
perfection. Only then could one think correctly, handle oneself
with grace, and continue one's education without direction. Children could not yet do the things that made life worth living.

So in the end, the integration of education with all of life did
little to elevate childhood in Greek thought. And there is reason
to think that children had rather a bad time of it in Athens. This
is not a reference to the practice of infanticide. The themes of
Greek literature, however, suggest some characteristic tensions
which must have borne heavily on the child. Scholars have remarked on the striking contradiction between the importance of
female figures in Greek mythology and the powerless position
of women in Athenian society. In other words, the social position
of mothers would never have suggested their psychological
dominance. To the extent that literature reveals psychological
preoccupations, it appears that Greek men were hostile toward
women and obsessed with them. Remembering their family patterns, we could guess why.

Consider that for the first seven years of life, while one's
upper-class father was hardly ever at home, the mother was
hardly ever away. In fact, she was forbidden to go out except to
religious observances or else with a chaperone. Couples seem
to have had little to talk about and few friends in common. Partly,

this was due to the fact that men typically married at around 30 years of age, picking girls who were only 16 to 18 or even younger. Husbands were fanatical about premarital virginity and fidelity in their wives, but they frequently neglected them to the point of eating and sleeping separately. We may well imagine that women resented this treatment, whether or not they admitted it to themselves. And apparently they focused their envy and resentment on their sons, in those first impressionable years. The boys were almost substitute husbands while the real ones were away. There was something a little scary about this attention, to boys of that age.

The common image of woman in Greek literature, the literature that these boys later wrote or commissioned from their poets, is a figure of determination or even terror. The female monsters of Greek mythology appear in much the same way as they appear in the dreams of those who suffer through similar family situations today. Among the divinities, goddesses are more intimately connected with the human characters than are the gods and are more resolute. While Zeus wanders aimlessly, philandering and throwing tantrums, his wife Hera doggedly works out her resentments through her many stepchildren. It was the goddesses who caused madness. Only the more virginal ones were benign. Athene, for instance, had to be transformed into an almost boyish figure before the Athenians could warm up to her. It is the same in Greek tragedies. Mothers are menacing figures, killing their children or getting them to avenge wrongs to the mother. And the menace usually has clear sexual overtones. Even the bogeymen of Greek folklore were female (bogeypersons, perhaps) and were characterized by ravenous sexual appetites.

This pattern is sufficiently consistent to indicate that Greek mothers were intruding on their sons' sexual awareness at such a time as to create lifelong fears. If one followed Freud's analysis, one would conclude that such pressure would tend to arrest psychological development at that stage. Narcissistic self-absorption can continue to disturb adult character. It may have been a powerful influence toward the exhibitionism and competitiveness of Greek society. It may also have diverted energies into the cultural activity for which the Greeks are famous. And it may help explain the homosexuality which was a feature of Greek life.

As these boys grew up, they started the cycle again. They avoided marriage until the family's reputation demanded it, and then they married girls half their age. The girls had likely been neglected, at least if they had any brothers. And so, because the wife was in no way her husband's equal, he felt justified in neglecting her in favor of the exclusively male society of public life. She, in turn, would live vicariously through her sons. The cycle seems to have become more pronounced as time went on. The various retellings of the Orestes myth, for example, come more and more to be dominated by the theme of matricide.

The Greeks sublimated these tensions in art and literature of impressive beauty. It would not discredit this art to think that it owed something to the repression of certain, basically sexual, energies. Every age has its own style of psychological repression. What is important is to see how constructively they were able to use these diverted energies. We are, however, reminded that artistic creativity has its price. The tragic view of life which the Greeks recognized so clearly, and their exhausting competition for recognition, shows a craving for the love their parents could not give. Their insecurity makes them the first men with whom we can identify.

The Hebrews likewise stand at the beginning of our history. Like the Athenians, they came to view education as a lifelong enterprise. It was a narrower education, to be sure, but it offered a more positive image of the child.

Most of our evidence for ancient Hebrew civilization is in the books which were their teaching materials. The Scriptures containing their laws, histories, and praises preserved the Hebrews' national identity even in the absence of a state of their own. This is the same as to say that their educational program was responsible for the survival of Hebrew society. For after the Babylonians destroyed their state (in 587 B.C.), and with their Temple and public buildings in ruins, they turned toward their children from a fear of vanishing from history.

Even before the exile made education crucial, there is evidence of sympathy for children. Many of their early stories concern younger sons, which is normally a sentimental reaction against the favoring of the first-born. Human families may favor the eldest, but it seemed that God often passed them over to give His higher blessing to a younger brother—the ingenuous Abel or Joseph rather than their jealous brothers; the wily Jacob, whose persistence was rewarded; or David, whose winning personality made him such a successful leader. Children could be important as individuals and not just as family heirs. The fact that the law required the Hebrews to "redeem" their first-born sons offers a parallel to their neighbors' practice of child sacrifice. Whether or not their own ancestors had practiced this, the Hebrews found a substitute—symbolized by Abraham's sacrifice of the ram in Isaac's place. The law institutionalized this practice, and later Jews understood that law to prohibit any form of infanticide. When later kings, perhaps Solomon, began the sacrifice of their own sons in the rites of Moloch, the chroniclers had no doubt that this was an abomination to Yahweh.

Education in those primitive times was the job of parents, with even the mothers playing a part. (Obedience was directed to mothers, too, by the fifth commandment.) Fathers were supposed to explain the national festivals, giving their historical as well as agricultural significance. At first, this was oral instruction and recitation. With the return from Babylonian exile the editing of the Old Testament was completed and instruction became literary. Hebrew had increasingly become a literary language, as the revived nation adopted Aramaic, the language of their neighbors. So schools began to teach the Hebrew Scriptures. The first synagogues were, in effect, schools where everyone—young and old—came to read and learn as well as worship.

This was something new among the world's religions. Before this, as in other religions, the Jews thought of the Temple as the center of religious life, and of sacrifices as the focus of worship. With the Temple in ruins the sacrifices ceased. Worship in the synagogue had quite a different character. Religion became a matter of thought and reflection rather than ritual behavior. And children went along, to begin a lifelong search for the truth contained in God's law.

We do not know when separate schools for children began. By the time of Jesus they existed in every important town, in connection with the synagogue. There was even an order from the High Priest in A.D. 63 that all boys, even orphans, must attend. So by then schools had taken over the burden of education from the family. With the Jews this did not mark a decline of interest in education, as it often does when societies delegate teaching duties to specialists or servants. For the pupils were being entrusted with matters of the utmost importance. Education began with the law of sacrifice and the praises of God, along with the proverbs which were particularly appropriate for the young. All this was sufficiently important that it called for memorization. After all, the laws all had a moral application, and action could not wait while one consulted a book. The study of Scripture was not meant to be simply literary, leading to speculation. Its goal was obedience. But in the end, the schools found that they could not contain adventurous minds that easily. So at age 10, those boys who showed some aptitude went on to study the traditions (in the Mishnah). After

15 a few continued with the theological disputations in the Talmud.

Children continued to be taken seriously by the Jews even after they were relegated to institutions of their own. For education never lost its place at the center of the nation's hopes. After the second Temple was destroyed (by the Romans in A.D. 70), the sacrifices ceased again. But education continued more intensely than ever, starting still with the law of sacrifice. For as one writer put it: "Sacrifices are pure; and children are pure; let the pure be occupied with that which is pure." Nothing could show the Jews' devotion to children better than this association of the two most precious things in their national life.

One can also see their devotion to children in the status of teachers. Those at the higher levels took no pay, but taught for the sheer honor of dealing with the law and with children. Or that was the ideal—actually there were ways of rewarding teachers for their effort. But no one wanted to attract mercenary individuals to the profession. Elementary teachers were looked down on precisely because they viewed teaching as a job and received pay. Unmarried men were not allowed to teach even at that level, for this calling was not to be a refuge for social misfits. Teachers were to be models and not simply specialists. Teachers of the law were the greatest men in Jewish communities— the first and perhaps the only time in Western history that teachers have had such status. It reflected partly a reverence for the law and partly their recognition of the importance of the rising generation. As they liked to say, it was as great a privilege to pass on the law to a child as to have received it from God on Mt. Sinai.

For those fortunate ones who went on with Talmudic studies, education never ended. In the final stages of that pursuit, teachers and students were considered partners in the search for truth. When they had gone through the books, they simply started over, expecting to find new depths of meaning. The Jews did not become speculative philosophers by this kind of study, but they did become scholars. And the respect that was accorded these rabbis, a respect greater than that due to one's own father, gave even their smallest pupils a status which today's child might envy.

Four

Rome and the Collapse of the Trustee Family

In Athens, as we have seen, the state was the center of everyday life for free men. The home managed only the necessities of life so that men could concern themselves with something higher, with human perfection as they conceived it. In Rome things were different. That state grew up around the family and the clan and consciously depended on them to raise the kind of children necessary to Rome's survival and power. The authority of the Roman family included even the right to execute its own members. Primitive Roman religion, which centered on the "genius" or spirit of the family, was very much like ancestor worship. But Rome had a long history, and family and state eventually found themselves at odds with each other. In the end, the growth of the state's authority had thoroughly undermined contemporary family structure, as states have often done since. Rome's story offers us an example of this seemingly inevitable process and of some efforts to avoid this form of social dissolution.

In the years of the Roman Republic, before the Christian era, Roman education was meant to produce those character traits that would make the ideal family man. Children were taught primarily to be good to their families. To revere the gods, one's parents, and the laws of the state were the primary lessons for Roman boys. Cicero described the goal of their child rearing as "self-control, combined with dutiful affection to parents, and kindliness to kindred." Mothers were obviously important to such training as this: Stories of the nation's heroes often give their mothers recognition for their part in building character. Plutarch recorded how the mother of the Gracchus brothers, for instance, coped with 12 children after being left a widow:

Cornelia, taking upon herself all the care of the household and the education of her children, approved herself so discreet a matron, so affectionate a mother, and so constant and noble-spirited a widow, that Tiberias seemed to all men to have done nothing unreasonable in choosing to die for such a woman; who, when King Ptolemy himself proferred her his crown, and would have married her, refused it, and chose rather to live a widow. In this state she continued, and lost all her children, except one daughter, who was married to Scipio the younger, and two sons, Tiberias and Caius, whose lives we are now writing. These she brought up with such care, that though they were without dispute in natural endowments and dispositions the first among the Romans of their time, yet they seemed to owe their virtues even more to their education than to their birth.

Tacitus also testified to the power of these women's example:

Of old our children were born of chaste parents and were reared, not in the chamber of some hired nurse, but in the lap or at the breast of their mother, whose chief glory was thus to stay at home and be the servant of her children. Choice was made of some matron from among the family's relatives, to whom were entrusted all the children of the same household. Of well-proved virtue, her influence was such that none dared utter before her an unseemly word or venture on an unbecoming action. Her presence, commanding awe and reverence, was there to check the children not merely at their lessons and serious duties, but even during their games and recreations. Thus, tradition tells us, did Cornelia train the Gracchi; Aurelia, Julius Caesar; Atia, Augustus for future empire. And the aim of all this stern formation was that whilst the child's character was still fresh and open and unspoiled by wrong, he should be taught to embrace the practice of virtue with all his heart; and that whether destined to be soldier, jurist or orator, his whole energies should be solely devoted to duty.

Such at least was the ideal of parenthood—one that showed considerable respect for the child.

After seven the boy became his father's constant companion. He helped him in his work, was his acolyte in religious observances, went along when his father visited friends, and could even attend the Senate if his father was of the Senatorial class. At least this is the picture given in the popular biographies of Cato and Augustus, for example. In the midst of the affairs of state, fathers insisted on spending hours with their sons and grandsons, teaching them swimming, riding, reading and writing, and the laws and history of Rome. Although some of these lessons were not thought appropriate for girls, fathers were expected to devote some time to daughters as well. Then, at about 16, the boy was officially introduced into society in a kind of coming-out ceremony. He adopted adult dress, became a full citizen, and went to live with some respected family friend for a year. This put him on his best behavior and probably helped to avoid the kind of tensions that are common between fathers and sons of that age. After that his apprenticeship was over.

This was not the philosophical education of the Athenians or the scholarship of the Jews. Neither was it the kind of puberty rite that crams the whole of one's preparation for adult life into one horribly memorable year. But it served Rome well in creating the competencies necessary for public life.

Rome prospered and began to acquire an empire after 240 B.C. This changed everything. Fathers were now often gone, fighting at the edges of the empire or administering the new possessions. Rome became an urban society, and the process of education became professionalized along with other aspects of life. Of course, it then ceased to be a training in character. The Romans did not yet have enough literary culture to justify keeping children in school from age 7 to 12. But teaching methods were so bad that after that length of time students still could barely read. Teachers were recruited from among the lowest ranks of society and were paid so little that most of them did other scribal work to make ends meet. Their frustration is amply shown in contemporary descriptions of the dreadful schools, meeting in the noisy marketplace with the teachers shouting the lessons and looking for excuses to whack students with their sticks.

By the beginning of the Christian era it was clear that the importance of the Roman family was declining. The Roman family concept had been what is called a stem, or lineage or trustee, family. That is, it was considered to be eternal, with the living members only acting as trustees of the family's name, honor, and wealth. The members' worship united them with the family ancestors, and their care for the family's property and its good name was their duty to posterity. Living patterns had often created extended households (although this is not necessarily implied in the trustee family concept), which added to the size and economic security of the unit. And if it appeared that the line might die out, families would adopt children to ensure that the name lived on. When family was taken this seriously, the father did not exercise his power—the *patria potestas*—to suit his whims; it was the family's power, delegated to him to use for the good of the family. The notion of selling the family's farm, for example, would have been unthinkable. No price could have compensated an unending succession of descendants for that loss.

But now, with the wealth of the empire pouring in and with Rome growing to be the capital of civilization and self-indulgence, parents were busy with activities outside the home. Of even more concern was the effect of luxury on the neglected younger generation. Cornelia's son-in-law, the great Scipio Africanus, reacted with something like horror:

Our free-born boys and girls are going with lute and psaltery to the training-schools of professional actors. There they mingle with lewd companions, are taught unseemly antics, and learn to sing songs which our ancestors held dishonourable for all who were not slaves. When I was first told this, I could not believe that men of noble birth were giving their children such lessons. But I was taken to one of the dancing-schools; and there, by Heaven, I saw more than fifty boys and girls, among them one whose presence made me grieve for my country more than all the others: a senator's son, the son of a candidate for office, not less than twelve years old, with castanets, dancing a dance which no shameless slave-boy could dance without dishonour.

If wealth were not enough to weaken family life, the state began to undermine the family's rival authority. It had some justification for doing so. The unrestricted right of the family head to enslave or sell family members could obviously be abused. Indeed, it seemed an abuse in itself, as families found that they could not count on fathers to take their responsibilities seriously. The state could claim that it was liberating wives and children from a tyrannical authority. But as the state extended the rights of individuals against their families, it also made it easier for the state to use those individuals for its own purposes. The wider clans, which had once performed military and political functions for the Roman nation, were replaced in these functions by the legions. Thus, citizens were freed to serve the state's all-conquering machine.

It is ironic that the wives and children who were to benefit from the limiting of the father's arbitrary power were not better off as a result. From all accounts, the powers fathers retained were exercised more capriciously than ever. Men lost the sense of responsibility that had once bound their decisions. Divorce became the rule rather than the exception—or so people said. Family property was squandered as the father pleased, leaving nothing to posterity. The birth rate went down to the point that there was real question whether the upper classes, at least, would leave any posterity.

The first emperor of Rome, Augustus (ruling from 30 B.C. to A.D. 14), was troubled by this situation. The frivolous attitude taken toward adultery, divorce, and infanticide offended him. He blamed the decline in self-discipline and political responsibility on a decline in family discipline. All this even threatened underpopulation at a time when Rome would have preferred to dominate its empire by its own native stock. Augustus's concern may have gone even deeper, to the fact that he had lost his own father at age four. As we shall see, he was just one of the many benefactors of children who had suffered a personal loss that might have made him sensitive to their plight.

Whatever the reason, Augustus introduced a number of laws designed to encourage family life and larger families, especially among the upper classes. He made it easier to marry by setting an age limit to parents' power to refuse their consent. Before, there had been no legal limit to the parents' right to refuse, and a son could not flout such a decision until his father's death. Augustus forced parents to give their daughters a dowry if they could afford to, in order to make them more attractive brides. In a sense, even these laws further limited the authority of fathers over their children. But at least they would have encouraged more families to develop and might have created a better atmosphere within the family. If there was little hope of saving the ideal of the trustee family, Augustus could at least hope to strengthen the conjugal family (that notion of the family which sees it as existing only from a couple's marriage until their deaths). Even that would be an improvement, in his view, over the atomistic individualism which threatened to dissolve all social bonds. Augustus levied penalties on those who refused to have children once they were married. They were forbidden to will their property or to inherit more than a certain amount from their own parents. Men with three or more children could receive higher government jobs and tax exemptions. Women with three children were granted certain civil and property rights. More "grounds" were required for divorce.

Augustus did not stop at legislation. He gave speeches on the importance of the family and tried to present his own family as a model for others. His concern was echoed by some of the emperors of the second century, who attempted to end infanticide and encouraged foster parenting of abandoned children. Historians consider this campaign to save the family one of the most notable efforts at social reform in all of ancient history. However, they differ on its effect: It may have reversed the decline in population among certain classes, but they doubt that it strengthened family bonds.

We cannot conclude, however, that the Romans were without a conscience about the sorry state of domestic life in their society. Writers criticized the emperors, each other, and even themselves for lapses from the old ideal of family life. That ideal was hardly known in Greek literature, where the family is treated largely as an economic arrangement. Plutarch, a Greek living in Rome around A.D. 100, was inspired by the Roman concern when he wrote his various works on education and family life. The Roman satirists, and especially Juvenal, show some sense that the sexual orientation of the empire period amounted to a kind of mania: When children followed that example, "treading deeper in vice, you will—oh, of course!—be indignant, rail with bitter noise, and make a new will." The figure of the neglected child was their symbol of the price paid for new sexual freedom. They obviously expected readers to respond with sympathy for the child. It was this conscience that Christianity would appeal to, as we shall see.

No one better exemplifies such a conscience about the treatment of children than Plutarch's contemporary, the educational writer Quintilian. His work, *The Training of the Orator,* is one of the most sympathetic appeals in behalf of children in all of ancient history. Parts of it were known even in the darkest ages of Western history, which gives the work unusual importance. By Quintilian's time Roman education was very different from what we have described, for as the Romans began to annex Greece (after 150 B.C.) they brought back Greek literature and philosophy. Having so little literature of their own, they were excited to learn that of the Greeks. And so another stage of education was added to the dreadful elementary schools. Children were sent on to the *grammaticus* to learn a foreign language and a borrowed literature. From that time until the twentieth century, the most high-brow education has always been the mastery of a foreign tongue.

Quintilian thought there was as much loss as gain in this literary emphasis. He himself was concerned with literature, but he thought education was incomplete if it lost sight of the family's goal of producing a good man. Like the luxury in which upper-class boys were raised, their education was actually corrupting them. His hope was that it could be reoriented, and even prove the salvation of Roman society. Among his suggestions were that the earliest years of the child's life were crucial. Education should start earlier than age seven, within the family. It should not be so hard as to give the child an aversion to learning. Rather, these early lessons would take the form of play—that embryonic notion of the kindergarten. Schools as well as tutors would be necessary for the child at a later stage, since education should be social. But even in schools, Quintilian hoped that teachers would be sensitive to individual differences of temperament and ability: "Among boys, good promise is shown in the far greater number, and if it passes off in the progress of time, it is manifest that it was not natural ability, but care, that was lacking." Beating, he thought, was usually unnecessary. A teacher who had made the effort to understand his pupil's individual needs and character could probably dispense with it: "I will content myself with saying that children are helpless and easily victimized, and that therefore no one should be given unlimited power over them." This ran counter to a more general tolerance toward "correction," which was justified by Cicero: "The more ingenious and clever a man is, the more teaching is vexacious and difficult for him. When he sees something which he himself grasps quickly being but tardily perceived it is torture for him." Punishment, then, showed a proper spirit in the teacher.

We are forever rediscovering Quintilian's sympathetic appeals, often without knowing that they go back so far. Renaissance humanists found a complete text of his work in 1416 and praised the wisdom of his direction. Unfortunately, even they found it easy to forget this good advice under the pressures of classroom teaching. Still, it is good to be able to report that there were concerned and thoughtful individuals in the midst of a society we think of as generally callous. Someone, perhaps Quintilian, inspired Trajan and later emperors and private citizens to endow schools for needy pupils, the world's first educational philanthropies. And from his time on, emperors interested themselves in education to the extent of prescribing the salaries that localities should pay teachers.

Professional interest in children may have been rising at the same time that families were failing, for it was not confined to teachers. The first extended treatise on obstetrics and children's diseases appeared around 130—the *Gynecology* of Soranus of Ephesus, a Greek living under Roman rule. There had been a few references to children's particular medical problems as far back as Hippocrates (400 B.C.). The writings credited to him make a number of observations about fetal development, about the various states of the tonsils in children, about weight gain and teething. He commented on several afflictions as they affected children, such as convulsions and epilepsy, recognizing that children might require different treatment. These writings are also responsible for the long tradition that human life falls into the seven-year periods of infancy (up to age 7 and the completion of teething), childhood (to 14 and puberty), adolescence (to 21 and a full beard), youth (to 28 and the end of growth), adulthood (to 49, a triple seven), elderliness (to 56), and old age after that. Cornelius Celsus, a Roman, had also described several operations then common for children. Soranus summed all this up, along with the kind of advice mothers-in-law then gave on how to salt the newborn, how to swaddle, bathe, and wean the infant, and how to choose a wet-nurse. Like Quintilian's work, this one was long cited as authoritative; as late as 1752 an English work on midwifery quoted Soranus as an expert.

There were Romans, then, who took up the child's cause. Roman society was at least self-critical in regard to the neglect of family responsibilities. To keep things in perspective, we need to say something of other societies of that time which were far more cruel toward their children. Romans did not seal up children in the foundations of buildings as many societies did, for instance, by way of dedicating the structure. Carthage, Rome's first great rival, was famous at that time for practicing child sacrifice. For a long time scholars believed Greek and Roman historians were exaggerating when they spoke of the Carthaginians' mass sacrifices. But in this century archaeologists have dug into mass graves yielding the charred bones of thousands of children four years old and younger. The Greeks and Romans were as horrified as we are. This may seem hypocritical, given the fact that they themselves did away with unwanted and unfit infants in large numbers. There was one difference, however: The Carthaginians sacrificed the children they wanted—the eldest sons of noble families. In an awful way this shows the "importance" of children to Carthage. The welfare of the nation was thought to depend on a supply of children for sacrifice. But it struck the Romans as intolerable that the state could command their destruction in order to keep up the power of their gods. Sacrifice indicated more heartlessness than simple infanticide, since many of the children had lived long enough for parents to become attached to them.

Quite apart from the cruelty involved, the killing of first-born children rather than the last-born surely had a negative genetic effect on Carthaginian society. Recent studies of the first-born indicate that they tend to be more intelligent and more achievement-oriented than subsequent children. Both heredity and family environment contribute to this advantage. Later children are more likely to carry a variety of genetic difficulties—beginning with the negative Rh factor—and would pass these on in larger and larger proportions. A long history of destroying the most favored would thus bring an evolutionary change. Also, we would expect that the upper classes, who were especially called upon to make this sacrifice, had been socially selected for some desirable genetic characteristic. Killing off precisely that class would increase the dysgenic effect on Carthaginian society. Beyond this, the higher expectations parents have of their first-born probably could not be transferred from a child who was four years old when killed. Those societies which have tended to kill later children, or have given the first-born a larger inheritance, have been practicing eugenics, in effect. By contrast, Carthage may have helped to defeat itself by this waste of its most precious resource.

One cannot help thinking that Rome, too, paid for its neglect of children and the family. Toward the end, the Western empire simply did not have the native manpower to fight its own battles. The emperors had long foreseen this. They blamed the falling population on a decline of commitment to the family. It may be that the decline of the trustee family was itself a result of the failure of other supporting institutions, especially the family-size farm. This would mean that the fall of the family was only one aspect of the decline of Rome and not itself a cause. It is to the credit of the Roman state that it recognized its own contribution to the weakening of family bonds and tried to revive a sense of family responsibility, only to discover how little the state can do to repair that institution.

Five

Christianity
and the
Reversal
of
Status

The spread of Christianity through the Roman empire brought a decisive change in attitudes toward children. As one might expect, the change was related to Jesus's own statements about children and to the revolution in values he promoted. In making the child the model of the life of faith, he exactly reversed the expectations of his listeners. For that reason alone the accounts of his teaching on children have the ring of truth. The attitudes expressed were so exceptional for that time that no one would have thought of inventing the stories.

They were remembered, apparently, because they had been a surprise, not because he had touched upon a familiar, sentimental theme.

Up to this point in our history, even the few authors who reflected on the child's needs had considered children to be only potentially human. This attitude may have helped when it came to disposing of unwanted infants. For classical authors accepted infanticide as the family's undoubted right, if not a duty in the case the deformed. The general public may be assumed to have been even more callous. In the later, Hellenistic, period of Greek dominance, families seem to have raised only one daughter, perhaps as a kind of family pet. Advice which must have been typical at the time can actually be read in a first-century letter from a husband to his wife: "If, as may well happen, you give birth to a child, if it is a boy let it live; if it is a girl, expose it." Rome also had a very high ratio of boys to girls—a telltale sign of infanticide. Infanticide was even a subject for jokes; the Roman comedies often involve attempts to do away with children and the cases of mistaken identity which came from bungling the job. The children who were rescued were abused in ways that boggle even our jaded minds. Children were sold into concubinage by their parents and might live with the children of those who were using them. Most Mediterranean cities had boy brothels, sometime including castrated males used as sexless prostitutes. Abandoned children were raised as gladiators or deliberately maimed to help in begging.

So when we come to the Gospel accounts, we do not have to allow for a conventional sentimentality about children. The attitudes which seem attractive to us were not a feature of ancient literature. Rather, they were part of the Christian sympathy for outcasts and women that was out of place at that time. From the very beginning, the prominence of women in the life of Jesus and in the history of the early disciples brought down either praise or ridicule on Christianity as a religion of the weak. Likewise, the association of Christianity with children has tended to discredit it among societies which do not accept Jesus's valuation of childhood, thinking it regressive.

Clearly, his comments on children were meant to shock even his followers into a new perception. The clearest statement was occasioned by an argument over which of the disciples or other religious luminaries would be the greatest in the coming Kingdom. "Truly, I say to you, unless you turn and become like children, you will never enter the kingdom of God. Whoever humbles himself like this child, he is the greatest in the kingdom of God. Whoever receives one such child in my name receives me." First, he was suggesting that the child's spirit was the very essence of the religious life—a life of wonder and dependence. Second, he was expressing the ideal of a society of service rather than of dominance. True religion was a faith like children express. And true greatness was in a life of service that could extend even to caring for children.

This was the most positive assessment of the child's worth up to that point, and perhaps in all of history. Other, similar episodes were reported in all of the synoptic Gospels in some form. Once, apparently on the Day of Atonement when children were brought to rabbis for their blessing, Jesus's disciples were trying to protect him from their clamor. His reaction was, "Let the children come to me, and do not hinder them; for to such belongs the kingdom of God." It is hard to imagine how odd these familiar sayings must have seemed at the time. For it would not have occurred to those listening that children were capable of the same religious status as adults, let alone an advantage in God's eyes. Jesus was jarring his audience into realizing that growing up is too often a process of narrowing self-interest. Children have an advantage in spiritual matters because they have not yet been consumed by mundane concerns. In another place, Jesus said in his exasperation that children understood him better than the teachers of his day. It was the perversity of adults that Jesus objected to, not that of children.

In the fourth Gospel, this teaching is taken to its logical extreme. There Jesus compares spiritual conversion not simply to childhood but to a new birth. The shock of the rabbi Nicodemus at this analogy is nicely preserved. He was offended by what we might call the regressiveness implied in that imagery. Jesus, on the other hand, was suggesting a new understanding of maturity. The life of faith required something of the child's awareness and simplicity as well as the adult's ability to be responsible. As in psychotherapy, there was a danger of regression here. But there was also the hope of a cure.

None of Jesus's references to children deal with exceptional cases. And here is where his followers strayed from his emphasis. What they added on the subject of childhood indicates that they could consider only an exceptional child as noteworthy. Luke recorded a story of Jesus himself as a child, amazing the teachers in the Temple with his precocity. Later apocryphal writings of the early Church included tales of miracles in Jesus's childhood. Thus began a tradition of such stories about the saints. St. Nicholas was supposed to have stood up at birth and to have fasted by taking the breast only once on Wednesdays and Fridays. The infant St. Ambrose was said to have had a swarm of bees fly into his mouth and then upward toward heaven, indicating his future greatness. Such a tradition had the effect of making normal childhood insignificant. It shows the prejudice against which Jesus contended. For he had realized that everyone finds, in childhood experience, the key to his or her spiritual development and happiness. Indeed, it was not until modern times, and especially in the writings of Rousseau and Freud, that something of this notion was rediscovered.

The epistles of the New Testament reflect a kindly view of childhood but do not develop Jesus's novel perspective. In fact, they tend to present the child as a problem: St. Paul made the successful rearing of children a test of their parents' fitness for authority in the Church. This was not to be done entirely through a hard line. He warned parents not to provoke their children to anger, because this would stand in the way of their spiritual development. And he put a limit on their authority over children by reminding them that parents were to provide for their children and not the other way around. All of this shows a sympathy equal to that of the most humane of the classical authors.

Where the Church went further was in the prohibition of abortion and exposure. Tacitus, a pagan, had remarked with approval that the Jews and the Germanic barbarians did not allow these practices. The Greek philosopher Epictetus had appealed to nature in asking how men could kill their offspring without remorse when sheep and even wolves did not. But other pagans, including Plato and Aristotle, thought "nature" made it a duty to expose sickly children. And in arguing with pagans, Christians had to find arguments for what was, to them, self-evident. When addressing pagans Justin Martyr observed that fathers who frequented brothels might unwittingly be served by their own daughters, since girls were sometimes rescued from exposure in order to be raised as prostitutes. The first Christian emperor, Constantine, made infanticide a crime (in 318). Later it was made punishable by death (374). We must not assume that the practice ceased just because there were edicts against it. But Western societies did begin to develop a conscience against disposing of children on the garbage heap. Of course, this added to the burdens of poor families who could not afford to feed all the children that came along. So the Church had to try to save the children abandoned on its doorstep. At first, it found foster parents for them, and later there were Church-run foundling homes.

Constantine and the other Christian emperors continued to issue laws designed to revive family life, as Augustus had done before them. Specifically, they forbade breaking up slave families and reduced the number of grounds for divorce. Beyond that, they encouraged parents who could not feed their children to put them up for adoption rather than to sell or abandon them, and secured the rights of those who raised foundlings or foster children against parents who might threaten to reclaim them once they could be put to work. These laws show a concern for the child's welfare that went far beyond the earlier anxiety about the upper-class family. But again, historians have doubted that they had much effect.

Oddly enough, the Church had no distinctive ideas on education. Even as Christian parents were coming to dominate Roman society, they were accepting more and more of the classical educational curriculum. Theologians objected to the immorality of the myths, as Plato had done, and they made fun of the quarrels among the proud philosophers of pagan times. But parents never considered the Church's catechetical schools to be a substitute for an ordinary grammar school education. Some of the more puritanical Churchmen argued that the Scriptures revealed all true wisdom and that a classical education was therefore unnecessary. But the prevailing view was that Christian children needed knowledge of the classics in order to refute the errors they contained. Even Tertullian, who was among the most uncompromising of the early theologians, said that one could not understand the Bible itself without a grounding in secular learning.

As a result, we see a merging of Judeo-Christian and Greco-Roman thought—the two main streams of Western civilization. Parents wanted the best of both for their children. The Church's only stipulation was that Christians should not teach classical literature unless they made clear their moral and religious objections to parts of it. In reaction, a new pagan emperor—Julian "the Apostate"—tried to recapture education for the old religion in 362. For the first time, schools were recognized to be ideological weapons. Through them, Julian tried to reverse the trend of the empire toward Christianity. The Church later claimed that he had barred Christian children from the schools, which was not strictly true. Rather, he excluded Christian teachers. After all, he asked, was it honest of them to teach what they did not believe, just for money? So Christians hastened to produce specifically Christian epics, comedies, tragedies, odes, and dialogues to replace the pagan ones and create an alternative literary education. Julian died in the next year, saving them the trouble of finishing this project. The fusion of cultures was resumed. So education remained primarily literary, for an elite. It became more bookish, if anything, than earlier Roman education. And, ironically, this desire to give Christian children the benefit of a traditional education saved pagan literature for Western civilization, for most of those works would not have survived to our day except for medieval copies made under the direction of the Church.

Historians have long sensed that Christianity was decisive in sentimentalizing the image of the child. Yet the notion of childhood innocence seems to conflict with another Christian teaching, the idea of infant depravity. The Church itself sensed the contradiction and began early to reconcile these views, which are so important for our later story.

Infant depravity, as it was eventually defined, meant that every individual inherits the guilt of Adam's original rebellion against God. The individual also inherits a tendency toward a personal rebellion. Jesus is not reported as having mentioned Adam when he discussed the subject of sin. As we have seen, he used children as symbols of a saving trust. St. Paul, too, made off-hand references to the innocence of children. But Paul also drew attention to the parallel between Adam and Jesus—the first bringing death upon the race by his desire to be a God unto himself, and the last bringing eternal life by his atoning obedience. No one developed this contrast into a doctrine that would associate children with Adam's rebellion until several centuries later. But the Church did baptize infants during that period, according to all available evidence.

That may strike us as odd. What could infants have done that would require this purification? In the fourth century this question arose in the Church. What could children be guilty of which would justify this practice, which was accepted as apostolic? Scholars now think that their puzzlement was the result of forgetting the earlier meaning of the rite. Baptism had not always meant primarily the washing away of sin. Christian practice was borrowed from the Jewish baptism of gentile converts or proselytes. And proselyte baptism had not been associated with specific moral offenses so much as with an identification of these gentiles and their children with God's chosen people. The whole family was baptized together, to show their new start in life and their ritual purity. In the Church also, it was inconceivable that parents would leave their children outside until they could choose for themselves. The end of the world might come too soon. And so children were identified with the Church in order to escape God's judgment on the world. Later, as other children were born into these Christian families, they were baptized too, as a kind of substitute for Jewish circumcision.

By the fourth century the Church had lost its sense that the end of the world was at hand. The only meaning baptism retained was that element which suggested purification or even the forgiveness of sins. For that reason, the less dedicated converts who were now flooding into the Church often deferred baptism until their deathbeds, rather than to commit themselves to lives of holiness. The clergy naturally took a dim view of this practice, which would allow a lifetime of indulgence and a last-minute repentance. But in arguing against it they had to explain why children had traditionally been baptized. Supposing that the sacrament marked God's forgiveness, they had to assume that the infant must somehow be guilty.

At this point, around the year 400, the Church began to debate the subject of the child's nature, a debate which engaged some of the greatest minds of that age. Pelagius argued that infants start life with a clean slate, as did Adam, and are responsible only for such sins as they themselves commit. St. Augustine countered with the view that all people were contained in Adam, as we might say that we existed as germ cells in the first human being. He thought that souls were generated by a natural process too, so that every soul in the world was contained in Adam's. Thus, all persons were indeed living in the first man and are therefore implicated in his original sin. Their later sins are simply the result of that rebellion, when humanity first decided for itself what was good or evil. Humankind now looks upon God as an enemy, and even children show the effects of this estrangement. They are out of tune with the universe and with their own true nature. As they grow up it becomes apparent that their emotions are warped, their reason darkened, their wills perverted. So from the start, they are incapable of any truly unselfish act. Augustine thought that baptism takes away the *guilt* of the original sin. But as children grow up the inherited *tendency* toward sin inevitably manifests itself. There must be something of a conversion, a change of direction, if one's self-centeredness is to be changed into a life of trust in God and charity toward others. Augustine's own autobiography shows that his views derived not only from a study of Scripture but from what he thought was common experience.

Infant baptism, therefore, was not the Church's response to a prior doctrine of infant depravity. Oddly enough, it was the other way around, as the doctrine arose to explain an earlier practice. The Church ruled in favor of Augustine and drew the logical conclusion that children who died unbaptized would go to hell. Such a teaching would seem to show an unconscious hostility toward children, if we assume that theological doctrines are rationalizations of secret wishes. But in fact, the Church was uncomfortable with this corollary. Theologians immediately began searching for arguments that would show that although unbaptized children might go to hell, they would not suffer there. A favorite argument was that the punishment for the original sin alone was simply a deprivation of the vision of God. The fires of hell were for volitional sins and therefore for adults. Unbaptized children would go to "limbo," where there was no remorse or torture. So while they might not go to heaven, they would never know what they had missed. It may well be that the doctrine of limbo which arose in response to that of infant depravity is a better indication of the underlying sympathies of the theologians.

At any rate, baptized children were safe. In fact, for the first seven years or so they were considered innocent, much as Pelagius had taught. Therefore, it was safe to indulge a sentimental view of children in those early years. The only difficulty was that childhood innocence had no strength against temptation and had to be protected. Naturally, protection took the form of outward restrictions and repression. This could be so severe that one would think the child was already suspected of some evil impulse.

Children can't seem to win. The Church had reconciled the most diverse views of the child's nature. Churchmen were even prepared to emphasize the more sympathetic one. But it appears that it doesn't really matter which view one takes. Believers in childhood innocence might not treat children any differently than those who emphasize their congenital waywardness. There were Puritans later who used the doctrine of infant depravity to generate parental sympathy for children, since it was the parents who had passed on this taint to their offspring. On the other hand, some of those who emphasized the innocence of the early years tried to protect children from their own awakening impulses and from outside influences. So either way might mean repressing children. But either notion could equally well lead to neglect. Those who thought children predisposed to evil might decide that, humanly speaking, nothing could be done to save them. And those who trusted to children's innate goodness might decide that there was nothing parents need do for them.

Clearly, the particular belief of a period does not necessarily tell us how children fared at that time. It is always easier to describe the official view of childhood than to say what effect it had. But historians have not always been careful to separate these two matters. The possibilities given above are not simply hypothetical. As we shall see, the Puritans were important for generating concern for children and for ensuring humane treatment for them, despite much that has been written about them. Some of them even observed that the doctrine of universal depravity forms a bond between the generations, since parents are thus responsible for their children's condition. It is also true that the Victorians, who exalted the image of childhood innocence, were, ironically, also guilty of raising repressiveness to something like record levels. But we are getting ahead of our story.

The different ways in which Churchmen could apply the orthodox view of childhood are nicely illustrated by two famous examples from the period. Around 400 St. Jerome wrote some letters concerning the raising of girls. They are very tender letters and concerned to make education pleasant. At the same time, they are highly restrictive. Jerome was worried about protecting the girls' innocence. For that reason he thought they should be kept strictly away from boys or from young nurses who might attract boys or cause the girls to think of themselves in a physical sense. Fancy clothes and even baths were forbidden. The girls should be raised with such a sense of dependence that they would be afraid to be alone. Even in attending church they should go at times when it was empty and there was no chance of their looking around for admirers.

These were directions for girls who were destined to become nuns. But after all, that was now the ideal for all girls. For those who emphasized the child's innocence, the task was to help preserve that innocence throughout all of life. Practically speaking, this meant that holiness of life became equated with sexual prudery. Virtue came to be considered something to protect, and the Christian life had gone on the defensive. Perhaps children suffered most from this doctrine of a merely negative innocence.

We see a very different attitude in St. Augustine, writing at the same time. In his *Confessions,* the Western world's first really revealing autobiography, he tried to go back to his own childhood. He realized that those years were crucial to an understanding of his development, and the episode that stuck in his mind was a time when he had stolen pears from a neighbor's tree. The story has become famous as an example of misguided moralizing. But Augustine was getting at something deeper than his early lust for fruit. As he remembered it, he was not even hungry and ended up throwing the pears away. He simply wanted the thrill of doing something bad. Young as he was, taking the pears was the worst thing he could think of.

To Augustine, this story demonstrated something about the nature of the young that ancient authors had never noticed: Children are motivated by processes as deep (and sometimes as perverse) as those that move adults. We tend to ignore our children, he thought, because they are too weak to carry out their wishes. If children were all six feet tall we would try harder to understand them. As it is, we hardly notice their true character because it is not a threat to our own desires. If there had been others of Augustine's ability to follow up this interest in child behavior, real progress might have resulted. For, suitably translated into a modern idiom, his view strikes us as a more realistic view than the hope of preserving an innate innocence by an ascetic life. He was certainly not saying that children are worse than adults. Rather, he was making the important and novel point that adult traits can be traced back to one's earliest years. No earlier writer had taken children so seriously as moral beings.

How such ideas affected the actual lives of children is a question that probably cannot be answered for that period. For the ideas could be adopted with varying degrees of emphasis to suit the parent's disposition. They could also be combined in varying ways, as when later Churchmen wrote introspective memoirs in imitation of Augustine but tended to represent the temptations of their youth as something external, in the manner of Jerome. What is clear is that Christianity directed increased attention to childhood. For the first time in history it seemed important to decide what the moral status of children was. In the midst of this sometimes excessive concern, a new sympathy for children was promoted. Sometimes this meant criticizing adults, as when those memoirs described coarse and worldly fathers. Such frankness would not have occurred to classical authors. So far as parents were put on the defensive in this way, the beginning of the Christian era marks a revolution in the child's status.

Six

A Dark
Age
and the
Revival
of Family
Authority

The fall of the Western Roman empire in the fifth century was the greatest trauma in the history of our civilization. Normally, one would not expect a civilization to survive such a catastrophe, and indeed it did not revive in quite the same form. One would, however, expect family structures to be strengthened as life reverted to more primitive conditions, and that appears to have been just what happened. When other forms of economic production and protection collapsed, the family had to provide social and material security. Whether children were better off within these increasingly powerful families may well be doubted.

The society of the empire had been largely urban. Urban economies tend to take over many of the functions kinship groups had performed, leaving the nuclear and conjugal family greater freedom. Then, the distractions of urban civilization may corrode even that minimum of family life. By contrast, the barbarian peoples who overcame the Romans still lived in an almost tribal situation. Even their primitive economies were organized around the family's combined efforts. These "Germanic" peoples, the ancestors of most modern Europeans, viewed their families much as the early Greeks and Romans had done—as eternal institutions, with the living members serving as the trustees of the family's life and assets.

The one major institution that did survive Rome's fall was the Church. Churchmen admired the barbarians for their devotion to the family and for their domestic virtues. They tended to idealize this more primitive society by contrast with Roman decadence. For while they believed that celibacy was the highest life, they thought the rest of the population was better served by the strong Germanic family than by the rampant individualism of sophisticated Roman society. Churchmen had been told, rightly or wrongly, that these barbarians did not allow infanticide and that mothers nursed their own children. Even the nakedness of the small children appealed to them, showing a more healthy and natural approach to life. Barbarian families seemed to be based on affection more than on economic considerations, as shown by the fact that the wife's dowry, which always served as a kind of insurance policy for widows, was paid by the husband rather than by the wife's family. Adultery was said to be unknown among them. Family loyalty might be a little excessive, as when wives and children came along to battles to cheer their menfolk on. But the Church thought it would be easier to civilize the crude Germanic family than to revitalize the feeble Roman one.

By the end of the darkest age of the medieval period (by about 1000) the Church had gone further in approving this way of life than it wanted to. What it was really aiming at was something between the all-powerful family that sacrifices individuals for the good of the group and what has been called the "atomistic" family that is held together only by the whim of the parents. The Church wanted to consider both the family and the individual sacred. It wanted a partnership bound by charity, the highest of Christian virtues. Granted, this commitment ought to be freely chosen by the individuals involved, but it ought not to be thought of as simply for their individual convenience.

The barbarians' families proved too stubborn for these reformers. On closer observation they tended to resemble the feuding families recently portrayed in *The Godfather.* The pattern of family power presented in that movie seems an aberration today, but it has been typical of the ruling groups in many periods of history. In that story, everything is done in the name of keeping the family supreme in the jungle world it inhabits. When necessary, this involves killing family members whose personal weaknesses threaten to drag the family down. Finally, the family as an emotional and spiritual union is destroyed in the effort to keep it strong, cracking internally from the strain of defending itself against outside enemies. Modern audiences, having a very different idea of the family, might assume that the fresh-cheeked girl being introduced at the family gathering is only marrying the boy she loves. But in fact she is marrying a family and enlisting in a struggle that will prove too much for her. The conjugal unit she had hoped to build disintegrates when her husband is forced to take command of the family's forces. By way of climax, the movie contrasts the family's Catholic profession and its actual practice by superimposing a christening rite on the massacre of the family's enemies.

There was a contrast in the sixth century, too. The Church was more civilized than its new members, who still carried on ferocious feuds. In parts of Holland a murdered family member was not supposed to be buried until the family had avenged him. It was not necessary to kill the guilty party; another member of the offending family would do as well. This is what family solidarity meant in those days. Understandably, the Church supported monarchies that would attempt to control such feuds. The Church also found that some of these groups still practiced infanticide. Deformed children were killed as the devil's changelings, and twins were sometimes murdered on the theory that they were evidence of adultery. The Vikings, the last of these Germanic groups to settle down, had a folklore haunted by the ghosts of dead children—probably the sign of a bad conscience. *Njal's Saga* indicates that the prohibition of infanticide was one of the biggest changes Christianity made in Viking life. The Church tried to be strict; there are records of French women being burned for the crime of killing their infants. But preserving these lives was a lot to ask of people who lived on the edge of survival. Eventually the Church allowed penances for it, taking into account the poverty of parents, accidents, and insanity, which became a common defense.

Compromises were also made for the upper classes. While elite families might not do away with unwanted children, they did pack them off to monasteries and convents to let the Church bear that burden. In fact, this may have been the main source of recruitment to the monastic life in the tenth and eleventh centuries. Children were sometimes dedicated to these institutions even before birth, for the good of the family, which could count on their prayers. The Church hierarchy was also filled with sons of the aristocracy, who were supposed to use their Church offices to promote their families' interests. Thus, while setting out to tame these rival families, the Church was itself undermined by nepotism and family ambition.

The record of the Church's compromises extends into marriage law. Church courts, which had the duty of regulating sacraments like marriage, had limited success in stopping child marriage, which was a traditional way of creating family alliances. The Church only ruled that girls could not marry before age 12 or boys before 14. Church law also tried to limit marriage between kin, which was often for purposes of strengthening existing family ties. But the marriage of first cousins was common among these people and the Church was powerless to stop it, despite Biblical injunctions against the union of such close relatives. Churchmen often successfully intervened to stop forced marriage, especially if a girl had expressed interest in becoming a nun. And there may have been many girls who were attracted to convent life, given the alternative of life in such families.

In ruling against the rights of bastard children, too, the Church seems to have bowed to the demands of the barbarian family. After all, discriminating against the child punishes the wrong person. But families have never wanted to share their wealth with illegitimate offspring. And so the Church courts (which also governed bequests) ruled that they could not inherit property. They also barred those of illegitimate birth from holding Church office. Having done that, the Church compromised once again by issuing special dispensations so that the rich might put their bastards into Church office. In due time there were illegitimate popes. The only surprising thing in all this is that the Church should have felt any embarrassment over it.

The period between the fall of Rome and the year 1000 is the most obscure in all of Western history. We can say little about the lives of children, aside from obvious inferences from the authoritarian family pattern common at that time. Educational institutions always leave some record of their activities, of course, but education was also at its lowest ebb in the history of our civilization. Only a few secular schools survived the political collapse, mostly in Italy. The upper class in Western Europe was a warrior aristocracy which saw no need for literacy. They trained their sons by sending them as pages to other men's courts, to learn to serve at table and on the battlefield. Their daughters learned the arts of needlework and of healing, along with the graces of music and entertainment so that they might enliven the evening with dances or chess or stories. Trade and government were in such a primitive state that there was scarcely a demand for clerks. Only the Church felt the need to carry on an intellectual tradition, so that the clergy could consult Scripture on matters of eternal importance.

The first stirrings of formal education among these new peoples came with the arrival of missionary bishops. One of their first orders of business was to take local boys into their households in order to train them personally for the priesthood. Sometimes they were given the sons of the chiefs themselves; in other places they inherited unwanted orphans. Later, when cathedral churches were set up in each bishop's town, the cathedral staff organized schools for the same purpose. They taught Latin for the purpose of reading the Latin Bible and the writings of the early Church fathers. They taught music (for chanting the service) and astronomy (for calculating the date of Easter). Some teachers who were lucky enough to have read books could not restrain themselves from teaching whatever they knew. They might add Greek and mathematics to the curriculum, out of a pure zeal for learning. For as bad as education then was, it appears that there were children with a real thirst for knowledge. These were later the scholars who compiled histories and encyclopedias which, pitiful as they seem now, helped to keep ancient learning from perishing altogether. Novice monks likewise helped in the effort toward cultural preservation by copying manuscripts. Time was set aside every day for reading as one of the duties and pleasures of the monastic life. Probably the only girls who learned to read were the novice nuns. All other children remained in an oral culture and therefore were subject to the influence of traditional pagan folklore alongside the newer Christian influences.

We do not know whether the few boys who were chosen for schooling felt themselves lucky or not, or exactly how their parents viewed the matter. Often, they were sent away from their families for the process. This was the pattern for all occupational training in Europe. Boys expected to leave home to live with their masters in learning most trades or crafts. Perhaps when the system was just beginning home life was sufficiently impersonal that the change made little difference in emotional terms. But in later years parents felt they had to justify the practice of sending children to live with their masters. There came to be a variety of explanations—to overcome the child's natural shyness, for health, to move up in social status, to pay off some debt to the master. Some of the children hated school. We have a lively account of the pedantry of the time and of one exceptional child's loneliness in the autobiography of the French abbot, Guibert (describing a tutor in the 1060s):

> Now the love that this man had for me was of a savage sort and excessive severity was shewn by him in his unjust floggings; and yet the great care with which he guarded me was evident in his acts. Clearly I did not deserve to be beaten, for if he had had the skill in teaching which he professed, it is certain that I was, as a boy, well able to grasp anything that he taught correctly. . . . For so uninstructed was he that he retained incorrectly what he had, as I have said before, once badly learnt late in life, and if he let anything slip out (incautiously, as it were), he maintained and defended it with blows, regarding all his own opinions as certainly true.

Obviously, some boys were clever enough to know better. Guibert went on to tell how the jealous cruelty of his classmates drove him to find consolation in books:

> Having steeped my mind unduly in the study of verse-making, so as to put aside for such worthless vanities the serious

things of the divine pages, under guidance of my folly I went so far as to read the poems of Ovid and the Bucolics of Virgil and to aim at the airs and graces of a love poem in a critical treatise and in a series of letters. . . . Hence it came to pass that, from the boiling over of the madness within me, I fell into certain obscene words and composed brief writings, worthless and immodest, in fact bereft of all decency.

Apparently no one had thought of censoring his reading.

The only notable attempt before 1000 to encourage a general literacy occurred in England. King Alfred (c. 900) tried to require that all free-born boys learn to read English, if not Latin. He himself helped to translate a number of essential works into English, including the first few books of the Bible. But that is as far as his campaign progressed, for he and his people spent most of the reign fending off Viking invaders.

Civilization remained in a perilous state for centuries. Europeans feared that the rampaging Vikings would snuff out the last embers of literary culture. With no assured future, it would be perfectly understandable if society had given little thought to its children. The Church appears to have recognized their importance to the extension of its influence. But we would hardly expect children to benefit greatly from their place in such a long-range strategy. Very likely there was no one who could afford the luxury of enjoying or encouraging children simply for their own sake.

Seven

Civilization

Begins

Again

After the year 1000 the last wave of barbarians settled down. For once there were no serious external
threats to Western Europe. Trade and town life, which are
essential to what is called civilization, had a notable revival.
There was more building in stone, which shows a certain faith
in the future. Population was increasing. A more settled and
peaceful life made families less defensive, so that the Church
could make some headway in its efforts to promote the ideal of
a more companionable family. These developments could not

help but change the position of the child in the family and in society.

Nothing could better symbolize the new atmosphere than the rise of certain holidays associated with childhood. St. Nicholas's Day (December 6) was fixed as the feast of the patron saint of children and scholars, and during the twelfth century it came to be thought of as children's day. After all, the most famous legends of the saint concerned his bringing murdered children to life and giving dowries to girls to keep them from being sold into prostitution. The latter story may even have started the practice of giving presents to children on St. Nicholas's Eve. In the cathedral schools a boy-bishop was elected on St. Nicholas's Day to rule until Holy Innocents' Day on December 28—the commemoration of the massacre of the children in Bethlehem. This little "bishop" was allowed to parade through the streets with his schoolmates, blessing houses and begging money. He even preached a sermon, sometimes written for him but always affecting childish sentiments. It was a time when children were allowed to relax in the middle of a long, vacationless winter. Adults thought these festivities charming and extended the practice to parish churches as well. But things quickly got out of hand. Children abused their freedom; they burlesqued the bishop's activities and indulged their delight in obscenity. Before the end of the twelfth century the Church was already trying to prohibit boy-bishops, but the practice proved too popular to stop.

These two holy days bracketed most of December, and so it was inevitable that Christmas itself would come to be associated with children. Traditionally, Christmas had not been a very important part of the Church's year. Rather, the emphasis had been on Christ's (adult) baptism as the beginning of his divine mission. The Apollinarian heresy, which denied Jesus's humanity, had awakened the Church to the need to celebrate his human birth. And now the Feast of the Nativity on December 25 became part of a more general recognition of childhood. Epiphany (January 6), which originally had commemorated Jesus's baptism, was so overshadowed by Christmas that in the twelfth century it was taken to refer to the visit of the Magi—a rather different manifestation to the world. All 12 days between these feasts were thus associated with the childhood of Jesus, and children everywhere had a recognized place in the festivities.

This new recognition of children coincided with certain social changes which allowed or encouraged the relaxation of family authority. For one thing, the rise of a market economy meant that people were forced to deal with others who were not their kinfolk. In many parts of Europe this was a new experience. Businessmen acquired obligations outside their own family group. When they moved, for economic reasons, it was no longer in tribes but as nuclear families. It was always easier for townspeople to move their businesses than for farmers to do so. And there would be the same freedom for each new generation of children, with an ever wider choice of careers and mates.

Thus, town life proved more conducive to smaller, conjugal families. As far back as historians can trace the history of these towns they have found the conjugal and nuclear family pattern— by the tenth century in France and Spain, for instance. As a social ideal, it still did not have the prestige of the extended aristocratic family. And it may be that most households were extended at certain points in the normal life cycle—right after a child's marriage or when only one grandparent was left, for example. But the trend in urban society was toward smaller, more intimate family groups. The chances of children eventually breaking free of such families to establish their own was greater than in the rural society surrounding them.

Another factor that helped lessen the power of kinfolk was the growing habit of keeping up with both the father's relations and the mother's. In ancient Rome the wife left her family altogether (they even called it "emancipation") to become a part of her husband's family. In Christian tradition, however, not only the woman but the man was said to "leave his father and mother, and cleave unto his wife" (both Jesus and Paul quoted those words from Genesis 2:24). Of course, the result of keeping in touch with both groups of relations was that the number of family bonds increased twice as fast as in a simple patrilinear system. But they must have counted for less. One can maintain only so many family obligations, beginning with the nearer relations on both sides. So children could now begin to chose from among those relations, defining their kinship circle as they pleased. When caught in family quarrels, the younger generation might now object that their obligations were unclear. This new freedom was symbolized when family names came into common use (from the twelfth century on) and we find girls sometimes using their mothers' maiden surnames. Joan of Arc, for instance, was sometimes called Jeanne Romée. The very fact that people now needed family names shows the decline of family. It had not been necessary to be labeled in this way in an earlier, more sedentary age.

The new political states also wanted to reduce the power of families, at least among the aristocracy, for the great families were the closest rivals to the authority of monarchs. When William the Conqueror tried to abolish the right of family vengeance in England (c. 1080), the nobles complained of this "tyrannical" interference in their affairs. But governments persisted, protecting those who deserted their families rather than serve in family feuds, for example. Aristocratic families did get their way in certain respects. Under weak kings they got the courts to recognize the family's right to pass on to their children the lands and offices which former kings had granted them. In some countries this principle of inheritance was extended even to daughters, who could not perform the military services which were at the very basis of the feudal bargain.

In addition, the Church was finally able to insist on what it took to be the proper standards of family life. The conjugal family, which seemed to be the model implied in Scripture, offered the best balance between responsibility and individual freedom. So the Church courts ruled that parents could not block a marriage forever by withholding their consent. (They could, of course, withhold an inheritance in such a case.) The Church insisted on the consent of both parties to the marriage, to save mere children from being forced into this step by their families. Only a public marriage before witnesses who could attest to the free consent of the partners was valid; therefore it was to be performed in the church porch and not in the groom's house, as was customary. The Church tried to prohibit the gift paid by the groom to the bride or her parents, for, like a dowry, this indicated a treaty between families rather than a union between individuals. Wives should not need property of their own to feel secure. Rather, the Church promoted the concept of community of property, which showed the moral and spiritual basis of the union. Finally, the Church insisted that divorce be handled in its courts and not by parents or kin, as before. It only failed in its effort to insist that a priest officiate at the marriage ceremony, according to the sacramental rite. The necessity for this was not established until the early modern period in many parts of Europe.

Recognition of the Church's authority in these matters increased as its values began to penetrate more deeply into European society. Peace, humility, mutual aid, and respect for the individual were beginning to compete with the older, aristocratic virtues of courage, honor, dominance, and group loyalty. And as it tried to soften a brutal age, the Church found that it could use the child's image in this task. Apparently there was sympathy for children which could be generalized for use in behalf of all the weak and needy. That sympathy was often only implied. One monk's chronicle of King Stephen's reign in England (c. 1130) recounted the story of a nobleman who gave his son as hostage and then proceeded to break his pledged word. When friends reminded him of what this would mean for his son, he shrugged it off, saying that he could always make more sons. Clearly, the writer expected the account to shock his readers. Churchmen found that they could enlist this sympathy for the child's plight to discredit the forces of oppression.

St. Bernard of Clairvaux (c. 1140), the foremost writer of his time, did the most to promote a sentimentalism which could be associated with the figure of the child. The infant Jesus and his mother occupied an important place in his devotional writings. Unlike earlier writers, Bernard was interested not by the power of the Virgin or Christ but by their humanity. Worshippers were reminded of the sympathy they could expect, born of fellow-suffering and weakness. It would appear that Europeans had found the leisure to remember God's love after centuries in which they had primarily admired His omnipotence. The child was the perfect symbol of their new tenderness.

Soon after Bernard's time, art began to play on this theme. The traditional pose for the Madonna and Child was with both facing front and the solemn infant Savior raising his hand in blessing. Other signs of his power might be present. But by 1200, the two were often pictured turning toward each other and smiling, with the infant caressing his mother or even nursing. (It is an odd fact that for several centuries artists were more likely to show the infant caressing the mother than the reverse, per-haps showing the inability of adults to be very giving.) Even more surprising to viewers was the fact that the infant Christ might be portrayed playing with a ball or fruit, like any other child. The ball or apple might have had a theological significance for the artist, representing the eternal soul or the remedy for Adam's curse. But to worshippers they must have suggested a more natural childhood even for the Savior. The same message is found in the scenes of him eagerly opening the wise men's gifts. One can hardly overestimate the importance of such a change in the symbolism of that illiterate age.

There is some question whether the Church's interest was in childhood generally or only in certain exceptional children. Medieval saints' lives commonly had something to say of the childhood years of those saints. But usually it is to indicate how very unusual they were even as children, as when St. Benedict miraculously fixed a sieve for his nurse. It was as though these children did not have personalities they could call their own. On the other hand, in some art—such as the scenes of Eve nursing her children or of Herod's massacre of the innocents in Bethlehem—ordinary children were treated more realistically even than the new, more natural Christ.

The Church did concern itself with matters of practical benefit to real children. Several books of child-rearing advice exist from the thirteenth century, which, of course, were by Churchmen. Because they could write, we know more of their attitudes toward children than we do of parents' concerns. Churchmen could be realistic in their treatment of children; one English clergyman described boys as

> living without thought or care, loving only to play, fearing no danger more than being beaten with a rod, always hungry and hence always disposed to various infirmities from being overfed, wanting everything they see, quick to laughter, and as quick to tears, resisting their mothers' effort to wash and comb them, and no sooner clean but dirty again.

Girls he considered naturally more obedient, quiet, and graceful.

The advice they gave was mostly concerned with urging parents to pay more attention to their children and to be more strict in their care. They praised women who nursed their own babies rather than leaving them to hired nurses. They made a host of practical suggestions, advising cradles for infants in order to avoid the danger of suffocating them in their parents' bed. Many offered directions on washing and other pediatric matters, and they repeated the older ideas on how to make education pleasant by the use of games and alphabet cards. They even suggested how discipline might be accomplished by love rather than by force. One German writer ruled out physical punishment altogether:

> Children won't do what they ought
> If you beat them with a rod.
> Children thrive, children grow
> When taught by words, and not a blow. . . .
> Evil words, words unkind
> Will do harm to a child's mind.

This was not a common sentiment at this time, however, for beating was still considered an essential part of child rearing and education.

Teachers sometimes suffered pangs of conscience and defended themselves by blaming parents for being too permissive. The sermon composed for one boy-bishop in 1558 joked that the age of innocence was now ending long before age seven and that this was forcing schoolmasters to be more strict. A few parents saw this as cruelty, however. A schoolmaster was fined £40 in 1480 for beating the son of a Bristol merchant. The students themselves could only dream of revenge, as one did in the following verse:

> I wold my master were an hare,
> And all his bokes howndes were,
> And I myself a joly hontere;
> To blow my horn I wold not spare,
> For if he were dede I would not care!

Churchmen sometimes warned each other against excessive discipline, suggesting that teachers confine themselves to switching the children or pulling their hair, for this did less real damage than kicking, slapping, or slugging.

The Church was more directly involved in the lives of older children. By the twelfth century, some schools were outgrowing their original role of training priests. Certain teachers began to broaden the horizons of education by pursuing more philosophical questions with their students. The schools that could attract famous teachers like Abelard drew students from all over Europe. Children, often around 14, came long distances to such great international centers as Paris, forming Europe's first universities. There they lived a bohemian life, taking care of each other as best they could. The surviving evidence mostly records their scrapes with the townspeople who so often took advantage of them, rather than giving us a sense of the intellectual adventure which must have accompanied this educational revival.

The Church had not overseen the rise of these universities, but it came to feel some responsibility for the students. Soon it was asserting control over the students' lives by providing hostels or dormitories to protect and discipline these youngsters. Later, when the Church became alarmed over the direction some of the debates might take, it also began to regulate instruction. As for educating girls, Churchmen were not agreed as to its desirability. Some, like Vincent of Beauvais, thought that upper-class girls should be taught to read and write. But others thought that only those destined for the convent would have any need for those skills. It had not yet occurred to anyone that there might be schools for girls.

Finally, the Church bore some responsibility for the episode known as the Children's Crusade (1212). Later accounts of this affair give a rather false impression of what happened, but they are quite revealing of contemporary attitudes toward children. According to those accounts, the crusade was the idea of two boys, Nicholas of Cologne and Stephen of Cloyes. Stephen, a French shepherd boy, was inspired by a vision of Christ announcing that the Cross and the holy places of Palestine could be recovered only by innocent children. So he bravely set out with a group that was said to have numbered some 30,000 boys and girls, many of them under 12. This crowd headed for the Mediterranean coast, expecting the waters to part like the Red Sea so that they could walk to the Holy Land. Their eventual goal was to appeal to the infidel Moslems to open the holy sites to Christian pilgrims. Nicholas guided a hoard of German children over the Alps into Italy on a similar errand.

Even these chronicles do not pretend that the crusade was anything but a disaster. Pope Innocent III was said to have approved the children's zeal. He was even then trying to interest Europe in a crusade and was reported to have declared: "The very children put us to shame. While we sleep they go forth joyfully to conquer the Holy Land." But the chroniclers do not hide the fact that the children were robbed, raped, and kidnapped along the way. And in the end, when the sea did not fold back, some shipowners who promised to take them across actually sold them into Arab slavery.

Where these histories exaggerate is in their glorification of the children's role in the incident. The earliest allusions to the crusade, which appear in local records, indicate that only a part of either group were actually children, though most were young. It also appears that the French episode was not connected with the German one and never considered going to the Holy Land. It was more like the crowds that wandered after certain miracle workers, or like the outbreaks of the "dancing madness" which probably led to the story of the Pied Piper of Hamelin. One such incident occurred in Erfurt in 1237, taking a large number of children away in a kind of religious ecstasy. The German crusade was in a tradition of popular crusades in which the poor had gone along with the armies and had represented the Christian virtues of humility and dependence on God—virtues feared lacking in the knights.

As the tale grew, the children's role came to dominate the story. This fit nicely with the cult of childhood which the Church was encouraging. The monks who had seen the crowds and first recorded the events had shown a marked hostility to these crusades. They were uneasy with any glorification of poverty, since it was so often an implied criticism of Church wealth. And the idea that God must use children where adults had failed was a slur on the earlier crusades. We know that the clergy in charge of the University of Paris had tried to discourage students from taking part. But later chroniclers viewed the episode in a new light. They had long been disposed to approve childhood generally, and now they began to remember the movement as an example of the innocent zeal of children—sad as the ending might be. The notion of children charming the fiendish Moslems must have inspired St. Francis in his similar attempt shortly afterward.

It may seem odd that a celibate clergy should have been so concerned with children in the Middle Ages. But perhaps the very fact that they were childless and that many of them had been left to the Church as "oblates" (or offerings) had directed their attention that way. A sense of loss may have caused them to focus on childhood and to show a sensitivity toward the children who were so abundant in that day. We need not suppose that all of the attention they gave to children was beneficial. But some of them were promoting the notion that love of children was a sign of good nature. It is a frequent theme in the legends of the saints.

Common people in this period left very little evidence of their thoughts—about children or anything else. The evidence they did leave with regard to children is not encouraging. One has only to think of our traditional nursery stories. Snow White, Hansel and Gretel, and the rest live very threatened lives. Many of these folktales were being elaborated in the Middle Ages. Medieval stories, as we find them preserved in contemporary manuscripts, show children primarily as the victims of adult misconduct—adultery, incest, abandonment. Many of the characters do not know their parents' identity, and plots often turn on a child's discovery of his or her parentage. Stepparents and other hostile adults often are bent on doing away with them. When the children are sometimes forced to kill the adults in the story, they are always justified in doing so.

The following examples from a collection of medieval English stories are chosen as typical rather than extreme cases. "Octavian" concerns the Emperor Octavian (Augustus) and his wife, who bears him twins. At first he does not accept the usual explanation for twins—that it is a sign of adultery. But the Emperor's mother convinces him by planting a cook's boy in the Empress's bed. Octavian then leaves his wife and the boys in a forest, where an ape takes one son away and a lioness the other. The mother finds the latter on an island, transported there by a griffin. The other boy changes hands several times before being taken in by a Parisian butcher. He never accepts the story that he is the butcher's son and proves his noble blood by showing exceptional courage (talking back to his foster-father) and initiative (trading the family's ox for a falcon for himself). Having established his right to the noble profession of soldiering, he distinguishes himself in a war and gains the love of the Sultan's daughter. As it happens, Octavian visits the Sultan just then and meets his son. Taking a liking to the youth, he questions him about his parents. When the truth comes out the family is happily reunited.

"Sir Degare" might have saved Freud years in formulating the concept of the Oedipus complex. It tells of a child who was conceived by an incestuous rape and exposed in the woods. The boy survives and at age ten goes searching for his parents. He is lucky enough to have a glove that will fit only his mother's hand, and his father's sword—which is missing its tip. The glove just saves him from marrying his mother. And he is only prevented from killing his father in a fight when the father recognizes the sword he is using and produces the missing point.

What could have made these stories and countless others like them so excessively popular? Of course, we cannot assume they literally represent social reality. Stories like these are still popular, after all, because they represent a psychological reality that is common to every age. Children fear abandonment even when there is no chance of its happening. All children's folklore contains the theme of cruelty and helps children to work through their fears. But there is a difference between then and now. These were not considered specifically children's stories then but were enjoyed by all age groups. Could this mean that such concerns were not successfully resolved by large numbers of adults? In addition, these stories were not fossilized relics, as they are today. They were constantly in the process of creation and revision by the adults who told them. Therefore we are probably justified in thinking that they come far closer to representing the true circumstances of childhood then than now.

The many tales of what witches and Jews were supposed to do to little children raise the same suspicions about those who told them. The Jews were accused of sacrificing Christian children and ritually drinking their blood. Witches were imagined roasting and eating children and using their fat and other byproducts to make the magic salves that they rubbed on their brooms. Those who suspected everyone around them of this kind of foul play may themselves have been haunted by the memory of dead children. At least it arouses our suspicion when infanticide is the first accusation they thought to use against outsiders.

The fact that the reader or listener was meant to identify with the child naturally softens this picture of the child's plight. The impact of such stories would have been lost entirely had there been no sympathy for children and no conscience against abandoning them. But what seems lacking is any alternative literature that shows a greater realism in the portrayal of child characters. Apparently even grownups delighted in stories of children of superhuman strength who might put whole armies of Saracens to flight. Others of these child heroes were endowed with incredible intelligence. That makes all the more surprising the one account that shows greater realism than the ancient tale from which it derived. Herodotus, the Greek historian, had described an experiment to see which was the natural language of humankind. An Egyptian and a Phrygian child were isolated at birth to discover what language they would speak without any social influences. The experiment was supposed to have ended when they used the Phrygian word for bread. In the thirteenth century, the eccentric German Emperor Frederick II tried to duplicate the test, and a chronicler recorded the sorry result:

> He bade foster mothers and nurses to suckle the children, to bathe and wash them, but in no way to prattle with them or to speak to them, for he wanted to learn whether they would speak the Hebrew language, which was the oldest, or Greek, or Latin, or Arabic, or perhaps the language of their parents, of whom they had been born. But he labored in vain, because the children all died. For they could not live without the petting and the joyful faces and loving words of their foster mothers.

It sounds like a description of what psychologists call "hospitalism." One wonders where the Emperor got the subjects for this experiment on the question of nature versus nurture.

Civilization began to reassert itself in the West during what we call the medieval period. One of the forces it had to contend with was the family. Families had been largely a law unto themselves until the other institutions of the medieval period arose to check the absolute power of parents. The Church now tried to awaken some notion of the child's individual worth. Political authorities sometimes extended their power in the name of protecting the individual. An increase in commerce made the family less significant in the economy. Schools grew, however slowly. In time, these institutions would struggle more openly for individual loyalties. Childhood would become a contested territory. For the moment, the West could congratulate itself that it was at least beyond the point of simply producing a future generation. It was already seeking to improve conditions for it.

Eight

Renaissance Childhood and Creativity

"Renaissance" is the name historians give to the period of history in which an interest in Roman and Greek literature stimulated a rebirth of art and speculation. In fifteenth-century Italy, and later in other parts of Europe, there was a truly marvelous outpouring of creative activity. Popular histories have perhaps made too much of all this, giving the impression that Renaissance thinkers made a greater break with the past than was the case. We are sometimes led to believe that the Middle Ages had been devoid of intellectual activity, when in fact the Renaissance grew out of the ferment of medieval thought. But the fact remains that there was a remarkable stirring in many fields of intellectual and artistic life.

One might expect that such creative people must have had remarkable childhoods. We would like to think that the period must have been an enjoyable time to live, if it saw this kind of progress. But there is another view of creativity, which emphasizes the difficulty and even agony of the process. After all, creativity at such high artistic levels involves seeing things from new perspectives. What would help a person develop this ability better than the feeling of being an outsider, or practice in overcoming some handicap? Just as sensitivity is produced by being rubbed a little raw at some point, so creativity may be induced by some tension. All in all, it may be more fun to watch the creative life than to be involved in it. The question is, which of these general conditions seems to have characterized the world in which the Renaissance artists grew up? Was it a time of general happiness and prosperity or not? And what can we say of family life at the time when Europe began to modernize?

In the first place, while the period was one of economic expansion, this in itself brought some strains. Economic disruptions were behind the search for new trade routes, resulting in the famous geographical discoveries of that time. Trade wars were endemic, especially among the Italian city-states. And even within these small states, powerful families were often dangerously at odds. The great merchant families, like the landed aristocrats of earlier times, took on a military character to protect their wealth and position. Even today one can see the family compounds within the Renaissance town. The houses of a kin group were sometimes built around a square so that they could be sealed off as a fortress. At first, the life of these family groups was carried on in the square rather than in the houses, which were sparsely furnished. But when the family ventured outside, to parade its power and wealth, even the children were part of the show. They were dressed as richly as adults for this competitive display. In the home they do not seem to have had this importance; inside the compounds cousins lived together under the eye of whatever adults could be spared for the task.

Judging from art and architecture, the nuclear family was taking on a somewhat greater importance among the upper classes during the fifteenth century. Bigger houses were built to accommodate more of the family's activities indoors. This meant excluding relatives, as the modern habit of privacy became the fashion. Larger interiors gave artists more work, so that the decorative arts became as important as religious art. In particular, these families wanted pictures idealizing the family, or at least the Holy Family. The demand for scenes of the mother-child relation became almost an obsession with Italians in this period. It was perhaps the single most important motif in Florentine art at the height of the Renaissance.

But again, we should not assume that this new devotion to the more immediate family meant devotion to children. Individualism did not extend to women or children in this age. The most dramatic evidence of social subordination is in the way girls were passed from their own families to those of their husbands. Despite the Church's efforts, the bride often had little to say in choosing her master and her new family. As in ancient Athens, the age difference between husbands and wives had grown so that Florentine girls first married at 18 on the average, and their husbands at 30, so far as fifteenth-century records show. This widening difference was due to the increasingly ruthless economic competition of the time, which led families to demand that brides bring higher dowries. For dowries had returned even in urban society, with the rise of a "merchant aristocracy." The bride's new family might use it as capital until the husband's death required its return to the widow. The price of marrying off one's daughters rose so high that many girls were sent to convents instead, but the richer families could demand older, more substantial husbands for the available girls. This age difference again meant little companionship in the union. Mothers would therefore invest more emotional energy in relations with their children at a certain stage, thereby reproducing the social and perhaps the psychological patterns of the Greeks. Thus Renaissance Italians found one more link with the Greeks whom they admired. And indeed there were increasing complaints of maternal domination, effeminacy, and homosexuality in fifteenth-century Florence.

The miserable experience of one Genoese girl, Giovanna Embrone, shows the plight of these diplomatic pawns. Giovanna's marriage was arranged to guarantee an agreement between enemy families. But the hostility proved too great for this kind of solution, so her brothers forced her to will her dowry to them rather than to her own daughter. This would bring it back into her original family. When they later murdered her husband, she tried to escape to a convent in order to be left alone. But the brothers appeared again, to keep the dowry from reverting to the Church. This meant persuading her to demand release from her vows, on the ground that she had been mad with grief when she took them. One would presume that the poor girl had left her daughter behind with her husband's family, since children belonged not so much to the parents as to the larger family; a son would undoubtedly have had to stay to take his father's place in the lineage.

The age difference between husbands and wives also meant that fathers were more likely to die when their children were still young. So it became fashionable for these fathers, 30 or even 40 years older than their children, to leave testaments of moral advice to make up for a lack of personal communication between the generations. Their advice related not to childhood but to family affairs. Children were important, but primarily as family heirs and not as individuals. With such responsibilities they could hardly expect to be coddled. If it seemed they would get the family into trouble, the family could get rid of them by legal "emancipation," so as not to be held accountable for their debts or crimes. On the other hand, if the family ran short of heirs, it adopted some, choosing relatives if possible. But blood ties were not as important as the family's fear of losing power, wealth, and status. Thus it was that after the Black Death, completely unrelated individuals joined to form artificial kinship groups rather than to exist without this family support. A search for power and security, rather than emotional attachment, was what kept families together.

Lower on the social scale, young people had more freedom. With less family money at stake, they often had more say in the choice of a mate. They tended to be a little older when they married, since they were not rushed into it by their parents. The families of skilled laborers in Italy were already conjugal and nuclear, and there was a larger element of sentiment in their relations. Artisans sometimes named their wives as heirs, for instance, whereas in aristocratic families children would have inherited the family property. And it appears that working-class husbands beat their wives more frequently than aristocrats. In an unfortunate way, even this demonstrates the greater emotional intensity of those families. For aristocrats did their fighting with fathers, uncles, and brothers in their more extended families.

While we might think of the conjugal family and nuclear household as more modern and desirable, the working classes did not consider it the ideal arrangement. It was too likely to break up when a parent died. Grandparents and other kin might not live close enough to help a family broken by death; the new family might have left home to find work, settling some distance from their relatives. Widows and widowers were forced to consider remarriage because of the economics of their situation, thus bringing strangers into the child's life. Faced with this insecurity, the extended households of the upper class remained the ideal.

As families prospered they tried to keep more of the family together. Sons were kept at home if the business could support them, and daughters might bring their husbands into the family home.

What can we say of the child's life in these circumstances? It began, rather unfortunately, with the nursing arrangements. Even the wives of skilled laborers, many of whom worked, preferred to hire wet-nurses rather than suffering the inconvenience of nursing their own children. Nursing was work for peasants, and sending infants out to nurse was one of the first luxuries women demanded. Some of the experts of the day protested against wet-nursing for the indifference it showed. But even they realistically proceeded to advise on how to choose a nurse. Following Soranus, they thought she should be healthy. But just as important, she should be of a good disposition, since they believed that the milk somehow contained the nurses' personal traits. One biographer noted that Michelangelo's nurse was a stone-cutter's wife, by way of explaining his interest in sculpture. This belief was one reason for not using animal milk. Only the poor were reduced to using goat's or cow's milk, and many thought that this might be the reason they seemed to share these animals' stupidity. As one contemporary put it, "A boy or girl nourished on animal milk doesn't have perfect wits like one fed on women's milk, but always looks stupid and vacant and not right in the head." Probably many nurses were forced to use animal milk when they went dry. Parents were unlikely to discover this, since they rarely visited their infants before it was time to take them home, at about two years of age. Illegitimate children were sometimes left even longer, for five or even ten years.

Obviously, women did not want children in order to enjoy them as infants. If parents were trying to protect themselves against the grief of an infant's death, this would be perfectly understandable. Neither did nurses pretend to go into the business for the love of working with children. It was a business and often took second place to other work. Thus they would often leave the baby swaddled just to keep it safe and out of the way. In short, wet-nursing meant neglect for all children. The nurse's own children would have reason to resent the intruder into their home. So the children of the rich might feel that neither of their first two families really wanted them. If a nurse became sick, the parents did not bring the infant home, but looked for another nurse. And when the child finally did come home she might not attach herself to the mother, but to an aunt, grandmother, or orphaned cousin.

Leonardo da Vinci is an example of a child who was displaced from several households in this way. His situation was complicated by illegitimacy. Being passed from his mother to a series of stepmothers further disrupted his life. This inevitably raises a point about Renaissance art. We have already said that the most common theme in that art was the subject of mothers and children. Leonardo himself contributed some of the most natural and joyful portraits of maternal affection in the history of Western art. His earliest drawings were of children and laughing mothers, and late in life he came back to this theme. The face of Mona Lisa began to fascinate him. He worked for four years on that haunting smile, with its mixture of seduction and reserve, and could never bring himself to part with the picture. Even then it did not satisfy him; he kept trying to reproduce the smile in later paintings, most notably in the "Madonna and Child with St. Anne." It even appears in his paintings of gods and men, as if to symbolize a lasting uncertainty over his acceptance. We may well imagine that it reminded him of the unhappy loss of his mother, the peasant girl whom he remembered from his earliest year.

It was in puzzling over Leonardo's life that Freud formulated his concept of narcissism. Leonardo was, for him, the classic case of the sexual disorientation which might result from an interruption of normal development by the loss of one's mother. In this case, it could explain his sexual indifference on the one hand and also his restless curiosity and the sublimation of vast energies in art and invention. Freud did not think his analysis discredited Leonardo's art. Great art transcends whatever conflicts may help produce it, as shown by its ability to speak profoundly to other periods with different psychological styles. It can justify a diversion of energy from more immediate forms of gratification by helping a society to live with itself and its particular psychological difficulties. But it may also give historians a clue as to what those difficulties were.

Leonardo was not the whole of "the Renaissance," of course, but his is the first name that comes to mind when we think of that creative epoch. No psychological explanation can account for his artistic powers, but it may explain his artistic *interests* and why his age needed to express these themes. The tender scenes of mothering which meet us everywhere in Renaissance art do not represent social reality very accurately. The fact that madonnas, both religious and secular, reached the height of their popularity in the Renaissance does not seem to have resulted from better mothering. It may well have been the reverse—a compensation for the loss of one's home. This would follow from the growing practice of paying someone else to care for one's children in their most demanding years.

The fact that artists had finally mastered the anatomic proportions of babies—with heads a quarter of the length of bodies instead of a sixth, as with adults—might lead us to suppose they were beginning to understand children better. But our suspicions are immediately aroused by the fact that their paintings do not show infants swaddled, though this was the universal custom. It was an idealized childhood which fascinated them, not the everyday reality. And it is not long before we find the telltale signs of sentimentalism. By the time of Raphael (1500), the children are almost too appealing, indicating a failure to resolve some aspect of childhood that kept bringing the artist back. The child characters in Shakespeare's plays have this same sweetness, too loving and brave to be quite real. As with other playwrights of that day, his children serve as figures of pathos, to enlist sympathy against the villains. It would aid this theory if we could show that Raphael himself was a victim of notable neglect. Unfortunately his biographer, Vasari, tells us: "Because his father knew of what consequence it was that the child should be nursed by his own mother and not left to the care of a hired nurse, he kept him in his own house that he might learn good ways." The fact that this seemed worthy of comment shows how untypical it was. Perhaps by Raphael's time the glamorized treatment of children had become traditional with artists and demanded by patrons. It would not always imply the indulgence of a personal need.

Some of the children in Renaissance paintings were simply philosophical symbols. For the little figures we call "cherubs" represented love or the gods of love, as they had in the Greek *erotes* and the *putti* of Roman art. Raphael gave them a theological significance, scattering them through the heavens to represent God's love, the great impulse behind all creation. Thus, these child figures formed the link between earth and heaven. They were a denial that space was empty or lifeless, as scientists were beginning to suppose. In their dancing and music-making these infants represented the joy of life that was God's gift. Renaissance artists also revived the use of adolescent figures, which the ancients had used to symbolize Eros himself. These pubescent figures appear, in exquisite poses, as the Angel in scenes of the Annunciation.

The new attention artists paid children did not break the pattern of sending infants away at birth. Moralists continued to write against this practice, answering a host of common objections which boil down to the fact that nursing was inconvenient and unfashionable. And yet one can find evidence of genuine sympathy for children at this time. Some parents were not indifferent to the death of their babies, despite high mortality. There are many examples like the letter describing an outbreak of plague in Italy around 1400: "At the same time in one bed were Antonia sick unto death and the other boy who died. Think how my heart broke, seeing the little ones suffer and their mother not well or strong, and hearing the words of the older one." On the other hand, we read that some parents had abandoned their children in the process of fleeing that plague. Historians can trade such examples of concern or neglect for any period in history. There were all kinds of parents, then as now.

Any discussion of childhood during the Renaissance should say something of the increased concern for education, which was a major thrust of the Renaissance. "Humanism" was, first, a rebirth of interest in Roman and Greek literature. The schoolroom experience should have been crucial to the birth of any such enthusiasm. However, we cannot say that schools were notably more pleasant in 1500 than they had been in 1100. Humanists loved to write on school reform and lamented the tradition of beating children for failure in their lessons. But there is nothing to indicate that beating declined. All the prints we have of schoolrooms then show a switch, usually a bundle of twigs, either in the master's hand or within easy reach. Often we see it in use. Some historians surmise that beating was on the increase in Renaissance schools.

There is no conclusive evidence on this point. But after all, students may have been having more trouble in school. The curriculum was more impractical than in the medieval schools, for classical Latin did not have the practical value medieval Latin had—in the law courts and in the Church. Classical Latin was a dead language which students were told would someday unlock the glories of ancient literature for them. In the meantime, it may have seemed a pointless drudgery. At the same time that education was becoming less practical, more children were being sent to school than ever before. The aristocracy now saw the need for a more academic training than they had once received as pages. But this meant there were more students who had little or no aptitude for schoolwork. In addition, proponents of the new education liked to speak of it as a toughening process, to appeal to an aristocracy that had always considered schooling to be effeminate as well as plebian. The training of the knight had always involved more agony than that of a priest. As education began to involve the knightly class it became a test of courage, and pain became a more recognized part of the toughening process. Even in the universities, regulations now had more to say regarding corporal punishment.

Teachers, for the most part, were still drawn from the same group of unemployed and unhappy clergymen as always. They were not much appreciated. As one Englishman put it somewhat later (in 1678): "Were the particular salaries of school-masters throughout the Land set forth in a table, it is not to be feared that their ample patrimony would excite the covetousness or envy of the reader." It is true that the Renaissance was the first time some individuals began to look on grammar school teaching as a real calling. And they produced works on educational method which were kindly, suggesting ways to make the process of language instruction as logical as possible and discouraging violent punishment. But all this may have made little difference in practice. Whenever we read of the students' actual life we still hear of tyrannical masters. Resistance to change is great, and masters who had been whipped did the same to their students.

Judging from autobiographies and other references, many in the early modern period could only speak with a shudder of the years spent at school. Richard Steele, in 1711, complained of the best of the schools:

No Man who has passed through this way of Education, but must have seen an ingenuous Creature expiring with Shame, with pale Looks, beseeching Sorrow, and silent Tears, throw up its honest Eyes, and kneel on its tender Knees to an inexorable Blockhead, to be forgiven the false Quantity of a Word in making a Latin Verse: The Child is punished, and the next Day he commits a like Crime, and so a third with the same consequence.

Steele thought that "the Sense of Shame and Honour is enough to keep the World it self in Order without Corporal Punishment, much more to train the Minds of uncorrupted and innocent Children." He blamed this cruelty on a lack of discernment of the child's abilities and natural disposition:

Let the Child's Capacity be forthwith examined, and he sent to some Mechanick Way of Life, without Respect to his Birth, if Nature design'd him for nothing higher; let him go before he has innocently suffered, and is debased into a Dereliction of Mind for being what it is no Guilt to be, a plain Man.

Steele represents a later, more reflective period as it outgrew the rigors of Renaissance education.

School often killed all interest in learning, so that graduates read almost nothing in the classical languages in later life. Still, it would be a mistake to think that more demanding schools affected all students the same way. The most prominent school in England in the middle of the seventeenth century was Westminster School under the notoriously brutal Dr. Richard Busby. It produced architect Christopher Wren, philosopher John Locke, poet John Dryden, and scientist Robert Hooke. One can hardly imagine these men doing any better in their respective fields as a result of kinder treatment. But one contemporary, John Aubrey, observed: "Dr. Busby hath made a number of good Scholars, but I have heard several of his Scholars affirme, that he hath marred by his severity more than he hath made." In general, Aubrey thought that "the common way of teaching is so long, tedious, and praeposterous, that it breakes the spirit of the fine tender ingeniose youths and causes 'em perfectly to hate learning."

All of which brings us back to our point, that the ability to be creative often develops through the experience of pain and disorientation. If the schools were in fact more severe, that very fact may have made some contribution to the outburst of cultural activity in the Renaissance. We would like to think that beautiful art and poetry represent a joyful and wholly natural response to life. But it may be that the beauty the artist creates largely represents a compensation for the lack of just such a natural response. It is notoriously easy to find some neurotic quality in almost any famous artist or thinker. Perhaps the same holds true for a whole society that is notable for its contributions to civilization. When Renaissance thinkers reflected on the creative process, they did not imagine it was simply an uninhibited indulgence of natural instincts, however they might talk of the artist's inborn genius. They did not think of art as self-expression, as the later Romantics held. Rather, art was hard work, building on the traditions inherited from the ancients. They believed art was sufficiently important that children should be steered toward it. Benvenuto Cellini recalled that his father had designed him to be a musician and composer and his younger brother to be a lawyer. In other ages that order would probably have been reversed. As it happened, neither boy entirely satisfied the father's wish, for Benvenuto became a sculptor and his brother a soldier.

Like the Greeks, men of the Renaissance knew the difference between excellence and self-indulgence. They expected nothing from their children until they had learned the artistic traditions of the past. And they and their children paid the price. Perhaps it should not surprise us that the theme of tragedy reappeared in their literature, after an interval of a thousand years.

To end on a brighter note, we should observe that these were the years when the toy industry was born, as one feature of the economic diversification of that period. Of course, there were toys before this, probably made by parents for their own children. Having parents make the toys may be the ideal way to arrange things. But if it is left to parents, it often will not get done. And so, whether because of greater demand, increasing wealth, or busier parents, the division of labor was extended to the commercial production of toys.

Most of the toys pictured in medieval illuminations could have been homemade—tops, kites (sometimes in the dragon shapes favored by the Chinese), pinwheels, hobby horses, and glove puppets (some with live birds sewn inside to make them move). But by the thirteenth century there were lead soldiers and horses and glass animals, which would have been beyond the technical capacity of most fathers. By 1400 we know there were professional toymakers in Nuremberg, making jointed wooden dolls. Nuremberg and Augsburg, in southern Germany, long remained the centers of the toy trade, exporting to Italy and France. By 1700 the Dutch were producing enough toys to export them to England and Scandinavia. Dolls were among the earliest items of trade between the English colonists and the American Indians. One of the earliest paintings from the New World shows an Indian child clutching a doll in grownup Elizabethan costume.

Again, we are reminded that toys were not exclusively for children. The costumed doll in that painting was like all others in being an adult figure, painted according to the latest fashion. The most elaborate ones, whose clothes were not carved but sewn, were used as fashion models in dress shops. When doll houses spread from Germany to the rest of Europe in the seventeenth century it is likely that they, too, were for adults rather than for children; they were astonishingly elaborate, with miniature furniture, china, and silverware. Even the furniture was often made of silver, which may be the reason many of the houses had locking glass cabinet doors on the front. We presume that children could look but not touch. The owners were probably grown women with a fondness for things in miniature.

The Renaissance saw certain advances in the cause of the human spirit. But children do not always share in our cultural advances. Indeed, any such advance is likely to mean new demands on them. We have seen nothing in the most characteristic features of the Renaissance to suggest a greater devotion to the child's welfare. Sentiment was collecting around the image of the infant and the adolescent, but there is no reason to believe this was of practical benefit to children. In fact, the indications of a more demanding attitude toward education show the price of progress.

Nine

Childhood Becomes Crucial: The Religious Reformations

The Renaissance of the fifteenth century had much to do with education, but at a rather high level. The religious reformations of the sixteenth century had more to do with elementary education and with children themselves and their family environment. For the reformers were interested in character formation at the earliest stages of life. Thus, they often seem more modern than the Humanists, who wanted to hurry children along until they could appreciate classical literature. In fact, interest in children first began to grow noticeably with the reformers' concern for the spiritual welfare of children and for the future of their churches.

The issue of religious reform was raised most dramatically in 1517 with Martin Luther's attack on the medieval idea that religion was the process of gaining God's favor by meritorious works. His own view, which he took to be the Biblical one, was that Christian faith was something more like the trust and dependence of a child. Luther had not always thought this. He had begun his religious search in the monastery, which seemed to represent the ideal of Christian self-denial. But after his break with the Church hierarchy he came to think of the family, not the monastery, as the real school of character. Family life was not second best for those without the gift of celibacy. It was the highest form of earthly society. Luther wanted families to worship together and for parents to be active in the religious education of their children. And he wanted them to learn to love their children, as God the Father loved them.

Unfortunately, even children would have to re-establish a right dependence on God, Luther thought. Recovering a proper love for God required nothing less than a spiritual conversion in every individual. He hoped that this process would prove less difficult by more careful attention to the childhood years. The inborn tendency toward spiritual rebellion seemed to grow as the years passed. So while children might have an advantage over adults in God's eyes, their development still required the most rigorous attention on the part of their elders.

There was still another reason for anxiety concerning children. Once Luther's movement gained momentum, Germany and later all of Europe was torn apart by ideological strife. For the first time since the later Roman empire, two religious cultures were fighting over the soul of Western civilization. And once again, it was recognized that the rising generation would decide the outcome of that struggle. The Catholic Church, too, turned its attention to questions of early character development.

Historians have long recognized that the evidence of interest in childhood increases markedly in this period. They have usually assumed that this was the result of an increasing repressiveness in European life. In effect, miserable adults made their children miserable by taking out their frustrations on the only group that was entirely in their power. In this view, the religious doctrines involved were largely incidental, of use in justifying the rising repression. Of course, there is always enough misery in the world to give plausibility to such an interpretation. It probably explains the attitude of many who were attracted to certain aspects of the new religious movements. But it does not explain the obvious sympathy of many others, including Luther himself. Anxiety over the future of the movement is sufficient to explain the general increase of interest in children among Protestants, while they differed widely in their attitudes toward them.

Luther, for example, was a fond father. He recognized that he had suffered as a child. He remembered being beaten by his ambitious parents for trivial offenses—"for stealing a nut," he once said. At school he was beaten for even less, 15 times in one morning "for nothing at all. I was required to decline and conjugate and hadn't learned my lesson." He hoped it had made him a more sensitive parent. It also gave him sympathy for teachers, and he advised them not to try to teach for more than ten years. He himself took great pains with the *Little Catechism* he composed for children (1529), thinking it one of his most important works.

But while Luther could be jocular in calling his children "little heathens," many other Protestants could not say this with a smile. They worried over signs of waywardness and thought children would have to fight against themselves and their fallen nature. The doctrine of infant depravity had not seemed so pressing when the sacraments of the Church were thought of as the essence of religion. But Protestants did not wholly trust the sacraments; they concentrated instead on an interior change. Scripture seemed to them to preach the necessity of an individual calling, a conversion that would free one from rebellion and selfishness. Whatever they practiced in the way of infant baptism, they still found the notion of the child's self-centeredness to be confirmed by common experience and took it as evidence of a flawed nature. So they waited anxiously for some sign that their children were being converted and became more concerned and more intrusive parents than we have met to this point.

Protestants were also the first group besides the Jews to feel culturally isolated within Western society. Where they were in the minority they could not count on the community to ratify their beliefs. They feared the cultural seduction of their children, as Christians had in the first centuries of the Church. Their children would have to stand on their own before God and against the world, and they knew this would be hard on them.

From such attitudes, historians have assumed the worst. One frequently reads that these early Protestants thought sin could be beaten out of their children. In fact, they were the first group that doubted that beating would save their children. The primary article of their faith was that only God's grace could save anyone. If they beat children it was for the same reason that everyone else did—to make them obedient and respectful. Obedience to God's commands was for one's own good here on earth. And God expected obedience from all His creatures, whatever their eternal destiny. But obedience did not ensure eternal salvation, because it fell infinitely short of true righteousness. Theoretically, then, Protestants recognized limits to the efficacy of beating. It was also an article of their faith that God might save the most hardened characters, so that they never need lose hope for their children. Just how they compared with other parents in practice is a question that has never been answered. For the main evidence we have is in the child-rearing books they wrote (to be described later). One can only infer their actions from such works.

It is even harder to say what these parents' subconscious feelings were. On the one hand, Protestants rejected the assurance the medieval Church had offered parents regarding their children. They could find no basis for limbo in Scripture, and even infant baptism became a theological problem for them. They wondered how it squared with the more obvious demand for a conscious religious commitment. But only fringe groups called Anabaptists were so consistent as to deny baptism until the years of discretion. The rest fell back on the analogy between infant baptism and Jewish circumcision. In this case, it may be that sympathy for their own children overcame logical consistency. They even proceeded to develop a theology of the two covenants of God, by which they asserted that their churches and even their families were in the same relation with God which the Jews had enjoyed as God's chosen people. Thus their children could be thought to be under God's special care, whatever this implied for the doctrine of God's arbitrary predestination. John Calvin taught that the covenant meant that the faith of Christian parents would save the unbaptized child. All of this looks suspiciously like a rationalizing of unconscious sympathies, as did the doctrine of limbo which it replaced. It is heartening to think that some such sympathy was growing, along with the new interest in children.

One might suppose that Protestants would have expected little good to come from educational efforts, given their belief in God's predestination. But here again, their practice offers a different picture. People had a duty to God whether or not they thought they were among the elect. Doing their duty was of benefit in this life, even if it guaranteed nothing in the life to come. And people could only learn that duty through searching the Scriptures. Thus it was that the Reformation became more important to the spread of educational opportunity than the Renaissance. Whereas Humanists had thought in terms of educating elites, often by individual instruction, the Reformers were more interested in the spread of primary education. It was not enough to prepare men for the priesthood and the professions and to make aristocrats more genteel; every Christian needed to be able to read the Scriptures for himself. Some went so far as to include girls in their plans.

Very early in the Protestant movement, Luther published an open letter "To the Mayors and Aldermen of all the Cities of Germany in behalf of Christian Schools" (1524). He asked them to support elementary education for as many children as possible, including girls (for whom there would be women teachers). Luther did not hold with the adage that ignorance is the mother of devotion. Rather, he believed ignorance was the mother of superstition, so he wanted the states of Germany to encourage enlightenment by enforcing school attendance, even against parental resistance. As he admitted, this was only partly due to a religious impulse:

> Even if there were no soul (as I have already said) and men did not need schools and the languages for the sake of Christianity and the Scriptures, still, for the establishment of the best schools everywhere, both for boys and girls, this consideration is of itself sufficient, namely, that society, for the maintenance of civil order and the proper regulation of the household, needs accomplished and well-trained men and women.

Following his advice, by 1530 Lutheran clergy and magistrates were establishing schools wherever they were in authority, in rural parishes as well as in towns. The Duchy of Württemberg has the distinction of establishing (by 1560) the first educational system in history, consisting of a network of elementary schools for both sexes, which fed into Latin grammar schools (for boys only). There students were introduced to the New Learning of the Renaissance. Some would go on to the university to prepare for the professions. Other Protestant states recognized the desirability of such schemes. Scotland struggled against its poverty to set up a system of schools that would reach all children, as Massachusetts Bay would do a century later. For the wealth or poverty of an area had little to do with its determination to offer a universal education. More crucial was the society's sense of historical and spiritual mission.

Of course this education was basically religious, at a time when religion seemed fundamental to all areas of life and thought. But it maintained contact with the traditions of Western education. Protestants quoted the same authorities as did the Humanists—Plato, Cicero, Plutarch, Quintilian, and Jerome. And they said the same things about stimulating children to want to learn, adding the same warnings against the overuse of corporal punishment. In general, they acted as if education could help produce Christian character, which had been the Humanists' hope as well. It is cheering to note that Luther did not see why the schools should not be fun as well:

> Now since the young must leap and jump, or have something to do, because they have a natural desire for it which should not be restrained (for it is not well to check them in everything) why should we not provide for them such schools, and lay before them such studies? By the gracious arrangement of God, children take delight in acquiring knowledge, whether languages, mathematics, or history. And our schools are no longer a hell or purgatory, in which with much flogging, trembling, anguish and wretchedness they learn nothing.

One can only wonder whether the new sense of educational mission actually realized these hopes, and for how long.

In Catholic areas of Europe one finds a rather different pattern of attitudes toward children at that time, which expressed a different theological perspective. Medieval Catholicism was built on the power of the sacraments, and Catholics accordingly relied on baptism and confirmation to safeguard their children. Their emphasis, therefore, was not on conversion or character change but on preserving the child's original innocence. And this often meant isolation and repression.

We begin to see these methods coming to the fore even before the Protestant revolt. Fifteenth-century French Churchman John Gerson defined the child's nature for later Catholic educators. Gerson, like Augustine, was generally pessimistic regarding children. But there was one subtle and crucial difference in his view. He believed that the child's instincts were only *inclined* to selfishness and lust and could be arrested or diverted before they became established. This put all of the burden on parents and teachers, who would have to cultivate the withered shoots of goodness in the child until they could blossom into virtues. Gerson did not go so far as to say that the child was innately good or had a positive resistance to evil influences. Indeed, he advised that children be kept away from others who seemed likely to spread the contagion of immoral tendencies. From long experience as a father confessor, Gerson was particularly concerned to shield children from sexual knowledge and activity. He wrote to awaken schoolmasters and confessors to watch children more closely and to encourage other interests. It seemed to him that boarding schools offered the best possibilities for regulating the child's development in a favorable direction.

Gerson recognized that Europe stood on the brink of an important cultural change. Even before the Protestant threat he suggested: "If you want to reform the Church, you must start with the children." But then, under the impact of the Protestant challenge, his followers made rapid headway in this effort to purify the child's environment. In the course of the seventeenth century, for instance, the custom of teasing small children with sex play was suppressed. At the beginning of that century, the child who became Louis XIII (a man notable for his sexual disorientation) had been masturbated by his nurses, who also kissed his genitals and had him feel theirs, and had frightened him by threats of cutting off his penis and nipples. He had observed sexual intercourse, had seen pornographic books, and had played sexually with his younger sister—all before age seven. Then, abruptly, he was thought to be old enough to be aware of what was going on, and such activity ceased. But by the next generation things had changed. Catholic reformers were able to impose the new proprieties even on the French royal court. All of this teasing was unthinkable at the court of his son, Louis XIV. The clergy had made parents wonder what children think and how they are affected by adults amusing themselves in this way.

The difference between Protestant and Catholic approaches is symbolized in the discussion over whether to expurgate the plays of Terence, which were commonly used for Latin instruction. Catholic educators did so, whereas Luther objected that children could not be protected from ribaldry but must conquer it instead. In practice, the difference between the groups may have been slight. But simply by ideal of celibacy Catholics presented virtue in defensive or negative terms. It was like a moral deposit, something one was born with and which could be stolen or squandered. The goal was not to increase this deposit so much as to protect it. And thus the repression of the child's impulses was more obviously encouraged by those who believed in the child's innocence than by those who took a more pessimistic view.

In certain respects, Protestant and Catholic reformers were agreed. Both groups thought that the child's training might begin much earlier than was traditional, pointing out that much was learned by age two. Protestants had more difficulty saying how greater attention to the child would help in attaining the ultimate goal of salvation, since no human means could ensure a super-natural conversion. Catholics were beginning to show much the same anxieties in this area; their concern over the child's state at first communion began to correspond to the worry of Protestants over conversion.

The most dramatic example of Catholic devotion to childhood innocence occurred in Italy. In the century before the Protestant Reformation, several religious societies were started in Florence to try to remove boys from a society which had come to seem rough and dissolute. The point of these confraternities, besides their special confessions and communions, was to keep the members from joining in the riotous festivals and games of the town. The boys were allowed to march in civic processions, dressed in white to symbolize their purity. They made a nice appearance, and the city fathers encouraged them to take a larger part in the ceremonial life of the community. So the fraternities were featured in the religious tableaus and dramas on feast days, and began to replace monks as the social repre-sentation of innocence. Meanwhile, Florentine schools were becoming more like monasteries, with the kind of concern over the chastity and gravity of the pupils that Gerson had expressed.

Toward the end of the Renaissance, when the friar Savonarola dominated the life of Florence (in the 1490s), he heightened the use of children as symbols of his purification of city life. Savonarola seems to have been the first important reformer to popularize the notion that the young would save the world. Of course, he did not have the kind of institutional or doctrinal changes in view that the Protestants would call for. To his mind social salvation depended rather on each person maintaining his or her baptismal innocence. His purpose in idealizing the young was to appeal to adults to try to recover some of the religious enthusiasm characteristic of youth, and to shame those who were too cynical to support his efforts at social rejuvenation.

Soon all of Italy was ringing with prophets and humanists announcing the birth of a new age—represented by youth—and the death of the corrupt "medieval" or Middle Age.

Savonarola was so successful in turning the young against the pleasures of Renaissance society that he opened up a generation gap. Children informed on parents who kept books on magic or indecent paintings, dice, or beauty aids at home. They were even protected by the police while breaking into houses to look for such things to add to the great bonfires of "vanities." When the traditional rulers of Florence were able to reassert themselves and execute the reformer, they naturally destroyed the political organizations of the young. But children continued to serve as symbols of civic righteousness. In 1504 Michelangelo offered the city his statue of the adolescent David to represent Florentine virtue.

These movements began before the Reformation. Later, when Protestantism threatened to overrun Europe, the Church was further stimulated to reform itself. And when it came to recovering lost territory, it relied on a number of new religious orders, all of which concentrated on education. The Ursuline Sisters, for example, offered schools for girls. The most notable of all the new orders, the Jesuits, became famous as educators. Their curriculum for grammar school instruction remained the standard by which other schools were measured until the nineteenth century. It combined the Humanist emphasis on classical literature with the medieval emphasis on logic and philosophy. Even more important, the *Ratio Studiorum* prescribed the teaching methods in detail, and Jesuit teachers were held to these methods.

There had been no lack of good advice for teachers in the Renaissance, but before the Jesuits there was no one to see that teachers followed it. Catholic Humanists like Erasmus and Juan Luis Vives wrote kindly works on educational method in the early years of the Reformation, around 1530. They revived the old suggestions on instruction by games and advice on the importance of the earliest years and of individual differences. Vives discussed teaching by induction and observation rather than simply by principle. All this is easier to advocate than to apply, and teachers were forever falling back on the method that had worked with them—recitation and fear. Now, after reviewing all the Renaissance advice, the Jesuits picked the features that seemed most promising and required their teachers to follow it. In certain respects they were innovators. They used games in instruction, had students produce plays, and introduced dancing as a form of physical education. Clergymen had criticized these activities before; the Jesuits turned them to good use. They soon acquired a reputation for excellence. Even Protestants like Francis Bacon praised their schools, and by the end of the seventeenth century there were some 800 of them scattered throughout Europe.

When Philippe Ariès wrote his modern classic, *Centuries of Childhood,* he expressed some surprise that the modern interest in childhood did not seem to arise because of some economic or medical advance, such as a decline of infant mortality. He noticed that the evidence of a rising interest came from the time of the religious reformations and originated with moralists and theologians. Somehow, he supposed, it must be related to the growing influence of Christianity on life and manners at that time. We can be more specific. A large part of the increasing attention to children was doubtless due to a contest for the religious allegiance of the rising generation. Even those who took their stand against Protestant reforms were becoming aware that many elements of popular culture were more akin to pagan traditions than to Christian practice. This made them more critical of what their society was teaching its children. And thus the rearing of children became a matter of more conscious consideration, making children one of the discoveries of that age of discovery.

Ten

The Nation- State Takes Up Child Care

In the sixteenth century, at the same time that religious reformations were occupying people's minds, the large nation-states were taking on more power than ever before. They were finally in a position to break down the regional loyalties that had been so important, to limit the authority of the Papacy in their political affairs, and to subdue the aristocracies that had once divided power with the kings. In France, England, and Spain especially, we can see the triumph of central authority at the expense of the once-powerful aristocratic families. As in imperial Rome, we can see real efforts by these states to perform some of the services for children which weakened families were now unable to provide.

The shift of power away from the family and toward the state is exemplified rather strikingly in the experience of England. In the late 1400s England had been the scene of a struggle for the throne among all the great families. This contest, the Wars of the Roses, ended when the Tudor family emerged triumphant. Henry VIII, the greatest of the Tudors, was the last king of England to punish a whole family for the treason of one member. The sole remaining member of the de la Pole clan, a small boy, was last seen being taken to the Tower of London. That practice, so common in the Middle Ages, had ended somewhat earlier in Florence and ceased a century later in France, marking the end of family power and accountability. By the time we come to the English Civil Wars of the 1640s we can see just how much things had changed. For these wars did not pit families against each other so much as split them internally. The conflict was not between rival dynasties but over the ideological issues that have characterized modern times. Political and religious ideas cut across family loyalties. In fact, every seventh aristocratic family in England was divided within the conjugal unit itself. That is, one family in seven—an astonishing percentage—saw brothers fighting brothers, or fathers at odds with sons. Clearly, the individual faced new choices and new uncertainties in this more modern age.

Monarchs tried to fill the place of a weakening family by making their states more paternalistic and by promoting their own image as the father of the country. A new cult of kingship emphasized that the monarch's first duty was the welfare of his people—his children, as it were. Kings made themselves the central focus of a new nationalism which took the place of older kinship loyalties. At the same time, the tendency of legislation was toward greater individual rights and away from family solidarity. For instance, by the 1530s in England the head of the family could legally sell bits of the family's property, divide it in any way he chose, or disinherit his children altogether. Even the French laws which allowed parents to disinherit children who married without consent should be taken as evidence of a weakening family. For in earlier times families could have dealt with this situation without calling on the state for its backing.

To see how these political realities affected children, we may observe the treatment of English orphans which the smaller nuclear household of modern times could not care for. The children of these families were in a more vulnerable position than those of more extended families, for the death of a parent might leave a nuclear household destitute. Accordingly, the state recognized a duty to maintain the weak and fatherless.

At the top of society this provision for children was anything but generous. The government's care of aristocratic wards was so unfeeling that it almost seems like part of a plan to reduce the wealth and morale of those great families. If a nobleman died, the king had a duty to see that his heir was cared for until the child came of age. But until the heir reached 21, the king or some guardian appointed by him was free to pocket the income of the child's estate and put him on short rations. More and more, kings looked upon this arrangement as a way to raise money for their increasingly ambitious projects. Henry VIII quadrupled his income from this source by auctioning orphans off to the highest bidder. The more the bidding process governed this system, the less likely the ward was to go to a relative. For even the child's mother had to bid along with the rest, and she was usually not successful. The percentage of aristocratic children who suffered from this system was quite high, due to the relatively short life expectancy of their fathers.

Those who had bought the wards were often not content with the income from their lands. Calculating the proceeds at the time of bidding had often left guardians with a narrow profit margin.

So they might try to sell the wards in marriage as well. The sale of marriages had long been customary in England, in the upper middle class as well as the aristocracy. When William Molynes had to move fast to purchase an estate around 1410, he took his wife's advice and sold his son's marriage to a London merchant as part of a loan arrangement. In this particular case, Molynes later broke the contract and thereby repossessed his child. Others were more callous. Stephen Scrope complained that "for very need I was fain to sell a little daughter I have for much less than I should have done." The lament was for the money lost, not for the daughter's feelings in the matter. But the same thing had happened to him as a ward of the king. He remembered his own guardian with bitterness: "He bought and sold me like a beast." Obviously he had not determined to do differently by his own child.

Guardians had the sole right to consent to any marriage of these wards. For the law now stated that boys needed an adult's consent for a valid marriage until they turned 21, while girls could escape at 16. Thus the guardians were eager to marry them off before that, and the law allowed marriage as early as 14 for boys and 12 for girls. Commonly, the ward was paired with one of the guardian's own children to keep the lands in his family. Or the guardian might be bribed to talk up a marriage into some other family. The child could refuse, of course, for his or her consent was necessary too. But few could resist the pressure or actual cruelty guardians employed. And if the child did refuse, he or she was forced to pay a fine to comfort the guardian in his disappointment! Under these circumstances it is not surprising to find that the aristocracy married fairly young—earlier than the lower classes, in fact. Early weddings were not the children's idea, unless they hoped thereby to escape some more repulsive match. Rather, such weddings represented the greed of their keepers or the anxieties of parents who wanted to see their children settled before they themselves died.

By 1600 there was some criticism of the wardship system, as monarchs used it more heartlessly. Scandals had come to light in which wards had been kidnapped or gambled away in dice games. This grew into a more general criticism of marrying children off for mercenary motives. Religious reformers especially were afraid that if marriage was not based on more personal considerations, it would continue to lead to adultery and desertion. Of course, there were always aristocratic conservatives who would justify the old practice of arranged marriages by citing examples of love matches that had gone sour. But attitudes were changing, to the point that Queen Elizabeth considered accepting an annual tax in exchange for her rights over wards. This proposal did not succeed, but at least mothers were given a month to scrape together their resources before others were allowed to bid on their children. It is heartening to note that the proportion of wards who went to relatives promptly rose from a fourth to a half.

When the Puritans came to power during the Civil Wars, they ended these practices. And even after their regime fell apart in 1660, wardship was not restored. We can hope that childhood became that much better for the children involved, though one cannot be sure. After all, some mothers had not cared even to bid for their children. The government sometimes refused guardianship to mothers on the ground that they were too flighty to be trusted. There have always been parents who were eager to escape from their children. The rich are able to act on that wish, and the aristocracy was proverbial for neglecting its children.

Lower on the social scale other arrangements prevailed. Town governments were beginning to take better care of the orphans of their freemen—that is, the local property owners. The Courts of Orphans which multiplied in the sixteenth century managed the child's property until he or she came of age and saw to it that the child was cared for. The court itself consented to the ward's marriage. But the temptation to put the money to use for civic projects was great, and when a few towns were unable to hand over the child's patrimony and the interest which should have accrued, parents began to make their own arrangements for guardianship by writing wills.

It was their money that had spoiled things for these children, causing people to think of them in mercenary terms. But most orphans had no inheritance to speak of, and when government took up the needs of these children the motive was more simply to help them. The most notable provision for orphans in sixteenth-century England was Christ's Hospital, founded in London in 1552 to care for some 400 poor children. The orphanage buildings were donated to the city out of the state's plunder of monastery property, but the operating funds were raised through philanthropy. It showed considerable generosity. We read that each child had a featherbed and that there was sometimes so much food that the children made themselves sick on it. Twenty-five women were hired to mother them. Boys and girls were taught some marketable skill, and the boys learned the three R's. When they were old enough, the boys were placed out as apprentices and the girls as domestic servants.

Historians are apt to complain that these children were only being taught to work and that the London government was merely ensuring a labor supply. In the context of the sixteenth-century economy this objection is unreasonable. The most the authorities could do was to help these destitute children escape careers in thieving, begging, or prostitution. As semiskilled workers they would be able to take care of themselves and thereby acquire some self-respect. In fact, the city fathers found that they were being too generous. Parents immediately began taking advantage of the orphanage, leaving their unwanted babies on the doorstep. Numbers soon rose so high that the governors had to refuse those children, legitimate or otherwise, whose parents could be found. They also tried to get other towns to make provision for their own orphans rather than to ship them all to London. Some towns did take up this responsibility, and they experienced the same overcrowding. The problem was simply beyond the resources of the towns, primarily because they were so vastly outnumbered by a rural population which took advantage of their efforts. These early orphanages simply could not take in all the children who now seemed to be unwanted.

Only the state could offer a solution as big as the problem. A series of laws directed every locality in England, rural and urban, to make regular provision for the poor. As they affected children, these "Poor Laws" concerned not only strays but those living with their families as well. By offering welfare payments the government tried to encourage destitute parents to keep their children rather than to abandon them to some public institution. As for orphans, local officials were responsible for seeing that they were taught a trade so that they would not be left paupers. So far as possible, officials tried to find foster families for them rather than to send them to workhouses. Once again, the pay to these foster parents was sufficiently generous that it invited abuse. Baby farming became a business, and there is strong suspicion that some of the babies boarded out were killed when the income was no longer needed or forthcoming. Parish officials did not ask questions; after all, they wouldn't have to pay again next year.

These efforts at maintaining poor children proved to be a burden. By the middle of the seventeenth century it is clear that stingier attitudes prevailed. Local officials were casting about for ways to save money on poor relief. Hundreds of orphaned children were shipped to labor-hungry America. Parishes economized by forcing the destitute to move their families into workhouses in order to qualify for relief. Even the children in these institutions were expected to work to help contribute to their own support, by spinning thread or making rope, for instance. By a statute of 1717 delinquents could be sent out to the colonies as punishment, saving the cost of rehabilitation and of further mischief. All this may represent a taxpayers' revolt, or a more businesslike approach to the problem, or even an attempt to broaden the benefits beyond what society could have afforded under the original system. It can hardly have been due to a rising population, for there was only a modest rise in the seventeenth century. And it was not due to a declining economy, for England was beginning a period of expansion. Attitudes once again showed their independence from any circumstances that would have justified them.

The many published proposals on how to economize culminated in a final solution, which appeared in 1729. After calculating the supply of unwanted children and the cost of raising them and lamenting the numbers of children aborted or murdered and the failure of all other projects, the author offered the following suggestion:

> I have been assured by a very knowing American of my acquaintance in London, that a young healthy child well nursed is at a year old a most delicious, nourishing and wholesome food, whether stewed, roasted, baked or boiled, and I make no doubt that it will equally serve in a fricassee or a ragout.

It was, of course, a satirical suggestion (by Jonathan Swift) and yet it seemed to him that one had to go that far in order to shock the complacent social planners whose calculations seemed to him so inhumane. Besides the condescension which there had always been toward the poor and helpless, there now seemed to be open resentment. This appears in the provisions of an act of 1662 by which only the parish in which one was born had a duty to offer relief. The reaction of constables was to keep an eye out for pregnant strangers who might struggle into a parish in order to ensure its support for their children. It sometimes came to a race to see if such women could be caught and hustled out of town in time.

The workhouses never managed to pay for themselves so they were purposely made as uncomfortable as possible, to encourage the families to take any work at all that would allow them to escape. Some of the workhouses, at least, had rules governing spanking and dismissed overseers for abusing children. Some of them made efforts to keep children separate from the drunks and vagrants who had to be kept there. But the workhouses cannot have been pleasant. Perhaps their worst feature was that people began to associate the pauper children with adult derelicts, as if the children were similarly headed for delinquency. This tended to justify the unsympathetic attitude society had adopted toward poor children. During the eighteenth century, when the population began to rise and there were more children to feed, conditions may have deteriorated still further. By then, workhouses must have been very like the cold hells Dickens described in the early nineteenth century.

It is curious that in the eighteenth century the public began to pride itself on its kindliness toward children. This was often said to be a sign of a good nature, which was something the fashionable classes began to value in that sentimental century. Though they resented paying taxes toward maintaining the poor, they were often willing to support charities that would benefit children. As proof of their kindliness, the two most prominent philanthropies of eighteenth-century England both concerned children. The first of these, the charity school movement, was a truly massive attempt to educate and domesticate the children of the poor. Many had realized that London was developing a criminal class—that is, one that bred its children to crime. It had also come to light that the number of churches left after the Great Fire of London (1666) did not begin to accommodate the soaring population of the city. So the religious and social foundations of the nation were thought to be tottering, at just the time when England was fighting for its life and liberty against Louis XIV. Accordingly, charity schools were founded which trained hundreds of thousands of children in religion and in the proper attitudes toward work, in hopes of turning these neglected children into loyal and pious English subjects. Boys were given at least four years instruction in reading and writing. Although some of the girls were not offered the same instruction, they learned basic household skills which good families would have taught, so that they could be employed as servants or even be marriageable. Both sexes were also taught the deferential manners which would make them attractive to employers and to society in general.

While many historians, again, think that this was very little to do for these needy children, critics of that time thought the schools were doing too much. They feared that the pupils were being filled with ambitions above their station, making them uppity or even rebellious. Not only the unenlightened thought this; some of the loudest critics were liberal and secular thinkers like Bernard Mandeville and Voltaire. It was one thing for these men to indulge in radical speculation among their friends; it was quite another for their footmen to organize for higher wages, as Mandeville put it. His friend John Trenchard expressed the objection most brutally: "What Benefit can accrue to the Publick by taking the Dregs of the People out of the Kennels, and throwing their Betters into them?" Perhaps the thing that galled these free thinkers most was the self-satisfaction shown by those who showered this bounty on poor waifs. Now that the fashionable world applauded generosity toward children, the intellectuals were quick to notice the smugness involved. In response to this criticism, the schools became rather defensive and began to emphasize work more than ever.

The second of the philanthropies involved the abandoned infants which seemed to be an increasing problem. In 1741 the London Foundling Hospital was established, in imitation of the famous one begun in Paris by St. Vincent de Paul a century earlier. Workhouses had been forced to take in these foundlings before, but the mortality rates had become a disgrace. In some workhouses, half of the babies accepted died. In one, near London, all 53 of those taken in during a five-year period succumbed. Many thought that better care would save many of these little lives. And so the wealthier classes did not wait for the state to force them to be generous. Händel gave concerts to help raise funds for the hospital, and the painters Hogarth and Reynolds lent it their support. Parliament offered public money if it would take in children from outside the city.

Once again, the effort to be generous worsened the situation. It took just four hours to fill the hospital, and mothers who arrived too late had to be restrained from throwing their babies down in the street in their disappointment. In the first four years of operation 15,000 children were shipped in, many of them half dead, and the administrators were forced to make society's cruel decisions. The rise in the supply of babies during this period may be largely due to the fact that poor and unmarried mothers no longer aborted or killed their infants, knowing that they could leave their problem on someone else's doorstep. As an unsympathetic contemporary crudely put it,

The Hospital Foundling came out of the Brains,
To encourage the progress of vulgar amours,
The breeding of Rogues and the increasing of whores.
While the children of honest and good husbands and wives,
Stand exposed to oppression and want all their lives.

In the end, the hospital had to become selective, turning many children back to the parishes they had come from. Actually, these children were more likely to survive than those left to the hospital, where the diseases of the metropolis spread among the unfortunate children collected there. For the parish children were often boarded with nurses in the country, where conditions seemed a little more wholesome. This practice did not, however, leave any monuments to enlightened benevolence such as the eighteenth century was fond of erecting.

Because the growing power of the state had helped to weaken the family, the state had tried to take up some of the responsibility families could no longer carry. The net effect, though, may have been to weaken the sense of family responsibility still further. As the state reached the end of its resources, the wealthier classes demonstrated their goodwill toward children by philanthropy. But even this sentimental indulgence may have had a negative effect if it blinded society to the growing abuses of that century. By the late eighteenth century parish children were being sent into the growing navy as "powder monkeys" and into the new factories, where they were worked until they dropped. For as Britain and the other states of Europe began their imperial and industrial competition, children were being given increasingly grim roles at the bottom of society. By ignoring such conditions, these nations had actually encouraged the abuses which they later tried to curb.

Eleven

Children
and
Progress:
An Early
Social
Movement

The modern world might be characterized as the time of social movements. Earlier ages had not seen these organized groups, which exist outside the recognized institutions of a society and seek to change them. They are a mark of the freedom and restlessness of our times and the plurality of modern culture. And because they do not have a base among the institutions of society, they seek their security in children. It is never long before movements realize that future success will depend on attracting the younger generation. Beyond that, the

supporters of a movement may believe children have an obliga-
tion to help in some way, since the changes being promoted are
for their benefit. Also, the movement's ideology will contain a
particular view of human nature, including definite ideas on what
childhood will be like in a better world. For all of these reasons,
the proliferation of social movements has been an important
source of the growing attention to children in recent times.

The initial organized groups promoting social change were
religious in character. The seventeenth century, in which the
first such movements arose, was an age in which all ideals and
attitudes were related to religious values and expressed in a
religious idiom. In the context of English history, for example,
the first reform movement was Puritanism. Despite the many
constitutional, ecclesiastical, and social changes of the previous
century, Puritans pressed for wider changes—changes in the
Church of England that would reverberate through all areas of
the nation's life. Many of them saw the wider implications of
their religious reforms and allied themselves with the most advanced thinking on the reform of law and politics, business,
education, and the arts.

Queen Elizabeth was not fond of Puritans. She was successful
in containing their attempts to force changes in her Church
through Parliament. After this political defeat, the Puritan faction
turned to other means of changing the nation, concentrating on
reforming the individual through education and persuasion. This
explains why, during Elizabeth's reign, we see numerous signs
of a new awareness of children among the Puritans.

For example, there was a revolution in the names they gave
to children. In medieval Europe children inherited the names of
their parents and relatives. And to avoid confusion the names
were varied by nicknames and pet name endings. No one considered that the names meant anything; they were just labels.
England had made do with only a few dozen Saxon, Norman, and
apostles' names for boys and a like number for girls. In Eliza-

beth's time all this changed. Parents began to use a great variety of Biblical names, and they showed that they knew the meanings of those names. For the names did have meanings; an appendix in the Geneva Bible listed the English equivalents. Sometimes Puritans simply gave their children those equivalents, and so we have the curious phrase-names like Grace, Prudence, Joy, Thankful, Praise-God, Sin-Deny, and Safe-on-High. These and even more exotic Hebrew names like Ichabod and Ebenezer were always associated with the Puritans. Playwrights, who represented the Puritans' worldly wise contemporaries, satirized them with characters named Tribulation Wholesome or Zeal-of-the-Land Busy, which were only slight exaggerations.

The point of this change in names was to symbolize a break with the past and with family tradition. Children would need new names in the new age the Puritans dreamed of. They did not think of children merely as family replacements but recognized that they were little individuals. Accordingly, they tried to give their children some direction as they set out in life. In Catholic France, which did not become a Bible-reading nation and was not then debating reform, the old ways of naming persisted.

Once Puritan parents had given their children these names, suggesting the children's personal destiny, they felt the need for books that would tell how to rear this new generation. From the time of Elizabeth to that of John Locke a century later, it was Puritans who published the great bulk of child-rearing advice. The books followed a pattern. All of them urged mothers to nurse their own children and answered the objections against that practice. All of them pointed out that learning began long before the school years and that parents should be careful to set a good example in those impressionable years. From the very first they complained that parents were too prone to indulge their children's whims—"cockering" them, as it was called. They warned parents against encouraging naughtiness by expressing their amusement, since they would have to beat it out of the child later. This especially has been used by historians as evidence that Puritans were more severe with children than were their contemporaries. But the Puritans' view was that in the long run a more consistent and thoughtful discipline would be less harsh than the usual practice. Everyone agreed that "correction," or spanking, would sometimes be necessary; the Puritans' point was that most parents were erratic. Spanking was by no means their first choice in discipline. The goal of punishment should be a change in the child's behavior, not the venting of a parent's anger. Therefore, they said, parents ought to be satisfied with "admonishing" the child if that would be sufficient to work repentance. They certainly recognized a difference between spanking and child abuse.

We are so accustomed to thinking of the Puritans as tortured and ferocious souls that readers may be suspicious of such a mild description of their advice. Historians and novelists in nineteenth-century England and America used "puritanism" as the scapegoat for all that they disliked about their forebears' ways. And by that time the descendants of the original movement had had plenty of time to sour in defeat. But to recapture the original flavor of the movement, one should read its earliest and most often reprinted statements, such as Robert Cleaver's *A Godly Form of Household Government* (1598) and William Gouge's *Of Domestical Duties* (1622). They give a rather different impression than the popular stereotype.

Cleaver took as his text "Chastise thy sonne while there is hope, and let not thy soule spare him to his destruction" (Proverbs 19:18). Readers prepare for the worst as they read that "foolish affection is indeed hatred, and not love." But most of what Cleaver has to say is by way of guarding against abusiveness.

The end in correcting must not bee to wreak and revenge thine anger or malice, or to revenge thy self for an injurie done, nor yet only the preventing of the like hurt by the like fault after-ward: but in zeal of Gods glorie, who is dishonoured by the lewdness of the offender, and in love to the partie. Thou must seeke by wise correction to reclaim him from such evill as bringeth danger to him, and make him more carefull of his dutie afterwards. Herein they faile who in correcting have no respect but to their owne commoditie [i.e., convenience]. For the matters that deserve correction, this is a rule, that there must be no rebuking, much lesse chastising, but where there is fault. For where any is unjustly corrected, besides the inju-rie, it hurteth him by hardening him against just correction, for he will think that it is the rash hastiness of his governour that putteth him to smart, and not his own desert.

The child must have the fault explained and be allowed to speak in his or her own defense. If a scolding will bring repentance, that should suffice: "Superiors must take heede of coming to the greatest remedies of correction too soone, for so they may soone mar the partie by over-sharp dealing, which by a wise proceeding by degrees might have been gained." Still, if all else fails, parents should not be deterred by fear of being thought cruel.

Gouge used a very different text: "Fathers, provoke not your children to wrath: but bring them up in the nurture and admoni-tion of the Lord" (Ephesians 6:4). He then began by reminding parents of the natural love that should motivate them.

The Fountaine of parents duties is Love. . . . Great reason there is why this affection should be fast fixed in the heart of parents towards their children. For great is that paine, cost, and care, which parents must undergoe for their children. But if love be in them, no paine, paines, cost, or care will seeme too much. Herein appeareth the wise providence of God, who by nature hath so fast fixed love in the hearts of parents, as if there be any in whom it aboundeth not, he is counted un-naturall.

Only after 50 pages, in which he describes the duties of parents to nurse, instruct, and care for children, does Gouge devote seven pages to discipline. In them he describes a middle way between permissiveness and severity:

> Reprehension is a kind of middle thing betwixt admonition and correction: it is a sharpe admonition, but a milde correction. It is the rather to be used because it may be a meanes to prevent strokes and blowes, especially in ingenuous and good natured children. [Blows are] the last remedy which a parent can use: a remedy which may doe good when nothing else can.

(We might note that Gouge's phrase "good natured children" could not be reconciled with many historians' descriptions of Puritan attitudes.) As for corporal punishment, Gouge suggests certain guidelines. The parent must be sure that the fault was committed and that it really was a fault. Then, "Correction must be given in a milde mood, when the affections are well ordered, and not distempered with choler, rage, furie, and other like passions." It should be proportioned to the fault and to the child's years. In the end, he says, it is better to err on the side of leniency: "They who offend in the other extreme, of severity, of the two are the more unnatural parents; they offend directly against the first branch of this text."

We have no real evidence of whether seventeenth-century Puritan parents took this advice or needed it, or to what extent they differed from their contemporaries. But because they were the first group to discuss child rearing at length and always dealt with the question of spanking, we have gained the impression that they invented it. The adage "Spare the rod and spoil the child" was common in the seventeenth century. But it was not particularly a Puritan saying (they would have preferred the Biblical counterpart from Proverbs 13:24—"He that spareth his rod hateth his son: but he that loveth him chasteneth him betimes.") The point is that Puritans shared the same instincts as other parents of their day. Where they differed was in the amount of thought they gave to their task. And this difference was a reflection of their social position as outsiders, thinking how to change traditional ways.

In this respect the Puritans were the first modern parents. Like many of us, they looked on their treatment of children as a test of their own self-control. Their goal was not simply to ensure the child's duty to the family, but to help him or her make personal, individual commitments. They were the first authors to state that children must obey God rather than parents, in case of a clear conflict. True, they probably thought this a remote possibility. But even to have imagined such a case showed an uncommon sense of the child's moral autonomy. The obedience they demanded was obedience to principle rather than to the parent's arbitrary authority.

Being critics of their society, Puritans were among the first parents who felt they could not rely on their neighbors or existing social institutions to help them socialize their children. For they had rejected the manners and morals which prevailed and felt isolated in their task of child rearing. Some even determined to leave England to found their own communities, and these always remarked that their children had been a main motive for their move. Those who stayed behind tried to rear their children to be "inner-directed" in the modern phrase—to stand on their own feet. The Puritan tradition is famous for fostering the kind of individualism that characterized the next several centuries, even after Puritan beliefs had faded. But they paid a price for their independence and uprightness in a greater anxiety about their children, which also seems modern. Earlier parents had trusted their impulses in raising their children, doing what had been done to them. Puritans resisted much that was traditional as well as their own impulses and thereby became conscious of just how problematical raising children can be.

Ralph Josselin, a Puritan minister of the latter half of the seventeenth century, confided his concerns over his children to a diary. Sicknesses were recorded, and providential deliverances, and weaning and breeching (which was when boys were taken out of gowns and put in pants). Punishments are not mentioned, and in general Josselin seems to feel constrained not to interfere too much. Despite misgivings, he did not overrule one daughter's choice in marriage, admitting the force of her objection that a particular suitor "seemed to her not loving, it was no small grief to mee, but I could not desire it, when shee said it would make both their lives miserable." A son gave him much more concern:

> John tooke his clothes and mony and in the morning unknown to any of us, or without a line to tell that he aimed at went away. Lord let him not outrun thy mercy. I will daily seeke to god to keepe him, to break his heart and deliver him from his own evill mind, and save his soule. Lord heare prayer, hasten an hour of love for him for Christs sake. Dec. 4: faire and dry. John returned, but lord change his heart, make us wise to win him to thee.

John continued to distress his parents by stealing, profanity, running away, and by reports of a growing "lewdness." But Josselin never lost hope that his heart might change, even after the boy married without his knowledge or blessing.

This concern was to lead Puritans to produce the first books written specifically for children and young people. We will have more to say on these books in a later chapter on the development of children's literature but may observe here that the great majority of English books addressed to children until well into the eighteenth century were by Puritans. All of them had a religious intent and sought to secure the adherence of young readers to Puritan doctrine, so most of them are pretty heavy going. But then as now, those who had enough interest to write for children showed some sympathy with their audience. It even occurred to them to try to be entertaining. There were religious allegories for children even before John Bunyan wrote *Pilgrim's Progress* for adults. Puritans composed religious verse, Bible story books, even morality plays. There were also stories about real children. These do not seem very real to modern readers, partly due to the fact that these children shared the social ostracism of the Puritan movement. They tended, as a result, to be censorious and uncomfortably pious.

The most notorious of them appear in James Janeway's *A Token for Children* (1671). All that historians have noticed in this book is the fact that these exemplary boys and girls all died young. It is therefore tempting to suppose that Janeway thought that the only good child was a dead one. But that was the opposite of his intention. For his point was that children could be examples even to adults. These youngsters had lived life fully and well, in its moral and religious dimension at least, before reaching their teens. The courtesy books which the Renaissance provided for children had simply told children how to be adults. Janeway was trying to tell them to take themselves seriously now, young as they were.

One of Janeway's stories strained belief even then, as he admitted. That was the account of a boy who, before the age of two, used to ask his parents about God. He objected whenever they tried to put him to bed without a time of family devotions and would shame them into fulfilling this duty. As he grew up he loved reading the Scriptures and grieved over the general corruption of his nature even when he had no specific sins to repent. His pleadings with God were sometimes so loud as to bother the neighbors. It is a relief to read that he did sometimes play with other children, but Janeway was more impressed with the fact that he would often be found praying by himself instead. Playing with others must have been a trial, so much did the boy dread hearing profanity or obscenity. At times, it "would even make him tremble, and ready to go home and weep." At age six, when he learned that he was dying, he expressed some fear as to his eternal destiny. But when friends reminded him of his prayers for forgiveness and a sincere conversion, he brightened up. The doctrine of the resurrection of the body still seemed hard to believe, but he allowed that "nothing was impossible to God." Several other stories in Janeway's book are nearly as repellent as this, but they are perfectly understandable given the circumstances of a persecuted minority. The attitude of disapproval, bookishness, emotionalism, and self-sufficiency of these children clearly reflect an effort to adjust to their outcast status.

The fact that Janeway concentrated on children who had died may again reflect the plight of the Puritan movement. Radical movements have always preferred dead heroes, who cannot backslide and discredit the whole group. But it must be said that Janeway's book is rather unwholesome. He enjoyed the thought of children weeping for their sins and lingered over the poignant deathbed scenes too long. The sentimentality of the work (it was the first baby-talk book in English) reveals a certain masochism. Perhaps this is to be explained by the suffering Janeway himself had endured. He had lost his livelihood for his beliefs, had seen all of his brothers die of tuberculosis, and knew that this would be his fate as well. There must have been people better suited to pioneer in the field of children's literature, but they had not gotten around to it. Apparently it took Janeway's peculiar position as part of a minority to make him sensitive to the difficulties children could face.

The need of the Puritan movement to perpetuate itself also brought Puritans to the forefront of seventeenth-century educational reform. During the English Civil Wars of the 1640s some Puritan educators put forward plans for universal education, for government aid to schools, and for a more practical curriculum. Obviously, they thought that a general enlightenment could only help their cause. Under this pressure, the government opened a number of new schools in remote areas of the country, founded a third university, and allowed scientific subjects into the universities. There was even talk of educating girls, of the need to train teachers, and to have government inspection of schools. All of these efforts and plans came to nothing when the Puritans and their allies lost control of the political situation and the monarchy was restored in 1660. Durham University was closed, the new science was de-emphasized, and a decadent Humanism again reigned supreme, out of fear of anything connected with Puritan "radicals."

Most tragically, England lost the opportunity to put the ideas of Jan Amos Comenius into operation, after bringing him from the continent to explain his educational philosophy. Comenius was Czech, the head of a sect called the Moravian Brethren. The formative influence in his thought was the Thirty Years' War, in which he had lost his family and all that he owned. As a schoolteacher, he hoped that education might be used to bring peace to the world and to increase the general happiness of humankind.

> Our first wish is that all men should be educated fully to full humanity; not any one individual, nor a few nor even many, but all men together and singly, young and old, rich and poor, of high and of lowly birth, men and women—in a word, all whose fate it is to be born human beings; . . . rightly formed not only in one single matter or in a few or even in many, but in all things which perfect human nature; that he should be able to know the truth and not be deluded by what is false; to love good and not be seduced by evil; to do what should be done and not permit what should be avoided; to talk wisely about everything with everybody when there is need, and not to be dumb in any matter.

Comenius recognized that this would mean a revolution in educational methods and goals. Society would have to begin thinking of education as the promotion of happiness—in this life and the next—and not simply as the mastery of Latin literature.

Comenius did not see why children should not be happy even in school, which had always been considered a painful ordeal. After all, school is a part of life as well as a preparation for life. Teachers need only start from where the children are in order to make education more agreeable and even pleasant. If they were to find out what children are interested in and what they already know, they could build on that. In fact, the children would teach themselves by observing and doing. Comenius was among the first to think of education as more than a schoolroom experience:

> It is many years since Quintilian said: "Through precepts the way is long and difficult, while through examples it is short and practicable." But alas, how little heed the ordinary schools pay to this advice. The very beginners in grammar are so overwhelmed by precepts, rules, exceptions to the rules, and exceptions to the exceptions, that for the most part they do not know what they are doing, and are quite stupified before they begin to understand anything. But we see that handicraftsmen do not proceed in this way. They do not begin by drumming rules into their apprentices. They take them into the workshop and bid them look at the work that has been produced, and then, when they wish to imitate this (for man is an imitative animal), they place tools in their hands and show them how they should be held and used. Then, if they make mistakes, they give them advice and correct them, often more by example than by mere words.

If formal education were more like this informal training, teachers would find that they did not need to beat their students to make them pay attention.

To help teachers Comenius published a primer—the *Orbis Sensualium Pictus* (1658)—with pictures on every page showing common things and everyday life. Beneath the pictures were captions in the vernacular and in Latin. The child would want to read these, since they described his world, and would puzzle out the words for himself. The originality of this little book was in starting from the child's experience rather than from the material she was to learn. Comenius also promoted the idea of the "class lesson" in which all the children in the room learned together. This was an innovation in an age when children stood in a line waiting to read or recite to their teacher individually. The class lesson would excite both teacher and class to greater effort and a higher level of expectancy. And we can credit Comenius with some notion of the kindergarten, or the "Mother School" as he called it, in which mothers would design learning experiences for their preschoolers.

Comenius's Puritan disciples were impressed with the practical and sympathetic nature of these ideas and with his plans for the later curriculum, which included more history, science, and vocational instruction than was usual. Unfortunately, he arrived just as the Civil Wars were breaking out, and Parliament never had the time or the funds to institute such changes. These ideas were discarded along with the rest of the Puritans' proposals when the Stuart kings were restored. When Rousseau hit on much the same notions more than a century later, he owed nothing to Comenius and had probably never heard of him. The time that elapsed was a measure of how far Comenius was ahead of his time.

There is no reason to think that the early interest of these religious reformers in children was the result of an excess of benevolence in their natures. Rather, it seems to have derived from their position outside society and their hopes for the future. Since that time, social and political movements have proliferated and have usually used the child as a symbol of the new humanity to be liberated through their reforms. Fascists, national liberation movements, civil rights reformers, nudists, and a hundred other reform groups have all given some thought to educational programs for the young. Whether children have benefited from this increase in attention is another question. It may have been uncomfortable to feel that they were responsible for the future.

In previous chapters we have seen several reasons for supposing that parents in the early modern period were becoming more anxious and the life of the child more constricted. The weakening of kinship ties had left the conjugal family more precarious, so that parents might be entirely dependent on their children for support in their old age. This made it more important than ever to give children an indelible impression of parental authority. In proper English households, children were supposed to stand or kneel in their parents' presence unless bidden to sit down, and to beg their parents' blessing night and morning. One writer (John Aubrey, no Puritan) remembered the 1630s as a time when

> The child perfectly loathed the sight of his parents, as the slave his Torturer. Gentlemen of 30 or 40 years old, fitt for any employment in the commonwealth, were to stand like great mutes and fools bare headed before their parents; and the Daughters (grown woemen) were to stand at the Cupboards side during the whole time of the proud mothers visitt, unless (as the fashion was) 'twas desired that leave (forsooth) should be given to them to kneele upon cushions brought them by the servingman, after they had done sufficient Penance standing.

We have seen reasons for thinking that the Renaissance emphasis on education had its painful side. Religious reformation had contributed a greater watchfulness and sometimes severity toward children. And now we see that visions of a new social order added to the divisions within society, for many parents felt they could no longer count on the whole community supporting the same values they hoped to inculcate in their children. A society which was becoming so diverse could not help but make parents feel more isolated in the task of child rearing. It is no wonder, then, that there was beginning to be more interest in and pressure on their children.

Twelve

The
Glorification
of the
Child

U p to this point in our story we have discovered very little appreciation of the child. In times of rapid change, people have worried about the coming generation. But it was the good of society that prompted their concern. Those who have taken the child's side or worked to make childhood itself a happy time have been quite exceptional. The eighteenth century saw a dramatic change in this regard, particularly in some classes in Europe. The child, or at least the child's image, was fully accepted and even glorified in the literature of that time. In later chapters we will see the extent to which this glorification did children any good and how far it only increased the demands on them. But first we must explore how this new sympathy was expressed, in hopes of accounting for such a change.

By the end of the seventeenth century, certain Protestant thinkers in England had grown out of sympathy with some of the classical doctrines of their faith. A few of them began describing their views in terms that were more complimentary to human nature, applying a humanistic view of humankind to childhood itself. The first to propose a serious re-evaluation of childhood were some neo-Platonist philosophers active at Cambridge University in the 1680s. Plato had written that souls are eternal and that children are born with experience of certain truths from their pre-existent state. This was how he explained the fact that some fundamental habits of thought do not seem to come from sensory experience. These are the concepts people were most agreed on, so he concluded that they were inborn. In *Phaedo* Plato discusses how growing up is actually the process of losing one's grip on these eternal verities and being caught up in transitory concerns. All this was a far cry from the doctrine that children inherited a mind that had been darkened by the Fall and needed rigorous training to set it right.

The Cambridge Platonists, especially Ralph Cudworth and Richard Cumberland, went a step further than Plato with their Idealist philosophy. They asserted not only innate knowledge in the child but an innate goodness. This went even beyond the notion of the innocence of the baptized child. For "innocence" may only mean a neutral state—neither bad nor positively good. These men postulated principles of innate "sympathy" or "benevolence" that formed the bases of conscience and sociable behavior. And thus we see the beginning of a view that was to become much more widespread in the next two centuries and bring the ideal of childhood to its height. Sentimental Victorians would adopt the view that children began as noble, unselfish, and joyous creatures until society crushed or corrupted their spirits.

Alongside these Platonic philosophers were others who had adopted what we might judge to be a more realistic view of children. In 1690 John Locke published his attack on innate ideas in *An Essay Concerning Human Understanding*. He attempted to show in detail how it is possible for all ideas to derive from experience rather than for some to be explained as innate. Similarly realistic was his general work on childhood, *Some Thoughts Concerning Education* (1693), which became the most popular book on child rearing in its day, with at least 26 editions before 1800. It had a European reputation, enjoying 16 French editions in that same period, as well as 6 Italian editions and translations into Dutch, German, Swedish, and Spanish. Books achieve this kind of popularity not because of their originality but because the public is predisposed to agree with their ideas. A work which contradicted very basic opinions would simply be ignored, however brilliant. But Locke did not have to wait to be discovered; the public was ready for his views.

We may assume that his audience appreciated his attack on the doctrine of infant depravity, for this was an obvious undercurrent in the book. Locke did not address this debate directly. Rather, he subtly undermined the doctrine by statements like the following: "Few of Adam's children are so happy, as not to be born with some bias in their natural temper which it is the business of education either to take off or counterbalance." By mentioning Adam's name he has reminded readers of the issue, but only to indicate that any "bias" is natural and not spiritual. And if such natural difficulties can be dealt with by education, religion need not come into the picture at all. Locke did not go on to idolize the child, as the Platonists were in danger of doing. He did not think it made any sense to say that children are naturally either good or bad. They are not capable of evil or virtue until they develop a will—that is, until they are capable of resisting their impulses. For until their actions are deliberate, children are nonmoral creatures. Intellectually, too, they are blank tablets, as Aristotle said in *De Anima.*

In effect, Locke thought children could be molded to one's desires. But this meant that parents had to be watchful that other influences did not create bad habits. Locke had much to say about nipping trouble in the bud. His advice about stubborn children sounds a good deal like that given in the Puritans' child-rearing manuals. Indeed, it appears that Locke's own parents had been of that persuasion. Like them, he insisted on obedience. It made family relations so much simpler. Locke was disgusted with parents who laughed when their small children fought and called names, only to find that they could not stand the brats when they became defiant adolescents. He had given much thought to "correction," having been a tutor if not a parent. His advice was to get spanking over with as soon as possible, so that the contest of wills did not go on and on. But he did not believe spanking is the main element in moral conditioning. It must be coupled with the use of shame. Without a sense of the shame or guilt of his or her action, the child will only be hardened in rebellion by physical punishment. Shame (and praise) help the child to internalize the parent's judgment. It impresses upon the child that the parent is not only more powerful but also right. Like the Puritans, Locke wanted the child to adopt the parent's moral position, rather than simply bow to superior strength or social pressure.

Locke went beyond the Puritans in advocating a toughening program, suggesting that children be made to wear leaky shoes in the winter to immunize them against colds. Here we are reminded that Locke was a physician by profession. Much of the advice in his book bears on pediatric matters that earlier child-rearing manuals had considered beneath them. He argued for loose swaddling, warned against sugar and snacks, and advocated strict toilet training. Other writers may have been afraid that dealing with these matters would be undignified. Locke had enough self-confidence to think he was dignifying the subject by his attention.

Like the Puritans, Locke did not find etiquette as important as the Renaissance courtesy books made it. He disliked the violence of the cult of heroism which dominated history and literature. And he thought that developing artistic, musical, or poetic talent in children would only lead them into a life of idleness and bad company. On the other hand, he does not sound like the Puritans when he advises parents to encourage their children's curiosity and play, or to begin to treat them as friends in their late teens, or to be careful not to break their spirits. Thus, it appears that the book may not have met anyone's expectations entirely, but that everyone would have found something in it with which to agree.

It is disappointing to find that Locke had given almost no thought to rearing girls. He could not have considered his instructions to be appropriate to them, since he approached his subject in terms of the specific roles upper-class boys would fill. It did occur to him to warn of the danger of strait-lacing girls into their bodices and other clothes. He had seen very harmful effects from trying to shape them in this way, and recalled seeing a tiny set of Chinese shoes that showed the unfortunate possibilities for disfiguring the body. When it came to discipline, Locke did not suggest a more lenient approach for girls. In fact, his most extreme example, of a child who had to be spanked eight times in one day (but never needed it thereafter), was a little girl.

Locke's work was much discussed in the eighteenth century, in periodicals and even in novels about family life. Most assumed he had said that children are naturally good, since he had denied the opposite. There was a line of philosophers who understood him better and developed his empirical psychology. But they were too subtle for the general public. Novelists catered to the more common understanding with characters who were simply and unaccountably good-natured. Tom Jones and Pamela, in the novels named after them, were born with innately good hearts which saw them through life despite the malice of their enemies. And in the end they were rewarded for this good nature, although they had as little to do with it as a Calvinist with his or her election. All this was reminiscent of the Platonic tradition, which persisted into the eighteenth century. It was still being elaborated at that time by philosophers like the third Earl of Shaftesbury. Shaftesbury (whom Locke had delivered as an infant and had tutored as a boy) argued that human beings are naturally motivated by generous and even altruistic instincts. Self-love, by his theory, is only part of a more general affection toward all of life. Children begin by loving themselves and then widen their sympathies as they learn more of the world.

The growth of a more optimistic view of human nature is one of the prominent and puzzling aspects of the eighteenth century. Perhaps by indulging a new sentimentality toward children, people were helped to feel better about themselves. They still had the example of harshness toward children before them, so they could take pride in their own benevolence.

We can see what the sentimental writers were up against, and their hopes for a more humane climate, in their discussions of corporal punishment. Experts had long argued against the practice where it was unjust or excessively brutal. But writers now felt confident that their readers were so repelled by the practice that they could be shamed out of it altogether. There was, by then, something embarrassing about the very desire to spank a child. In 1735 the *Gentleman's Magazine* ridiculed teachers who "foam in ecstacy at the sight of a jolly pair of buttocks." It wondered about one famous flogger who became so eager to punish his pupils that he tried to talk boys into taking a flogging in advance, promising to overlook their next offense. The most telling criticism was that there was something sexual at the basis of this sadism. For why did some schoolmasters pick on the prettier boys, and why did they say that it was because of their concern for them? "What shall we think of such liking?" By 1780, at least, some English schools announced that they did not administer corporal punishment, obviously expecting this advertisement to meet with public approval. Of course, such schools were free to expel unruly boys.

With so much debate over the child's nature it would appear that child-rearing practices were diversifying in eighteenth-century England and America. No longer was there a common tradition in each class but rather several contrasting approaches as the social structure became more fluid and as religious diversity grew. Descendants of the seventeenth-century Puritans and Dissenters seemed even more anxious about their children as their sects dwindled in numbers, and they expressed this in their discussions of obedience. The phrase "breaking the will," which was not very current in the seventeenth century, seems to have increased in popularity. The classic statement of this view is John Wesley's:

> If you are not willing to lose all the labour you have been at to break the will of your child, to bring his will into subjection to yours that it may be afterward subject to the will of God, there is one advice which, though little known, should be particularly attended. . . . It is this; never, on any account, give a child anything that it cries for. . . . If you give a child what he cries for, you pay him for crying: and then he will certainly cry again.

Other religious leaders, however, were becoming self-conscious and defensive about strictness. In the 1730s Jonathan Edwards, the New England theologian, admitted: "What has more especially given offense to many, and raised a loud cry against some preachers, as though their conduct were intolerable, is their frightening poor innocent children with talk of hell fire and eternal damnation." But he protested that he did not make up doctrine to suit his wishes. "As innocent as children seem to be to us, yet if they are out of Christ, they are not so in God's sight, but are young vipers, and are infinitely more hateful than vipers, and are in a most miserable condition, as well as grown persons." As a father Edwards seemed much less ferocious. An admirer testified that

> he was careful and thorough in the government of his children; and, as a consequence of this, they reverenced, esteemed, and loved him. . . . When they discovered [i.e., displayed] any considerable degree of will and stubbornness, he would attend to them till he had thoroughly subdued them and brought them to submit. And such prudent thorough discipline, exercised with the greatest calmness, and commonly without striking a blow, being repeated once or twice, was generally sufficient for the child; and effectually established his parental authority and produced a cheerful obedience ever after.

Locke would have approved. We may take it as the ideal practice at that time, whatever may have happened when observers were not present.

Edwards obviously felt that his preaching went against a tide of sentiment for the child which would sweep away effective discipline. It is easy to cite examples of this affection. A New England parent wrote his father in 1716 of the death of his grandson: "A sensible, quiet, meek, yet cheerly-tempered child, strongly-natured, hearty, fat. How often have we pleased ourselves with the thoughts of your seeing this your pretty grandson who had so manly, beautiful and graceful a look; but Providence has ordered otherwise." Churches filled with such parents found ways to adjust their theology to reflect this sympathy. By the time of Horace Bushnell's *Christian Nurture* (1847), the child's depravity was implicitly denied. Conversion was redefined as a gradual and painless process which could begin in infancy. Ideally, Bushnell taught,

> The child is to grow up a Christian, and never know himself as being otherwise. . . . The Christian is one who has simply *begun* to love what is good for its own sake, and why should it be thought impossible for a child to have this love begotten in him?

These various moral approaches were all some distance from the usual practice in upper-class households, which were more oriented toward the enjoyment of life. The genteel accepted and indulged their children as they accepted themselves, ignoring what they did not wish to see. But as Locke had observed, if parents were seriously crossed, they might punish the child severely, and the more so as they had allowed the waywardness to become rooted. A different kind of training was appropriate to children in this class, for their job would be to rule others, not themselves. One Virginian recorded such parents as saying that "to curb their children is to spoil their genius." They represent an older tradition, raised without self-consciousness or guilt, unlike the more modern, intense manner of the Puritans. William Byrd, the wealthy Virginia planter, showed some of this smugness in his comments on the death of a two-year-old son: "My wife was much afflicted but I submitted to His Judgment better, notwithstanding I was very sensible to my loss, but God's will be done." This was the same man who made a nephew drink a cup of urine to cure him of bed-wetting—not an uncommon remedy.

With a greater variety of approaches, observers were learning to keep their thoughts about other people's children to themselves. One Englishman in 1767 complained in a letter of the children in a country house he was visiting. A crowd of six of them received all the delicacies at dinner from a mother who imagined that they were all afflicted with weak stomachs. A little daughter was allowed to drink all the cream at breakfast and put her fingers in the sugarbowl "because she was once sickly." Others pestered the visitor, destroyed his belongings, and made conversation impossible. And to top it all, he overheard his host say that "I am a mighty good sort of a man, but that I cannot talk to children." This was a mortifying comment in an age when it was becoming common to say that affection for children was evidence of a good nature.

By this point it will surprise no one to hear that the most determined efforts of historians to discover the actual facts about parental discipline indicate that it has changed very little over long periods. Linda Pollock, in *Forgotten Children: Parent-Child Relations from 1500 to 1900,* used English and American diaries and memoirs to reach the rather disappointing conclusion that debates on childhood and a growing devotion to the child's image did not seem to affect how these parents "corrected" their children. Granted, she could only study those parents who were sufficiently literate to record their activities. But they would also be the ones who were bookish enough to be aware of all the new advice. Through the period she examined, Pollock noticed only one momentary increase in reported physical punishment—in the early nineteenth century, particularly in English schools.

Attempts to pin down a date for the transition from a "moralizing" to an "accepting" attitude toward children have proven futile. One can find a rather frightening and unsympathetic "Calvinism" well into the nineteenth century, in certain parts of the English-speaking world especially. By that time generations of repression may have resulted in a subculture of sadism. But the novelists who portrayed such villainy were picking on an undefended target. In any event no generalizations can be made in the face of regional, national, class, and denominational differences.

The book which is most often treated as the dividing line between the dark age of childhood and the beginning of an enlightened concern appeared in France in 1762—Jean-Jacques Rousseau's *Emile*. Obviously, this citation overdramatizes the effect of the book and the suddenness of the change. But the work is remarkable nevertheless. No book can change deep-rooted attitudes by itself, but it may catalyze a change. And all of Europe was stimulated by *Emile*, the story of a tutor and the boy in his charge.

The opening sentence itself was revolutionary: "The Author of Nature makes all things good; man meddles with them and they become evil." Earlier writers—whether Catholic, Protestant, or free-thinking—had thought that human institutions were necessary precisely to counteract the flaws of human nature. Rousseau asserted just the opposite, that nature was the source of all good and that human institutions were the cause of the evil in the world. He realized his break with past ideas and felt that he had to quarrel with everyone. He even attacked Locke for having seen education as the creation of useful habits. Useful to society perhaps, but what about the development of the individual? The child will have to live with nature as well as with human society. And he must live with himself. Society seemed bent on alienating the individual from himself by forcing him into a mold. It would be far better, Rousseau thought, to let the child learns directly from a beneficent nature. In that way he will always be in tune with nature and maintain his self-reliance, his enjoyment of life, and an inborn benevolence toward his fellow-creatures.

Contrast that with what we do with our children, Rousseau demands. Civilization begins by swaddling the child, the first of our many forms of bondage. Then the child learns rejection, when his mother sends him away to a wet-nurse. It is true that mothers pretend they would like to nurse the child themselves. The growth of sentiment has made us hypocritical about our callousness. But mothers are easily dissuaded from the idea of nursing, perhaps by fathers who also dislike the inconvenience involved. Thus the whole moral world of the child is upset. The moral reformation of the world would depend on reverting to the ancient pattern, the mother nursing the child and the father teaching him, as in early Rome.

Rousseau proceeds in his fictional narrative to describe how a wise tutor might manage the job of raising a child more naturally. He begins at the beginning, with an effort to imagine the blooming, buzzing confusion which the infant encounters at birth. Rousseau even sensed that there was a language of childhood, involving the whole body and characterized by tone and stress. No one before him had shown anything like this awareness of just how different the world would seem to the child, nor of the different meanings he might assign to his surroundings.

Emile's tutor does not try to rush the boy into accepting some particular view of things. He is permissive in the sense of letting the child learn his lessons as nature presents them. Teacher and pupil are equals in their search for knowledge, the teacher trying to sustain their mutual wonder at the wisdom and variety of nature and opening the child's eyes to what is around him. Rousseau does caution that the tutor must not be the child's slave, for that would only teach the child to be a tyrant. He should be given liberty, but never power. And if this liberty allows him to break a few things or make mistakes, that is a risk that must be taken. For he must be allowed to be active if he is to be constructive. His activity follows a God-given impulse and is evidence of the curiosity which will motivate his learning.

Until this time, writers had worried that society would not be able to curb the child's will and make him well-mannered and studious. Rousseau was the first to make people worry that they might break the child's will and kill his natural curiosity. Before his time the power of natural instincts had seemed a little frightening; now people became preoccupied with the crushing power of society. Nothing is more characteristic of modern attitudes than this feeling that society has the advantage in its struggle with human nature. Rousseau was the first to accept the child's impulses fully, as necessary to any healthy functioning and even as the basis for moral development. Impulses are not the root of any evil, according to Rousseau, unless they are either frustrated or encouraged in the wrong direction. Unfortunately, he thought, that was just what families and schools were doing.

Rousseau certainly does not give the impression that children were being neglected in his day. Quite the contrary. Adults were constantly fussing over them—doctoring, swaddling, concocting indigestible foods, making elaborate and inappropriate toys, correcting their speech, keeping them from hurting themselves, and teaching them things they could not begin to understand. After all this the child does not know who he is. Moral training is conducted in an anxious and artificial climate—by precept, when the child actually learns morals by example. Nature itself will teach a scale of values based on simple prudence. The child will learn how to behave so that others will be nice to him, without being brow-beaten. For the child's self-love, far from being a defect in his character, is the very basis of his code of honor and fair play. In fact, whatever malice we may see in children is not innate but is their resistance to being forced along the path of virtue. The wise tutor will find that he never has to beat the child, but can trust nature to administer the proper punishment. For instance, when Emile lies, his tutor simply stops believing anything he says, until the boy learns the value of honesty.

Only when Emile reaches age 12 does the tutor begin formal academic education. By that time Emile is demanding to learn to read and to be taught science and mathematics. In Rousseau's view, this desire is the key to pedagogy. Most of the problems of education are problems of motivation, as teachers try to rush things. They talk of geography before the child knows the way around his own backyard. They teach history before the child understands anything about adult motivation. They try to reason with children, as Locke advised, so that children pick up the trick of arguing and think that skepticism is the same as sophistication. It would be far better, Rousseau thought, to let questions arise naturally. Children would not need Locke's learning games and alphabet blocks, for method would not matter. When a child is self-motivated, the teacher cannot keep him from learning. Comenius had held similar views on the need to build on the child's own questions and his understanding of life. No doubt it would have spoiled things a bit for Rousseau had he known that he was not being entirely original.

By age 15 Emile is seeking the broader moral education which is to be found in literature and history. And by 22 he wants to see the world, and so he is taken abroad to learn about politics and economics at first hand. By 25, when he and his tutor return, he is ready to take his place in public life.

One of the most striking things to readers of that day was the fact that Rousseau did not seem to care whether Emile ever learned the manners of a polished gentleman. This was not an oversight on Rousseau's part. Like the Puritan he was at heart (born in Calvinist Geneva), he rejected polite society as a fraud. In any event, he believed high society was doomed and predicted that France was on the edge of a revolution. Indeed, *Emile* was written for the purpose of creating a more natural being who would fit in with the more natural society which Rousseau foresaw. In the end, this revolutionary approach to education and social problems became almost religious in its seriousness. The climax of the book is the famous "Creed of a Savoyard Priest" in which Rousseau describes his own beliefs. Even for Rousseau, who was generally suspected of being a skeptic, a concern for children became, finally, a matter of religion.

At the end of the book it occurs to Rousseau that Emile will be marrying, and that he has said nothing about educating girls. The perfect man will need a perfect wife, and so Rousseau adds a section called "Sophy, or Woman." It is a shock. His sexist theme is that "woman is specially made for man's delight." For that reason there is no need even to teach girls to read. Their minds ought not to be awakened, except to think what other people will want them to do.

This is bound to raise the question of Rousseau's character, which is a topic of some importance in our history of attitudes toward children. For he is representative, in certain respects, of many of those in the next century who sentimentalized childhood. As sympathetic as he was toward children, the motives behind his ideas and their actual effect were unfortunate. Rousseau did not have satisfactory relations with women. His own mother had died when he was born, and he never married. His liaisons with aristocratic admirers led to unpleasantness, because he was so uneasy around anyone whom he could not dominate. His only lasting relationship was with an ignorant working-class woman. By his own account he left each of their five illegitimate children at a local foundling home. As a tutor, too, he had been a failure, frequently being overcome with rage at his pupils' insubordination and ignorance. His paranoia may have driven him to suicide, though there is uncertainty surrounding his death.

These matters are not raised to disparage his philosophy of education or his very real contribution to an understanding of the child. Rousseau was the first author to accept and affirm the child fully. His was not the idle nostalgia of a poet for his own childhood, but a genuine effort to get inside the child and learn his needs and limits. We have noticed that many of those who are important for a history of childhood had problems stemming from their own experience as children. But Rousseau's problem was more troublesome because it was disguised. Even historians are too ready to overlook the signs of trouble in someone with such apparent sympathy for children.

The problem was that Rousseau felt guilty and ashamed of his paranoiac desire to dominate others and thereby reduce their threat to him. This shame is what prompted him to design an educational method which did not rely on authority. But in fact the authority is only hidden. Emile's tutor uses nature itself to subdue the child, manipulating him through his environment. As a result, he feels free to dominate the child more completely than if he had to acknowledge his use of power. There is even a hint of sadism when Rousseau repeatedly rejoices to say that the child is suffering only at the hands of nature and only for his own good. Summing up the beauty of his scheme, he points out: "There is no subjection so complete as that which retains the appearance of liberty."

Something of this sadism helps explain the sentimentalizing of childhood which reached its height in the nineteenth century. Like Rousseau, authors used sympathy for the child as part of an attack on society. The new individualism was distinctly anti-social, and expressing the pathos of childhood became a favorite way for authors to vent their hostility toward a burdensome civilization. As we shall see, the child in the Victorian novel became more and more innocent and appealing in order to provide a growing contrast with a heartless society. Actually, the sentimentalism which gathered around child characters became increasingly false because it had little real connection with children. The growing number of children who were dying in fiction did not represent social reality. In fact, child mortality rates were falling. These figures of suffering children represent the authors' memory of themselves and were the focus of their self-pity. The fact that writers disguised their hostility by identifying with a childlike innocence allowed them a clear conscience. It even justified their righteous indignation, since cruelty toward children was now an unanswerable accusation.

It is difficult to believe that Rousseau himself cared anything for the actual effect of his work, so long as it helped establish his literary reputation. He made no attempt to answer the practical problems involved in his educational program and secretly ridiculed those who tried to rear their children by his precepts. The work is largely a self-advertisement, as Rousseau takes time to quarrel with everyone and overturn all previous ideas, proving that he and he alone is right. If taken seriously, the book would make the job of the sensitive parent all but impossible, with its frequent warnings that some slip—say, a laugh—"may destroy six months' work and do irreparable damage for life." This was just one more way Rousseau found to raise feelings of guilt in those around him. Perhaps it is fortunate that he never gave the world a demonstration of the kind of father he would have been.

There were those who struggled to put Rousseau's ideas to practical use. Johann Basedow, a German, opened a truly experimental school in 1774, in which he tried a variety of teaching techniques. He was a pioneer in that he took the development of the child's intelligence as a conscious aim and was not satisfied with the mastery of subject material. Basedow also produced some elementary textbooks which were reminiscent of the *Orbis Pictus*. Johann Pestalozzi likewise tried to use some of Rousseau's insights in his school in Switzerland (1799). He combined the notion of starting from the objects of the child's own world with a rather excessive insistence on analyzing everything down to its basic elements. His pupils busied themselves practicing all the possible curves and angles before being allowed to draw pictures. Reading was also delayed until all the combinations of vowels and consonants had been mastered. Pestalozzi succeeded as a teacher in spite of his methods, by his enthusiasm for children. Observers came from as far away as the new United States to be inspired by this rugged and disheveled old character. Both Basedow and Pestalozzi tended toward a greater sentimentalization of the child than had Rousseau and a greater indulgence of self-expression, perhaps as a compensation for their own orphaned and difficult childhoods.

Educational reformers could seldom agree in detail, so none

of the Rousseauist schools survived the deaths of the founders. Governments were slow to institutionalize any of their reforms, although Prussia hired some of Pestalozzi's assistants as advisors. One of these was Friedrich Froebel, founder of the "kindergarten" and the proud author of *Mother and Play Songs* (1843). At about the same time, still another German, Johann Herbart, formalized educational method into five steps (reflection, presentation, association, generalization, and application). It took some such formula to give shape to teacher-training programs and begin the professionalization of that calling. Herbart's scheme provided the element of consensus needed for institutionalized progress.

If Rousseau had little immediate impact on education, he did stimulate the finest brains in Europe to consider the nature of childhood. The greatest philosopher of the day, the Prussian Immanuel Kant, was so taken with *Emile* that he missed his regular walk for several days while reading it—a major event in his methodical life. Scientists, too, began to turn their attention to solving the riddle of the child's basic nature. Who was right? Locke, who denied innate characteristics, or the Platonists and Rousseau, who emphasized the nature or capacities that the child brought into the world? They did not want to decide this question of nature versus nurture simply according to their personal preferences. But how could they settle the matter objectively?

It occurred to some of these scientists that they might do so by studying "feral children"—those raised by animals or without companionship of any kind. Since the mid–seventeenth century there had been published accounts of children discovered running wild in the woods and showing no signs of human behavior even after capture. Linnaeus, the Swedish scientist who is largely responsible for our modern system of biological classification, had published the details of ten such cases. It surprised some that the supposedly innate characteristics of human nature were not more secure. Rousseau himself admitted that the wolf-children gave evidence of the power of environment and conditioning, which seemed to argue against the developmental timetable he had described. But the other side was just as puzzled when they found that even years in human society did not necessarily produce speech or other signs of reason, or even upright posture. Why couldn't conditioning reverse those early habits? The simplest answer was that all such children were idiots—born incapable of speech—and that parents had abandoned them for that very reason.

None of these cases had been studied closely over any length of time until a wild boy was caught in France in 1798. A celebrated psychologist promptly pronounced him a congenital idiot. But a physician, Jean Itard, asked that the boy be put under his care so that he could prove that he was capable of education. Victor of Aveyron, as he was named, was judged to be about 11, and he made remarkable progress emotionally and socially. He changed from a surly, snapping beast into a sensitive and helpful lad. His first tears were the culmination of a massive moral development. But it surprised Itard to see just how much change was needed before Victor began to resemble a human. He actually had to learn to be conscious of pain and of changes in temperature. Itard had to admit that five years of work had not brought any progress toward speech, even though Victor made some progress in reading and writing. It appeared that, although the capacity for speech is innate, the skill had to be developed at a particular point in the child's life or else the opportunity would be lost forever.

Questions of the child's nature had turned out to be more complicated than anyone had supposed. The crowds that turned out to watch Victor expected that in a few months he would have picked up enough of the language to offer some striking observations on his life in the wilds. Instead, they were disgusted by his convulsive movements and his indifference or hostility toward all efforts at attention. Even scientists saw fewer signs of intelligence in him than in a dog. They could not have guessed at the skills which had allowed him to survive the years that he had been glimpsed by farmers. They were unable to imagine the trauma of abandonment and utter isolation, or the effort required to unlearn all of his earlier patterns of behavior.

Itard recognized the source of the spectators' disbelief. It was that same hostility toward civilized society which Rousseau had expressed, the hostility that was to make children the heroes of so many Victorian novels. It was part of that turning from civilization to nature which was such an important part of the Romantic era. Victor disappointed them because they would have preferred to think better of human nature. Itard himself reluctantly concluded: "Man is inferior to a great number of animals in a pure state of nature, [which is] a state of vacuity and barbarism, although it has been falsely painted in colors the most attractive." He rebuked Rousseau by pointing out that "the moral superiority which has been said to be natural to man, turns out to be the result of civilization." This was an unwelcome lesson to an age that wanted to owe everything to nature and nothing to society. With faith in religion beginning to wane among the enlightened, it would not do to have the child, their main symbol of beneficent nature, changed into something beastly. The glorification of the child was one of the reasons further progress toward a scientific understanding of the child was delayed until Darwin's time, when humankind's animal nature was taken more seriously.

Thirteen

The
Business
of
Entertaining
Children

Historians differ widely on when children's literature began, because they differ on what qualifies as a children's book. Some refuse to consider works that were obviously written for children to be true children's books if they cannot imagine any child enjoying them. But we have seen that different eras have had their own ideas of what childhood is really like. We may be as mistaken in our way as they were in theirs, and there may be no way of telling what children in the past thought of what was offered them. But in a study of attitudes toward children, even rather unattractive works may be evidence of what children were thought to enjoy and of what was thought to be good for them.

Many of the stories we now associate with children are preserved in some form in medieval manuscripts. Almost as soon as printing developed, some of these appeared in books. For example, William Caxton introduced the printing press in England in 1477, and some of his earliest productions were *Reynard the Fox* and *Aesop's Fables.* It is not clear that these stories or books were originally meant for children. After all, the books were very expensive at first. Also, we know that all age groups enjoyed such stories in those days. Colbert, the greatest man in Louis XIV's government, relaxed in the evening by listening to what would now be called nursery tales. We gather that before literacy became widespread everyone listened to the same stories. What has changed since then is that adults have "grown up" and have left these stories to children. Partly, this has been the result of literacy, which develops the critical abilities but shrivels the imagination. The old nursery tales required no intellect to speak of, but to enter into a fairy tale or animal fable would require the kind of imagination only children possess nowadays. It may be that adults were more childlike in the early years of the modern era.

In the course of the sixteenth and seventeenth centuries it appears that the fables, fairy stories, and nursery rhymes that appeared in medieval sermons and romances came to be the property of younger readers. *Robin Hood, The Seven Wise Masters,* and *St. George* hardly needed to be simplified for them, but they were printed more and more cheaply. We gather that they were not in great demand among adults any longer, or at least not among the more prosperous classes. Still, there was a large market for the "chapbook" versions, which sold for as little as one penny and amounted to one folded sheet making 16 or 32 pages. They were, in effect, the equivalent of our comic books, with their crude woodblock pictures and paper covers.

It was perfectly appropriate that these stories should become the child's own literature, since they so frequently involved the youth of their heroes. Of course, childhood and youth made up a larger proportion of an average lifetime then than now, and it may be that readers thought it was also the more interesting part of life. The characters seem in no hurry to grow up. Take *Bevis of Southampton,* for example. Bevis was sold by his mother to the Turks, which was only to be expected of mothers in medieval stories. But the Saracen king grew to like him, as did the king's daughter. Bevis staunchly refused to renounce Christianity, however, and was forced to leave the court and become a knight-errant. The rest of the story relates the exploits of the boyish and exuberant Bevis, his horse Arundel, and the famous sword Morglay. Together they face evil men and monsters, dragons and giants all over the known world. When at last they find their way back to England Bevis is in time to help defeat the Vikings and win an English princess. Adulthood would have been an anti-climax to these adventures.

Bevis, like many of these stories, sounds like a garbled version of a chivalrous romance. Unfortunately, in the sixteenth century there were many who disapproved of this life of chivalry. Renaissance Humanists objected that such romances glamorized a life of idleness, violence, and adultery and gave a militaristic tone to society. The Humanists offered children something else to read, in the courtesy books or conduct manuals which described proper courtly behavior and the way to rise in the world. These could be said to be the first books expressly written—or at least adapted—for children. It is odd to think of the first children's books warning their readers against nursery tales, as these sometimes did.

Other serious-minded authors concurred. Puritans agreed

with Humanists as to the ill effects of the chapbooks. And St. Teresa of Avila (describing the 1530s) complained of her mother's taste in this regard:

> She was very fond of books of chivalry, but this pastime did not hurt her so much as it hurt me, because she never wasted her time on them; only we, her children, were left at liberty to read them; and perhaps she did this to distract her thoughts from her great sufferings, and occupy her children, that they might not go astray in other ways. It annoyed my father so much that we had to be careful he never saw us. . . . So completely was I mastered by this passion, that I thought I could never be happy without a new book.

Religious reformers were even suspicious of the Humanists' courtesy books. After all, what are courtesy and good manners but hypocrisy? And what did such books teach besides grasping after worldly advantage? These reformers did not see the need for anything but religious reading. If children wanted adventure, there was plenty of that in the Bible. Fairy tales were rejected even more strenuously, as the source of serious superstition. Rather than admit such influences, Puritans made suggestions as to the best parts of the Bible for children to begin on, and even tried their own hand at books for children. Most of the English books produced expressly for children up to the eighteenth century were from this source. As John Aubrey remembered it:

> When I was a child [in the 1630s] the fashion was for old women and mayds to tell fabulous stories nightimes, of Sprights and walking of Ghosts, etc. This was derived down from mother to daughter, from the Monkish Ballance which upheld Holy Church, for the Divines say, Deny Spirits, you are an Atheist. When the [religious] warres came, and with them Liberty of Conscience and Liberty of inquisition, the phantoms vanished. Now children feare no such things, having heard not of them.

At another time, he credited printing with the decline of fairy tales as the common entertainment of all ages.

Before Printing, Old-wives Tales were ingeniose, and . . . the ordinary sort of People were not taught to reade. Now-a-dayes Bookes are common, and most of the poor people understand letters; and the many good Bookes, and variety of Turnes of Affaires, have putt all the old Fables out of doors: and the divine Art of Printing and Gunpowder have frightened away Robin-goodfellow and the Fayries.

Looking back, the discouragement of fairy tales seems to have been a mistake, whatever the reasons for it. Psychologists can show how they serve useful, even vital, functions. Fairy tales are not about reality—nature or society—and the child does not become confused by supposing that they are. Essentially, they are about the child's own impulses and feelings and help to clarify his or her inner life and identity. The characters can be shown to stand for various feelings that are troublesome to all children. A girl loves her mother but sometimes experiences the mother's rejection, so it may help to split that figure into an idealized mother and a cruel stepmother. The child's anger can then be expressed without guilt. Dragons often stand in for the father, as one can tell from their usual activity in monopolizing the women in the story, so that a boy can project his feelings of anger toward them when it would be too scary to admit such feelings toward father. The marriage or the coronation which closes the story represents the child's hope for achievement, independence, and a triumph over present inferiority. Thus the stories promote confidence about life, even while acknowledging the anxieties common to all children. Their universal lesson is that even the meek, the small, and the young can succeed in life. Simply to tell the child this, in so many words, will not have the impact that the story has, however fanciful it may seem.

The objections critics have voiced, then and now, miss the point. It is true that characters triumph by magical means. But the stories are effective at a time in life when all means seem equally magical, when nature itself seems animate. The magic represents hope, which needs to be encouraged if the child is ever to face life with confidence. A social realism, by contrast, would simply seem defeating in a children's story. It is also true that the stories do not seem to teach moral lessons (unless an editor has added them) and often encourage trickery. But in fact they offer something that must precede moral development, by encouraging the child to choose sides. By sympathizing with one character and against another, the child acquires the habit of identifying with those he or she wishes to emulate. And whereas one might ordinarily be expected to choose the most powerful figures as one's models, fairy stories encourage just the reverse. To introduce moral issues before the child is sure of his or her moral identity would be futile and even disturbing. Of course, fairy tales do not have only those functions we have mentioned. The same story might strike the same child very differently at different times. Boys and girls may differ in their preferences. And we cannot say that because a story *could* have met a certain need that it *must* have done so. In general, however, it seems that the instinct which allowed these stories to circulate was wiser than the reason which tried to rule them out.

By 1700 some were already rejecting censorship. Charles Perrault, a famous literary figure of his day, published the first *Tales of Mother Goose* (this title was actually a subtitle for *Histories or Tales of Past Time, With their Morals*) in 1697. They became the rage of the French court. Apparently adults had grown away from these stories to the point that they now seemed quaint and charming. Adult sophistication had increased, and there seems to have been something of a reaction in favor of a sentimental cult of the primitive and the childish. This fad can also be seen in the practice, popular in England around 1700, of applying nursery rhymes to contemporary politics, which has led some writers to the mistaken notion that the rhymes were originally written as political jingles.

Historians of children's literature are right to take Perrault's book as a milestone, since it put the stamp of cultural approval on nursery folklore. But many people at the time continued to be shocked. The blood-thirsty tales horrified Puritans and everyone else who was trying to take childhood more seriously. On the face of it, the stories are pretty unsavory. Consider the eight tales that Perrault chose, and the cruelty which is their major theme. "Sleeping Beauty" is about a fairy's curse on a baby princess. True, the rest of the story tells of the efforts of all and sundry to counteract that curse. But even after Beauty is married to her Prince, her mother-in-law, an ogre, tries to eat all their children in turn. "Red Riding Hood" concerns a much-beloved daughter and granddaughter who is eaten up all the same. And Perrault did not use the happy ending which appears in later editions of that story. Mercifully, Blue Beard has no children, but only because he murders his wives too soon. "Cinderella" and "Toads and Diamonds" are both about good girls who are hated and persecuted by jealous families. Things work out well for the heroines, and the mean sisters get what is coming to them. But this result comes about through the wisdom of fairies, not of sympathetic humans. "Puss and Boots" concerns a boy whose family leaves him nothing but a cat for his inheritance, though it proves to be a very remarkable cat. "Riquet with the Tuft" is the account of two genetic casualties—the world's ugliest prince and the world's dumbest princess—who are magically enabled to correct each other's deficiencies when no one else can help. Most horrifying of all is "Little Thumb," about a family so poor that the parents try several times to lose their seven children in the forest. To be sure, the parents do feel badly about this, and the children don't seem to hold it against them. When Little Thumb ingeniously finds the way home, the children are welcomed back because they have managed to bring some money with them. But later, when they are abandoned again and are captured by a nearsighted ogre, they only escape when he butchers and eats his seven daughters instead. And nobody laments those daughters.

Even Perrault felt a little uneasy with these stories. He felt constrained to attach morals to them, which a modern psychologist would insist would limit the child's imaginative use of the stories. But at that time many thought that even the morals did not redeem them. They also denounced *The Arabian Nights* (which French publishers discovered shortly afterwards) for being crammed with gore. Not that this criticism stopped publication. English editions of *Mother Goose* and *The Arabian Nights* appeared in the early years of the eighteenth century. For it was discovered that there was money in the business of entertaining children.

The only way to beat this commercialism was to join it. Reformers began to produce something that could compete in appeal but would have a more wholesome effect. The most successful of these books was *Divine and Moral Songs for Children* (1715) by the English Dissenter Isaac Watts. The book saw 75 editions in America alone before 1800, far more than the Bible itself. Of course, it was popular because adults bought it to give to children, but the same was true of *Mother Goose* after all. It was very accomplished verse and probably gave children a good deal of pleasure. Unfortunately, like much of the well-meaning children's literature of the eighteenth century, the book was eventually imposed on children. And that spoiled everything. When Lewis Carroll parodied some of Watts's verses in *Alice in Wonderland* (1865), he could count on the fact that his readers would know them by heart, having been forced to learn them. They had become a national institution.

In a sense, these literary endeavors were a step backward. The reformers' books were meant to inform children about the real world and to teach moral lessons. But in their efforts to remove whatever was evil or frightening in the stories, the reformers were failing to meet an even deeper need—the need for a way of coping with childhood fears. Ignoring these fears would not keep them from arising in the child's mind. Rather, it left the child with the feeling that only he or she had such fears and must repress them. The realistic solutions to life's problems which authors presented must often have made children feel even more helpless. And thus we can say that, despite all their good intentions, these writers could not compete with folklore in psychological sophistication. For folktales were created by the collective experience of the thousands who had added to them, or at least had selected certain ones for preservation. The traditional stories had met needs which were not even recognized as needs by early experts.

Of course, there continued to be light entertainment for children despite the moralistic authors. By 1744 the first English book of nursery rhymes—*Tommy Thumb's Pretty Song Book*—appeared. It would have taken people by surprise. Books had always been held in respect, yet here was one that was filled with nonsense. Whoever published it did not have the nerve to give his or her name, calling it the work of "Nurse Lovechild." But someone had recognized the delight children take in simply playing with words and rhythms and tried to meet them on their own level.

By the end of the eighteenth century there was enough children's literature that people were writing *about* it. Most of these critics did not stop at making recommendations as to what children liked or should like but went on to write children's books that embodied their principles. Generally, they showed the influence of Rousseau. Some, like Thomas Day, went to extremes to follow his advice, even in personal affairs. Having been disappointed in love, Day decided to raise a girl on Rousseau's principles in order to ensure a perfect wife. He picked out two orphans of about 12 to raise by a rigorous training program, encouraging them to be loyal, logical, and fearless. Both of them failed the course. The disappointed Day later died from a fall from an unbroken colt while testing his belief that kindness would tame any animal. Such was his faith in a benevolent Nature, which was very much the principle behind his interest in children. Another of these early child experts, Maria Edgeworth, had herself been reared by a disciple of Rousseau. Her brother had even been exhibited before Rousseau, who appears to have been uninterested in the products of his advice. In this case, the boy grew up so wild that his disillusioned parents packed him off to boarding school and later disowned him altogether. But Maria maintained the family tradition by writing children's stories of admirable realism and sympathy.

These and other liberal-minded authors of the late eighteenth century brought new themes and attitudes to children's books. Adults were portrayed as friends, whereas before they were simply authority figures. Kindness to animals became an important element. Orphaned and poor children were held up as models to the pampered children of the rich, as in Day's *Sandford and Merton* (1783). Pride in wealth or social rank was disparaged, in the tradition of Rousseau. The girl characters with whom the authors (mostly women) identify are not usually pretty or even witty; it is enough that they are sensible, obedient, and kind.

No doubt these authors worried too much about the effect of fright or frivolity or fairies on the child's mind. We, in our turn, may worry too much about the lack of a sense of fun in their writings. We feel sure that children must always have hated being preached to. But many of us could probably echo what Harvey Darton observed in his classic history of children's literature. While rereading *The Swiss Family Robinson* (1812), which had been one of his childhood favorites, he was surprised to find that it was basically a religious work. All Darton had remembered were the adventures, forgetting entirely Father Robinson's constant moralizing of the day's experiences. It is impossible to say how children reacted to the books they were given or how they used them. Of course, any statement that attempted to speak for all children would have to be false.

A moralistic literature did not imply that children were still considered evil by nature. But it did suggest that the world was full of evil influences. The more that writers regarded children as naturally innocent, the more efforts were made to protect them from a threatening world. In England the campaign to expurgate literature for the use of children began in 1807. Thomas Bowdler and his sister Harriet published *The Family Shakespeare* in that year, with the hope that they had removed "everything that can raise a blush on the cheek of modesty." Charles Lamb and his spinster sister Mary brought out their *Tales from Shakespeare* in the same year, with much the same intention. They did not want to keep children from reading the classics. Indeed, they hoped the book would encourage parents to expose their children to great literature if they were assured that any suggestive words had been removed. The expurgators even convinced themselves they had improved the classics, raising them to a higher artistic plane by refining their language. They had discovered that some seventeenth-century editions of Shakespeare had added smutty dialogue in an effort to please jaded audiences. This encouraged them to claim that later editors were the source of all that they found objectionable in his plays and that they were restoring Shakespeare's works to his original intentions.

It was an odd situation. Older generations have often worried about the morals of the young. But around 1800 people began to worry about the morals of their parents. Henry Fielding's own great-granddaughter expurgated his novels. Even the Bible was sanitized—by Noah Webster, who used his vast vocabulary to find euphemisms for words like "belly," "lust," and "stink," which had not bothered readers before. As time went on, the Bowdlerizers became more and more meddlesome. By the early twentieth century they were not satisfied with substituting words but were leaving out whole sections. They had long since ceased leaving asterisks where they had tampered with the text, for fear of encouraging curiosity. By that time, movies were becoming a source of concern, and in 1907 the city of Chicago took the lead in establishing government censorship in the interest of children.

Inevitably, there was a reaction. In the 1920s scholars began to recover all the ribaldry. Unfortunately, children have largely stopped reading the classics and therefore do not profit from the scholars' efforts. Censorship did not exactly stop, but it did change its focus. Nowadays, the concern is with removing racist and sexist slurs. It seems that there will always be some tampering with the books our children read, so long as we hope children will live up to a higher level of conduct than they would discover in an entirely realistic literature.

In the midst of the moralistic stories and the expurgated classics appeared a new kind of children's book—original tales or rhymes written to enlarge the stock of traditional nursery lore. In England, the first of these light-hearted works appeared in 1807, in William Roscoe's *The Butterfly's Ball* and Catherine Dorset's *The Peacock at Home.* With their large print and engraved illustrations, they made quite a contrast with the chapbooks and their often irrelevant woodcuts. These new books made no effort to improve children, any more than the folklore rhymes had done. And as they caught on, the traditional rhymes were printed in this generous format. For the first time, pictures were more important than the text. It is rather jarring to note that publishers hired children to hand-tint the engravings. Like the provision of slave "play children" for the master's own children on the American plantations, this is a reminder of the class differences in the history of childhood.

Even in the early nineteenth century not everyone approved the new, more frivolous literature for children. Americans especially complained that the nursery rhymes were too inane, the folktales too brutal, and the fairy stories too pagan. Puritan attitudes had been so prevalent that Samuel Goodrich could recall the horror of his chance introduction to Red Riding Hood and Jack the Giant-Killer. Having been raised in a serious-minded Connecticut home, he assumed that they must be true. After learning differently, he tried to save other children from the same experience by writing the popular "Peter Parley" stories. Americans were also shocked at the English for allowing children to hear Grimm's fairy tales (first published in German in 1812). Fortunately, the discovery of these tales, cruder than Perrault's, again led to more original children's stories, including the first made-up fairy tales (in the 1840s).

By this time, entertaining children had become big business. Some English publishers maintained themselves primarily on their production of children's books. The toy industry, too, showed the growing importance of children to the European economy. London, the largest city in Europe at the time, had no toy shops in 1730, but by 1780 there were many. One might find rocking horses to replace the older hobby horse, soldiers and forts, dolls for every pocketbook—made of everything from cardboard to china. There were Noah's Arks for homes which would not allow secular play on the Sabbath, and even mechanical toys to match the growth of the clockwork industry. By 1800, Bestelmeier of Nuremberg was producing a catalog of nearly 500 toys.

Already, experts were complaining that toys had become so elaborate as to leave nothing for the child's creative imagination. Maria Edgeworth suggested that just paper, scissors, and paste would make a better gift, for they would stimulate creativity, while more sophisticated toys might only stifle it. The educational impulse soon became strong within the industry. The first jigsaw puzzle (which appeared in 1762) was a map to teach geography. There were educational card games and board games to teach vocabulary, music, history, and astronomy. And there was even a morality game, designed in France, in which the players' counters are sent to the stocks or prison for landing on certain vices. It may well have been acceptable for Sunday play in strict households.

The businesses which developed in response to children's needs did not let parents forget those needs. Even economic development helped ensure that adults pay more attention to the young. And increasingly those businesses helped to shape the notions of childhood. By 1800 the publishing industry had established the principle that children's books do not have to make sense to adults, that children's minds are not simply smaller versions of adult minds. Parents were made aware that some things are suitable for children and other things are not. Indeed, this truth was insisted on too strenuously by the expurgators and the experts. Most important, adults were encouraged to accept amusement as good in itself. It was part of the child's right to a happy childhood. The widespread acceptance of such a right marks a milestone in the history of childhood. It shows that parents had begun to wonder what their children would like, as well as what would be good for them.

Fourteen

Concern
for
the
Child's
Survival

If the growth of population were simply a matter of medical advances or rising agricultural production, there would be no need to raise the subject in a book on attitudes toward children. But there is reason to believe that attitudes also played a part in the population revolution of the eighteenth century. Our present population problem began in that century, when levels began to rise all over Europe. No one explanation seems to cover all the areas which experienced this growth. But where the evidence is most complete, the rise can be associated with the new sentiments regarding children.

To go back to a beginning, by 1300 Europe contained all the people the land could support. That was because land was used for so many purposes and used so inefficiently. Seed grain only multiplied itself a few times over by harvest time, so that much space was necessary just to produce the seed needed for the next year. Some land had to be left fallow at each planting to avoid soil exhaustion. Wood was the main building material and also the main fuel, so land had to be left to forest. The fibers for clothing were grown, too, keeping still more land out of food production. Population had reached the point that more children would have been a genuine burden. Europe, with its conscience about infanticide, was faced with the threat of real scarcity.

In 1348 came salvation in the form of the Black Death. For those who survived its repeated outbreaks, it was a blessing. As population fell, so did the prices of land and food. Once again, the poor could welcome the children that Providence sent. And as the plague lost some of its virulence, population began to rise again, from 1450 to the early 1600s. That was the period of the Renaissance and Reformation, of important political and economic changes. Having more children, or at least keeping more of them alive, was part of the expansiveness of that exciting age.

Early in the seventeenth century population growth slowed noticeably, in some parts of Europe at least. War, malnutrition, and certain infectious diseases were responsible in part. But in England, at least, it has been found that the birth rate fell as well. Parents may have been limiting the number of births as they realized that population growth was threatening their standard of living. They had always had some ideas about how to accomplish this. Ancient medical texts suggested a variety of methods, and prostitutes passed on their own notions on the subject. Perhaps parents were simply practicing abstinence. In any event, baptismal records show that families were spacing their children out.

Almost certainly, the late marriage patterns in some areas of Europe were one means of reducing the number of births. Among the English aristocracy, for instance, the average age at first marriage in 1600 was 21 for women and 26 for men. And those averages went up in the course of the century. Surprisingly, people lower on the social scale married even later. The usual pattern in seventeenth-century England seems to have been 23–24 for women and 27–28 for men. In Normandy the pattern in the 1730s was similar. Fewer than half of all men and women (42 percent and 44 percent, respectively) reached marriageable age (27 and 25 on the average, respectively). And the average family had only 4.1 children, one of whom died in infancy. All this has come as quite a surprise to historians who had imagined that large families were the rule and that Shakespeare's fictional Juliet was fairly typical in eloping at 13.

Late marriage obviously cut down the number of children that would be born. It may have been adopted for just that reason, especially by those who lived on the very edge of survival. In the seventeenth century it became more common not to marry at all, rather than to reduce the family's resources by paying a dowry or splitting an inheritance. In England, at any one time, half of all women in the child-bearing years (15–45) were either not yet married or already widowed. One might suppose that such a situation would result in a mass of illegitimate children. But oddly enough, the rate of illegitimate births recorded in England, which had been 5 percent of all births in 1590, had fallen to 2 percent by 1710. It could be that a more hard-hearted or desperate age was doing away with more children, especially bastards, without even seeing them baptized.

Whatever the explanation, it is clear that children were not welcomed as indiscriminately as they had been in previous centuries. Widows were considered the most desirable wives, not only because they were more likely to have some cash savings but because they were less likely to bear more children. The poor recognized that children were not an economic asset, whatever historians have said to the contrary. After all, they left home for apprenticeship or domestic service at just the time they became old enough to be a real help around the house. Thus the rearing of these children through their first few, unproductive years was one of the ways in which the poor subsidized the rich. That may have been a major reason that the poor had the fewest children. In 1700 in England unskilled laborers had, on the average, only 2.3 children at home, whereas more prosperous workers, the middle classes, and even the gentry had about 2.9. France, Flanders, Holland, and other parts of Europe showed similar patterns.

This reluctance to have children meant deprivation even for those who were born. Since they came so late in their parents' lives, and since life expectancy was so short, postponing families meant that children were likely to be orphaned. In Normandy the average parent died at age 51, and an average child lost one parent at 14. Thus children suffered for their unpopularity.

Sometime around 1750 things changed. Europe's population, which was around 140 million at that time, began to rise. It reached 190 million by 1800 and perhaps 265 million in 1850. Initially, this had nothing to do with advances in medicine. But it did have to do with a fall in the death rate, especially the death rate among children. For the fall of mortality meant not that adults lived longer but that fewer infants died. Most likely this was the result of better diet. A warming trend, new crops, agricultural improvements, and better transportation of food to meet local shortages all improved the nutrition of Europeans and thereby increased their resistance to infectious diseases. This raised the chances of survival of all groups, but especially infants and children. Historians also suspect that infanticide dropped in that period. That would also appear as a fall in the death rate, but it is more like a rise in the birth rate in showing a more accepting attitude toward children.

The new sentimentalism that was becoming apparent in literature at just that time may have led to greater efforts to keep children alive. For the deaths of infants had often meant not actual murder but the failure of parents to make rather modest efforts to preserve life. Typical of the older carelessness is the example of a seventeenth-century French family. As a precaution, it had a midwife christen a very sickly daughter as soon as she was born. The infant was an hour old before she cried. But the next day, for no good reason, the tiny thing was transported to church to be baptized again. And when she survived that, on the following day she was carted some 18 miles to a wet-nurse. Given the roads of the day, it is no wonder that the poor girl died of the ordeal. Even the diarist who recorded the story observed that a quieter atmosphere would have improved the child's chances. The spread of more humane attitudes in the eighteenth century reduced the likelihood of such treatment. Similarly, they may have been responsible for the decline of swaddling at about this time.

There was a rise in the birth rate as well. Of course, better nutrition would have increased the likelihood of conception. Also, in England at least, a greater proportion of women were marrying, and they were marrying earlier, no longer avoiding the child-bearing years. These new marriage patterns reflect greater economic opportunities. But they also reflect a choice. Greater wealth might have been used for various things. Among the first things chosen in this period of economic expansion was larger families. Starting one's family earlier increased the likelihood of a longer life with one's children. Age at first marriage fell. The English birth rate reached its all-time high in the 1810s.

One is bound to say, however, that the more accepting attitude toward children which we can detect here was rather shallow. The growing number of children conceived sometimes only meant less self-restraint. In England, illegitimacy went up to 6 percent of all births by the first decade of the nineteenth century. Families might not do away with unwanted children any longer, but they were abandoning them to foundling hospitals in greater numbers than ever. A third of all children born in Paris in the 1770s were left in foundling homes, and a third of these were the children of married couples. The same figures still held true for the 1810s. The chief of the Paris police estimated that only 3 percent of all children born in his city were nursed by their own mothers.

Parents felt less restraint on family size as industrial growth began to open new job opportunities in the 1780s in England and somewhat later on the continent. So long as Europe had been primarily agricultural, the availability of land had restrained the size of families. But now it appeared that economic opportunities were growing. Parents did not have to calculate their children's chances in the world of work so narrowly as they had done. By the time Thomas Malthus wrote his *Essay on the Principle of Population* (1798), he seems to have assumed that people had always married as early as possible and had their children willy-nilly. In fact, this attitude—whether the result of affection or carelessness or both—was something rather new in European history.

Most social theorists did not worry as much as Malthus about the population increase. They thought their nations needed more people. Improved agriculture could feed more, growing industry required more, bigger armies and navies depended on more, and overseas empires could be consolidated only by an emigration of Europeans. National ambition encouraged large families throughout the nineteenth century. This is not to say that the experts talked parents into breeding more children. But at least the attitudes of social theorists were not in conflict with those of parents. Couples who had always wanted more children may have been glad to be assured that there would be opportunities for them all. For once in history, Europeans felt free to indulge any wish they may have had for children.

The history of medicine has not yet entered into this discussion of population growth, because medicine was not yet of great importance to the infant death rate. Capping wells, collecting garbage, and other public health measures could have saved many more lives than medicine, for the existing knowledge of cures was not sufficient to affect mortality rates. In fact, it has only been in this century, with the use of antibiotics, that there has been a marked decline in the kinds of infectious diseases which once took so many children's lives. Nevertheless, there were developments in pediatric medicine throughout the early modern period. And while they may have made little change in children's health, they do show a professional concern for children, a concern which was leading to permanent institutions devoted to their physical welfare.

The pediatric knowledge of the ancients had been lost to Europe throughout the Middle Ages, but it was preserved by the Arabs who had overrun the Greek cities of the Near East. Two of the most prominent of the medieval Arab philosophers, Rhazes and Avicenna, made commentaries on those pediatric texts. Few people in Europe could follow these developments, since a knowledge of Greek was so rare before the Renaissance. But with the invention of printing, pediatric advice began to reach a much wider audience of doctors in Latin translation. Soon there were translations in the vernacular languages for parents. In 1473 the first of these appeared, a German work by Bartholomaeus Metlinger, which quickly went through eight editions. It was shortly followed by works in Italian, French, English, Dutch, and, by 1551, Spanish.

These Renaissance books made no advance over the classical authors. In fact, their authors often boasted that they were following the Greeks to the letter, only simplifying things for a popular audience. For example, they described the salting of infants even though they admitted that this had not been practiced for ages. The books take up an enormous range of childhood complaints. A typical table of contents would show concern over children's diarrhea, cramps, coughs, sores in the mouth, shortness of breath, earache, diseases of the eye, fevers, stomach aches, swelling of the head and glands and navel, sneezing, sleeplessness, hiccups, vomiting, bad dreams, convulsions, hoarseness, constipation, worms, chafing, epilepsy, consumption, palsy, kidney stones, crossed eyes, teething, bed-wetting, burns, scales, shingles, measles, and smallpox. Writers could not yet identify the connections between symptoms and were afraid to go beyond the ancients or trust their own observations. But they did not imagine there was much more to be learned. One of the few areas of uncertainty was the efficacy of charms, amulets, and astrology. Ironically, these would probably have done less damage than the medicine of the day.

By 1650 European doctors had begun to shake off the authority of the past. By that time it was clear that they knew more than the Greeks in several of the sciences, including anatomy. And around that time doctors identified a number of diseases that offered a complex of symptoms—rickets, diphtheria, infantile scurvy, chorea, congenital syphilis, scarlet fever, whooping cough. They were obviously reaching for explanations that would go beyond the mere listing of symptoms, though they were not able to offer cures. In the meantime, they abandoned some of the revolting prescriptions of an earlier day. For instance, the practice of rubbing hare's brain on the gums to help in troublesome cases of teething was replaced by the more straightforward approach of lancing the gums.

There were those who thought that increased medical attention was doing children more harm than good. John Locke said so, and he was a doctor. One must sympathize with parents who were distressed to see their children suffering. But in the absence of real cures, a growing sympathy for children led, in the eighteenth century, to an indiscriminate use of painkillers. Some medical writers accepted the use of opiates as a matter of course, realizing how little doctors could do for children. But there seems to have been a growing intolerance of pain, which overrode the objections of others. As drugs and distilled spirits became widely available in that century, many parents simply doped the fussy or active child rather than have to attend to him or her. This practice was increasing just as swaddling decreased; it was, in effect, the new way of immobilizing the child. Again, it is ironic that the problem grew as sympathy for children was growing and was partly a result of that concern.

Mothers could have done more than doctors to improve their children's chances of survival simply by nursing them instead of hiring others to do so. In the eighteenth century medical writers began to collect statistical evidence to support their stand on maternal feeding by comparing the mortality in country districts where it was the usual practice with towns which resisted their advice. They had given up the argument that milk transmits character traits, which they had once used to discourage the use of lower-class nurses. Instead, they went back to something like Plutarch's theory, that nursing would create a greater bond within families and bring satisfaction to parents as well as to children. But resistance to nursing at home persisted, so a compromise was effected—hand-feeding with animal milk. This was not exactly new. Cows' horns had been used as baby bottles at least as early as the medieval period, but the eighteenth century saw a great rise in the use of metal or clay pots for this purpose. Mothers were more willing to keep their children at home if they could feed them this way. Unfortunately the pots, with their long, curving spouts and their leather or sponge nipples, could not be washed well enough to be safe. Of course, at that time people were not aware of the need for cleanliness, much less sterilization. Even when glass nursing bottles began to be used, around 1800, the possibility of sterilizing them went unrecognized. And doctors would still have lacked any notion of the need to sterilize the milk itself, which can be a very dangerous food when exposed to the air. For the time being, the new compromise only benefited mothers.

Doctors were on the right track in attacking the traditional practice regarding supplemental foods. In 1748 William Cadogan of the London Foundling Hospital wrote a small tract (distributed by the hospital) to discourage mothers from forcing solid foods on their infants. It was common to give newborn babies something called "pap"—flour mixed with water or milk to the consistency of bookbinder's paste and baked lightly. For parents could not believe that milk was enough. Infants were also fed sugar, oil, even masticated roast pork, to save them from malnourishment. Naturally, all of this complicated children's digestion considerably and must have contributed to the incidence of diseases like rickets that are linked to malnourishment.

The fact that a physician like Cadogan was willing to offer his advice free, in the interest of public health, was even more important than the fact that he was right. Earlier books on child care were the work of publishers rather than doctors and were motivated by mercenary considerations. Perhaps for that reason earlier writers had been unwilling to offend their readers by attacking traditional ideas, as Cadogan did. Doctors themselves had been notoriously secretive, unwilling to give free advice if it might threaten their livelihood. So it was something new for medical writers to make serious suggestions for improving the general health of the next generation. Experts were becoming aware that cleaner water, cleaner clothes, and better diet would make a far greater difference to the child's chances than more widespread medical care. They did not, however, change the habits of centuries overnight.

Some sent their suggestions to the government in the hope

of speeding their acceptance. In 1784 Dr. William Buchan tried to interest the British government in a plan that would have discouraged the hiring of wet-nurses. The state was to pay poor mothers to nurse their own children, promising them a certain amount every year for each child still alive. Besides giving these mothers more leisure to care for their own, this practice would also keep them from taking in the children of the rich. As long as their children survived, they would not be able to nurse extra children, nor would they need an outside income so desperately. As a result, the rich would be forced to keep their own children. Buchan thought the government could easily afford the plan, since the economy would benefit so greatly from the larger population that would result. He also suggested that the government itself should train girls in "the proper management of children," to combat widespread ignorance on that subject. Thomas Paine made similar proposals in the 1790s. Unfortunately, Paine's association with the French Revolution helped discredit his suggestions. In general, child welfare programs were stigmatized as radical interference with the family in this time of social and political reaction.

As yet, we have noticed no particular relation between the level of technology and child welfare. Attitudes were still more important as late as 1800. Britain was passing France as the foremost world power, but it lagged behind many other states in implementing measures that might have improved the child's chances of survival. It was an Englishman, Edward Jenner, who discovered the technique of smallpox vaccination in 1798. But while Bavaria, Denmark, and other states began to make such vaccination compulsory in the early years of the next century, Britain did not do so until 1853. London, the biggest and richest city in the world, must have been one of the most inhospitable for children. From 1730 to 1750, 75 percent of the people of greater London died by the age of five. By 1770–1790 things had improved to the point that 51 percent died by that age. This change was without benefit of medical advances or government programs. It could have resulted simply from better mothering and increasing concern. And still it was a sorry record, even in comparison with very primitive peoples. By 1810–1830, after the introduction of smallpox vaccination, the child mortality figure was 32 percent.

England could have been in the forefront of pediatric medicine, for Europe's first children's clinic was opened in London in 1769 by Dr. George Armstrong. Over the next 12 years he treated some 35,000 children. One would expect that Armstrong and his assistants would have forged ahead of the rest of Europe in the treatment of children's diseases by specializing in this way. But he had no successors when he closed in 1781. The next such clinic did not open until 1787, in Vienna. English political and medical institutions simply did not support this interest, so it remained a matter of individual concern. Even at that, though, there was some progress. Michael Underwood's *Treatise of the Diseases of Children* (first published in 1784) showed changes in every subsequent edition—something new in pediatric manuals.

The lead in children's medicine was taken by Germany, as it forged ahead in science generally. The first pediatric journal was in German (in 1834). The scientific study of infant nutrition began around 1840, with Johann Simon's comparative analysis of various animal milks. The first professorship of pediatrics (1845) and the first professional society of pediatricians (1883) were in Germany. Germans initiated the first important work on sterilizing milk and on infant formulas, around 1880. These advances in medicine did not have an automatic or immediate effect on most children, for attitudes were still important in the application and spread of the new knowledge. Germany, for example, continued to have one of the higher infant mortality rates in Europe despite its position of medical leadership.

One would suppose that as an interest in child care became

more professionalized, progress would come at a steadier rate. But discoveries were forgotten and rediscovered, sometimes 30 years later. Time was lost on false leads. Disagreements and professional jealousies got in the way of research, and study was necessarily hampered by the moral objections to experimenting with children. Beyond all this, we must remember how fearfully difficult some of these questions are; scientists are still analyzing the properties of milk, for instance. There was progress. Children's clinics began to spread throughout Europe in the 1840s. By the 1880s even Spain and Russia, on the fringes of European civilization, had their own pediatric journals. But popular attitudes showed some resistance to change. Scientific evidence of the superiority of breast-feeding over existing alternatives mounted, yet hand-feeding continued to spread. No doubt many parents thought they were protecting their children against the fantasies of quacks.

Local governments often took the lead in trying to break down these prejudices. Municipal day care centers spread, first in the French industrial cities in the 1840s and later in the rest of Europe, in an effort to save children from the neglect that threatened their health and development. New York City began to distribute booklets on child care in 1874. By 1900, milk distribution centers had appeared in Paris, London, Hamburg, New York, and Barcelona, selling pasteurized milk at cost, sterilizing bottles, and instructing mothers on infant care. National governments followed this lead. Several European states forced mothers to stop work for a couple of months after giving birth, starting with Switzerland in 1877. Germany adopted a plan to pay mothers to nurse their own children, so that they could postpone their return to the labor force. France had established 500 child welfare clinics by 1907. The introduction of compulsory education gave these states a much wider opportunity to intervene in child health and nutrition.

To some extent, governments had to be frightened into a

concern for child welfare. By the 1870s the fertility rates in all of Western Europe were declining noticeably, in a period of intense national rivalry and imperialistic competition. Just as colonies, armies, and industries were absorbing more people than ever, it appeared that the supply was dwindling. France's population, which had never gone up as rapidly as the rest of Europe's, seemed actually to be declining, and there was fear of national extinction. Some governments were satisfied to think that they were ensuring that all children born would actually grow up. But other nations tried to encourage higher birth rates. At a time when racial explanations of history and culture were taken very seriously, breeding the right kind of people became a duty to the state and to world progress. Even in such a polyglot nation as the United States, President Theodore Roosevelt exhorted native-born Americans to have more children in order to preserve the national character and power of America against the threat from recent immigrants.

Despite the wishes of political leaders, birth rates continued to fall after 1900 and have tended downwards ever since. Again, this had little to do with a new technology of contraception but largely represents a change in attitudes. Artificial means of birth control were not widely used until well into the twentieth century, in the 1940s in England for example. They do not seem to have been needed. Catholic Ireland, in which contraceptives are still only available by prescription and abortion is not available at all, maintained considerably lower birth rates than the United States until the 1960s and lower rates than those in (Protestant, and presumably more liberal) Northern Ireland until 1970.

While we cannot be sure just how the decline was achieved, we can guess the motives for it. Children were an economic drain on their families for longer than ever before. Child labor laws and compulsory school attendance kept children at home but prevented them from contributing to the family's income. Also, the social security programs of the late nineteenth and early twentieth centuries made it unnecessary for the poor to think of children as their main defense against misfortune, unemployment, or disability. It may be, too, that the new parents did not think that the larger families of the Victorian era had been entirely satisfactory and wanted to give their own children more individual attention.

There have been times, especially in the sixteenth and nineteenth centuries, in which Europeans felt free to accept as many children as Providence provided. But at other times societies have found ways of keeping the numbers down. Nor did the world have to await scientific progress to save the bulk of its children. The highest levels of infant mortality were never necessary. Children have always been something of an option. The only revolutionary change which modern medicine has offered us, very recently, is the expectation that all our children will survive and the confidence to invest our affections in them. But again, whether this will ensure that they will stand higher among our values will also prove to be a matter of attitude.

Fifteen

The High
and Low
Point
in the
History of
Childhood

One of the puzzles of our history is the fact that the greatest exploitation of children coincided with the greatest glorification of childhood. Obviously, we have to consider a class division between those children who formed the backbone of industrialization and those whose pampered lives rested on that labor. But there is a sense in which even the idolization of childhood among the upper classes was exploitative. Even for the favored few it might seem like the best and the worst of times. Although their suppression was more subtle and was disguised as kindness, it could be deeply destructive.

In one way or another, the experience of all classes was related to the central factor of the nineteenth century—industrialization. The Industrial Revolution began in England and is usually said to have started around 1780. It was soon apparent that industrial technology could use unskilled labor, and lots of it. So, naturally, the millowners thought of using children. Children could start tending the new machines immediately, without the apprenticeship training of the old crafts. As cheap as they were, they became more attractive laborers than their parents in the eyes of employers. By the 1830s the cotton mills, the great symbols of English economic dominance, depended on children for nearly half of their labor force.

Of course, children had worked before. Sometimes it had been dangerous work, aboard ships or as chimney sweeps, risking death by falls from rigging or roofs. Evidence of cruelty to chimney sweeps (driving pins into their feet or lighting fires to make them hurry) induced England's Parliament to pass acts to protect them (in 1788 and later). But the authorities could not be made to enforce them. As late as 1816 the Society for Superseding the Necessity of Climbing Boys was reporting revolting cases like the following:

In the improvement made some years since by the Bank of England in Lothbury, a chimney belonging to a Mr. Mildrum, a baker, was taken down; but before he began to bake, in order to see that the rest of the flue was clear, a boy was sent up; and after remaining some time, and not answering to the call of his master, another boy was ordered to descend from the top of the flue, and to meet him half way. But this being found impracticable, they opened the brickwork in the lower part of the flue, and found the first mentioned boy dead. In the mean time, the boy in the upper part of the flue called out for relief, saying he was completely jammed in the rubbish, and was unable to extricate himself. Upon this a bricklayer was employed with the utmost expedition, but he succeeded only in obtaining a lifeless body. The bodies were sent to St. Margaret's Church, Lothbury, and a Coroner's Inquest which sat upon them returned the verdict, Accidental Death.

Little girls, also, could be worked unbearably as lace makers and handloom weavers. But usually children's work had been with their families and had been intermittent, varying with the child's age and the seasons. Children had not worked as steadily or as regularly as they now had to work on the production line. In fact, no one had ever worked such long hours before the introduction of machinery. Agricultural labor had followed a seasonal rhythm, and the fluctuations of market demand had forced extra holidays on craftsmen as well. The preindustrial mentality had been to work as hard as necessary to maintain a traditional standard of living, and then to try to enjoy one's leisure. But the new mill-owners saw no reason to limit their profits as long as the machines could run.

Children suffered the most from the new conditions of life. The bleakness of their lives is most eloquently expressed in the Parliamentary investigation which finally began to look into the situation in 1832, after more than one generation had lived through the new conditions.

Have you ever been employed in a factory?—Yes.

At what age did you first go to work in one?—Eight.

How long did you continue in that occupation?—Four years.

Will you state the hours of labour at the period when you first went to the factory, in ordinary time?—From 6 in the morning to 8 at night.

When trade was brisk what were your hours?—From 5 in the morning to 9 in the evening.

With what intervals at dinner?—An hour.

How far did you live from the mill?—About two miles.

During those long hours of labour could you be punctual; how did you awake?—I seldom did awake spontaneously; I was more generally awoke or lifted out of bed, sometimes asleep, by my parents.

Were you always on time?—No.

What was the consequence if you had been too late?—I was most commonly beaten.

Severely?—Very severely, I thought.

Will you state the effect that those long hours had upon the state of your health and feelings?—I was, when working those long hours, commonly very much fatigued at night, when I left my work; so much so that I sometimes should have slept as I walked if I had not stumbled and started awake again; and so sick often that I could not eat, and what I did eat I vomited.

Did this labour destroy your appetite?—It did.

In what situation were you in that mill?—I was a piecener . . . taking the cardings from one part of the machinery, and placing them on another.

Will you state to this Committee whether piecening is a very laborious employment for children, or not?—It is a very laborious employment. Pieceners are continually running to and fro, and on their feet the whole day.

Do you not think, from your own experience, that the speed of the machinery is so calculated as to demand the utmost exertions of a child, supposing the hours were moderate?— It is as much as they could do at the best—they are always on the stretch, and it is commonly very difficult to keep up with their work.

State the condition of the children towards the latter part of the day, who have thus to keep up with the machinery?—It is as much as they can do when they are not very much fatigued to keep up with their work, and towards the close of the day, when they come to be more fatigued, they cannot keep up with it very well, and the consequence is that they are beaten to spur them on.

And is it your belief that if you had not been so beaten you should not have got through the work?—I should not if I had not been kept up to it by some means.

Does beating then principally occur at the latter end of the day, when the children are exceedingly fatigued?—It does, at the latter end of the day and in the morning sometimes, when they are very frowsy, and have not got rid of the fatigue of the day before.

What were you beaten with principally?—A strap.

Anything else?—Yes, a stick sometimes.

In those mills is chastisement towards the latter part of the day going on perpetually?—Perpetually.

So that you can hardly be in a mill without hearing constant crying?—Never an hour, I believe.

When you got home at night after this labour, did you feel much fatigued?—Very much so.

What did you do?—All that we did when we got home was to get the little bit of supper that was provided for us and go to bed immediately. If the supper had not been ready directly, we should have gone to sleep while it was preparing.

You have already said it had a considerable effect upon your health?—Yes.

Do you conceive that it diminished your growth?—I did not pay much attention to that; but I have been examined by some persons who said they thought I was rather stunted, and that I should have been taller if I had not worked at the mill.

What is the effect of this piecening upon the hands?—It makes them bleed; the skin is completely rubbed off, and in that case they bleed in perhaps a dozen parts. . . . The hands never can be hardened in that work, for the grease keeps them soft in the first instance, and long and continual rubbing is always wearing them down, so that if they were hard they would be sure to bleed.

Were there girls as well as boys employed in this manner?—Yes.

Were they more tenderly treated by the overlookers, or were they worked and beaten in the same manner?—There was no difference in their treatment.

You seem to say that this beating is absolutely necessary, in order to keep the children up to their work; is it universal throughout all factories?—I have been in several other factories, and I have witnessed the same cruelty in them all.

Were the children of the slubbers [overseers] strapped in the same way?—Yes, except that it is very natural for a father to spare his own child.

Did it depend upon the feelings of a slubber toward his children?—Very little.

Can you speak as to the effect of this labour in the mills and factories on the morals of the children, as far as you have observed?—As far as I have observed with regard to morals in the mills, there is everything about them that is disgusting to every one conscious of correct morality.

Do you find that the children, the females especially, are very early demoralized in them?—They are.

Is their language indecent?—Very indecent; and both sexes take great familiarities with each other in the mills, without at all being ashamed of their conduct.

Do you connect their immorality of language and conduct with their excessive labour?—It may be somewhat connected with it, for it is to be observed that most of that goes on towards night, when they begin to be drowsy; it is a kind of stimulus which they use to keep them awake; they say some pert thing or other to keep themselves from drowsiness, and it generally happens to be some obscene language.

Could you attend an evening-school during the time you were employed in the mill?—No, that was completely impossible.

Did you frequently sleep nearly the whole of the day on Sunday?—Very often.

At what age did you leave that employment?—I was about twelve years old.

Why did you leave that place?—I went very late one morning, about seven o'clock, and I got severely beaten by the spinner, and he turned me out of the mill, and I went home, and never went any more.

Were all the mills in the neighborhood working the same number of hours in brisk times?—Yes.

So that if any parent found it necessary to send his children to the mill for the sake of being able to maintain them, and wished to take them from any mill where they were excessively worked, he could not have found any other place where they would have been less worked?—No, he could not; for myself, I had no desire to change, because I thought I was as well off as I could be at any other mill.

And if the parent, to save his child, had taken him from the mill, and had applied to the parish for relief, would the parish, knowing that he had withdrawn his child from its work, have relieved him?—No.

So that the long labour which you have described, or actual starvation, was, practically, the only alternative that was presented to the parent under such circumstances?—It was; they must either work at the mill they were at or some other, and there was no choice in the mills in that respect.

What, in your opinion, would be the effect of limiting the hours of labour upon the happiness, and the health and the intelligence of the rising generation?—If the hours are shortened, the children, may, perhaps, have a chance of attending some evening-school, and learning to read and write; and those that I know who have been to school and learned to read and write, have much more comfort than those who have not.

From your own experience, what is your opinion as to the utmost labour that a child in piecening could safely undergo?—If I were appealed to from my own feelings to fix a limit, I should fix it at ten hours, or less.

And you attribute to longer hours all the cruelties that you describe?—A good deal of them.

From what you have seen and know of those mills, would you prefer that the hours of labour should be shortened with a diminution of wages?—If I were working at the mill now, I would rather have less labour and receive a trifle less, than so much labour and receive a trifle more.

These children could not look forward even to retirement from this labor, much less a vacation each year. Michael Crabtree was describing his whole life, unless he could breed enough children to live off their labor. And there were worse stories than his, especially from the mines, where eight-year-old girls dragged carts of coal through wet tunnels on their hands and knees. Friedrich Engels caused a sensation when he asserted that the grim circumstances of this economic system allowed factory owners to use their girls as a "harem": "In ninety-nine cases out of a hundred, the threat of dismissal is sufficient to break down the resistance of girls who at the best of times have no strong inducement to chastity." And he cited evidence for stunted growth, spine and bone malformation, and the premature aging which made factory children old at 40. Some doctors were saying, Engels claimed, that factory districts would soon be producing "a race of pigmies," by a sort of evolutionary decline.

Not everyone wanted to hear such stories. Some simply did not believe that things could be that bad and assumed that radicals were coaching the witnesses before Parliament. They preferred to believe Andrew Ure, who described his experience of seeing child labor in very different terms:

> They seemed to be always cheerful and alert, taking pleasure in the light play of their muscles—enjoying the mobility natural to their age. The scene of industry, so far from exciting sad emotions in my mind, was always exhilarating. It was delightful to observe the nimbleness with which they pieced the broken ends, as the mule-carriage began to recede from the fixed roller-beam, and to see them at leisure, after a few seconds' exercise of their tiny fingers, to amuse themselves in any attitude they chose, till the stretch and winding-on were once more completed. The work of these lively elves seemed to resemble a sport, in which habit gave them a pleasing dexterity. Conscious of their skill, they were delighted to show it off to any stranger. As to exhaustion by the day's work, they evinced no trace of it on emerging from the mill in the evening; for they immediately began to skip about any neighbouring playground, and to commence their little amusements with the same alacrity as boys issuing from a school.

Others were sympathetic to the idea of regulation but did not know how far government could tamper with the economy without endangering British development and prosperity. For it was often said that it was only in those last hours of the evening that the mills maintained their competitive advantage and returned a profit. In any event, Michael Sadler, chairman of the investigative committee, lost his next election. And while there was a Factory Act in 1833—which prohibited children under 9 from working in textile mills, limited children under 13 to nine hours per day, and required mills to provide six hours of schooling per week—the law was widely ignored.

Even the parents of these unfortunate children conspired to circumvent such laws, for they were in a quandary. Sometimes they were so distressed at their children's suffering that they attacked sadistic foremen. But often they served as foremen over their own children and were forced to use the methods just described. Given the state of wages as industry replaced the crafts, these parents could not afford to leave their children idle. They might even be fired before their children in slack times and be dependent on the children's wages. Some admitted breeding more children to send to work, now that children were a more obvious economic advantage. For they could make a more immediate and noticeable contribution to the income of a factory family than they had on the farm, especially where farms were small. The new demand for child labor made it desirable to keep children with the family rather than to send them out to apprenticeship or service. But in the process, home life was robbed of any joy.

The revelation of the plight of small children in the mills and mines and rural labor gangs began to take effect only because certain persons would not let the matter rest. The seventh Earl of Shaftesbury devoted his life to promoting child labor legislation and, what was more important, to seeing that it was enforced. To Shaftesbury, the suffering of children was not remote. He himself had been the victim of harsh and insensitive parents and knew what misery was to a child. For even as heir to an earldom, he had been so ignored that he actually suffered from cold and hunger. Shaftesbury was determined that his own ten children would remember a better and happier life. And he hoped that his efforts would make all homes more attractive places.

But politicians could never have carried the day against vested interests had there not been a considerable sympathy for children in society at large. Those who did the most to crystallize that sympathy were writers and artists. Children became an obsessive theme in Victorian culture at the same time that they were being exploited as never before. As the horrors of life multiplied for some children, the image of childhood was increasingly exalted. Children became the last symbols of purity in a world which was seen as increasingly ugly. Unfortunately, those who were seriously expected to maintain the innocence of angels had as hard a job as the factory children.

We can think of the exaltation of childhood as part of the Romantic movement, which was coming to dominate art and literature around 1800. Romanticism was a glorification of the artist's individuality and creativity as against the settled forms of poetry and painting. It was also a glorification of nature as against industrialization, which was thought to be drying up the sources of human sympathy. Artists wanted to be more open to the inspiration of nature, to feeling, and their own instinctive genius, even if it meant rejecting their society. The child was seized upon as an obvious symbol of the creative and original impulses of the artist, since children are largely ignorant of society's conventions. Children are at one with nature, confronting it directly and not through the filter of "reason." And this was just what the Romantic poets were trying so painfully to recapture.

William Blake's *Songs of Innocence* (1789) and William Wordsworth's *Ode: Intimations of Immortality from Recollections of Early Childhood* (1807) are only the most famous of the many works from that time celebrating the child's vision. Both of them saw adulthood as a deprivation of the child's emotional and spiritual response to nature. They find a rather sentimental counterpart in Joshua Reynolds's many paintings of children, especially his "Age of Innocence" (1788). For Wordsworth, the child seemed to know intuitively things that adults, with all their intellect, can hardly recover. He expressed this in terms of the Platonic doctrine of the pre-existence of souls:

> Our birth is but a sleep and a forgetting:
> The Soul that rises with us, our life's Star,
>   Hath had elsewhere its setting,
>   And cometh from afar:
>   Not in entire forgetfulness,
>   And not in utter nakedness,
> But trailing clouds of glory do we come
>   From God who is our home:
> Heaven lies about us in our infancy!

Wordsworth felt that the loss of this glory—as it "fades into the light of common day"—was inevitable and common to all periods of history. But Blake represented the more general feeling that contemporary society was making the child's situation worse than ever before. Urban life, mechanization, and a puritanism gone sour had turned the child's life into a nightmare. For Blake, children were the very symbol of love and goodness. But the church which proclaimed these values denied them in its rejection of childishness. The family, which should have been a nurturing institution, was likewise an agent of repression. Schools busied themselves in crippling children's minds. All of the institutions that should have been promoting children's welfare were making them hostile to the world and alien to their own nature, which was to affirm life and God. Blake put this most poignantly in "The Chimney Sweeper":

A little black thing among the snow,
Crying " 'weep!" 'weep!" in notes of woe!
"Where are thy father and mother? say?"
"They are both gone up to the church to pray.

"Because I was happy upon the heath,
And smil'd among the winter's snow,
They clothed me in the clothes of death,
And taught me to sing the notes of woe.

"And because I am happy and dance and sing,
They think they have done me no injury,
And are gone to praise God and his Priest and King,
Who make up a heaven of our misery."

Neither Blake nor Wordsworth was regressive in his devotion to childhood. Each wanted to go back to his own early experience in order to begin again, and not simply to escape from an unpleasant world. Both were convinced that the "progress" of their day was headed in the wrong direction and that society needed to recapture a childlike vitality. But as this theme became hackneyed, Victorian novelists lapsed into a simple regressiveness in their use of child characters. They introduced these vulnerable creatures as a contrast to a villainous society which had grown materialistic and impersonal. With these authors, there is not the same sense that regaining the child's perspective will bring new life. Quite the opposite; their child characters usually die. One is left with the feeling that they are better off dying in their innocence than growing up in a heartless world.

Such stories do not seem to have much to do with the actual suffering of contemporary children. Most of the characters are not from the working class nor do they face the social ostracism once suffered by Puritans. Child characters were dying in record numbers in fiction even as actual child mortality was declining. This is no doubt why the books seem so false; they represent not real children but the authors' self-pity. A stagnant nostalgia for childhood did not solve the problems children faced in Victorian society. In fact, it became part of the problem, for by elevating the image of the child, these authors disguised their ambivalence toward childhood and created unrealistic expectations concerning children.

With some of the authors, we know beyond doubt what was happening. Charles Dickens's *Oliver Twist* (1838) was the first of the stream of novels emphasizing the plight of children. Dickens kept going back, in his later novels, to relive and resolve his own childhood loss. He remembered having been happy in his early years, until his father was taken to debtor's prison and he was sent to work. The desperation of his parents was frightening, and the family's disgrace wounded him deeply. Of course, the end of schooling was a severe blow to a precocious child. Whether or not his earlier childhood had been as idyllic as he remembered it, this trauma haunted his later life. He became preoccupied with trying to understand how he could have suffered so deeply in those few months around age 12. The enormous success he enjoyed never softened that memory.

Dickens's fixation on childhood loss was typical of Victorian England. A whole society could identify with his nostalgia and pathos. The death of Little Nell, in the original serialized version of his *Old Curiosity Shop* (1840), was a national event. Obsession with a sentimentalized childhood, which is now recognized as a flaw in Dickens's work, was at that time a main reason for his popularity. The other popular authors who followed his lead also found that they could not handle the emotions that collected around their imaginary children. At mid-century, George Eliot's *Scenes of Clerical Marriage* would have been typical: "Nearest her mother sits the nine-year-old Patty, the eldest child, whose sweet fair face is already rather grave sometimes, and who always wants to run up-stairs to save mamma's legs. . . . Then there are four other blond heads—two boys and two girls, gradually decreasing in size down to Chubby." By 1900 Marie Corelli's *Boy* is representative of a much larger literature: "Lifting a pair of large, angelic blue eyes upwards, till their limpid light seemed to meet and mix with the gold-glint of his tangled curls, he murmured pathetically—'Oh, Poo Sing! Does 'oo fee ill? . . . Oh, Poo Sing!' "

With some honorable exceptions, such as *Huckleberry Finn* (1883), the children are simply not real. They do not develop in any convincing fashion. In fact, they usually do not develop at all. Their innocence is too fragile for the real world, and they die to punish cruel adults. Using the child's point of view was the best means of magnifying all that the authors found distasteful in their society. For in truth, children cannot ignore what adults have trained themselves to overlook. But in the end the child's environment is pictured as so uncongenial that he or she could not be a symbol of development. Instead, the child is simply a victim—of commerce, of industry, of organized religion, of family authority, of stingy poor relief, of urban indifference. A few of the children do help to redeem bad situations; Eppie is able to do so in *Silas Marner* and Tiny Tim in "A Christmas Carol." But most are sacrificed to no purpose, in what one historian has called a "national non-fertility rite."

How can we explain sadism masquerading as morality in this way? Why do these authors almost seem to have enjoyed abusing their own fictional creations? It would seem that something inside these authors had been killed in childhood. Of course, some repression of our instinctual desires is necessary if we are to live with each other and is common to all periods. The child fears abandonment, and so he or she represses occasional hostility toward parents for fear of losing them. There is no possibility of escaping such repression altogether. For by the time one could explain to the child that his or her fears are groundless, the child would already have begun repressing certain thoughts and experiencing guilt over them. But Victorians must have suffered more than was necessary. The guilt they felt over their desires was such that they responded by creating characters who had no guilt and no questionable desires.

As these authors and their public began to wonder about certain Christian doctrines, the cult of the child and the worship of the natural became almost a religion. Eliot alluded to this when she remarked that although we do not see angels anymore, children now perform the same services. American philosopher Emerson expressed a similar notion in saying "Infancy is the perpetual Messiah." And so, to protect this vision of innocence from corruption, the child characters were killed and their purity embalmed. Authors could not think how to picture the transition from innocence to maturity without introducing the forbidden interests which dominated the adult world. Real children would have been too frightening for these authors or their public. For real children would have reminded them of the impulses they had helped to repress in themselves. Such portrayal would have raised anew their guilt at those desires and reminded them of their own part in suppressing them. In short, it was too painful to face the fact that they had helped to murder the child within them. They preferred to think that society alone was responsible and that they had been innocent of all offense when it happened.

There is no question that Victorian writers were trying to sympathize with children. But their very idealization of the child must have made many parents even more repressive of questionable behavior in their children. We must believe that Dickens did much to awaken the public conscience to the hardships working children faced. But even he seems to have sensed that working-class children often suffered less, psychologically, than many of their betters. For in large part he was portraying the sad and loveless lives of the children of the rich.

If the Victorian idealization of childhood grew out of repression, and encouraged further repression, we still have the question of the original causes of that repression. Historians have tended toward social explanations. They observe that the growing middle classes were taking themselves more seriously now, and that their newfound self-esteem was bound up with a more repressive code of moral conduct than they saw among either the poor or the aristocracy. Beyond that, the ugliness and incomprehensibility of industrial life encouraged a retreat from life. In primitive societies technology was an extension of body functions and concepts, which even children could understand. But with economic specialization and a baffling technology, both children and adults lost any real understanding of the material basis of their lives. Bewilderment and fear made parents segregate their children from the adult world, to the point that many acquired an early distrust of life.

Children were introduced to the myth of childhood goodness through the children's literature which flourished during this period. The nineteenth century had begun with high-minded authors who taught children the evils of pride in wealth and social station. But as the century wore on, the child characters themselves were increasingly placed in the position of teacher. It was not they who needed redemption but their elders, who began to be pictured as ineffectual, insensitive, and even cruel. As in the novels of the day, many children's stories concern the child's appeal to adult consciences. If the attraction of their innate innocence is not sufficient to work a change in adults, then the children may sicken and die as a punishment on them.

For Victorian writers, children were the guardians of virtue. So it followed that the fictional children dying of these mysterious wasting diseases would go to heaven. For heaven was theirs by right and not by God's mercy. Indeed, the whole notion of religious education was becoming somewhat problematic in view of the child's innate goodness. Thomas Paine had expressed the view that "a system of religion that has anything in it that shocks the mind of a child cannot be a true system." And so it was that in the children's stories teachers and parents are sometimes struck dumb under their children's angelic gaze. It is the child characters who sit in judgment on religion rather than the other way around. "They come to us from heaven, with their little souls full of innocence and peace," wrote the American religious reformer Lydia Maria Child in 1831, "and, as far as possible, a mother's influence should not interfere with the influence of angels." One would think that this idolatry would have been a challenge to the churches. But, as Gillian Avery has observed,

> it comes as a shock to realize that the first presentation of children as virtually sinless comes in "Sunday" literature, the pious tales that might be read when the ordinary story books had to be laid aside. Here, thirty or forty years before it became seemly in ordinary juvenile fiction, children are not only shown as better than their parents, but are frequently the instruments of the parents' salvation.

The stories of Mary Louise Molesworth in the 1880s and 1890s may serve as the culmination of tendencies which went back almost a century. She described an English nursery world in which adults (and especially fathers) have a rather shadowy existence. Nurses, servants, and shopkeepers exist to show unfailing patience and kindliness to children. The children are pictured as naturally sweet, frank, generous, spirited, and devout. Mrs. Molesworth's favorite character type is "the little friend of all the world," the child who melts the hearts of all who met him or her. Prettiness, which earlier authors had considered an invitation to vanity, was apparently now required of the child characters. For now that goodness was assumed in all the children, they had to have other charms in order to interest the reader.

Why did these authors deny the ambivalence they surely felt toward children? If we grant that children are often appealing but exasperating and tiresome at other times, we are left wondering why Victorians tried so hard to forget those less lovable characteristics. Perhaps we have a clue in the stories themselves. For it was just as children reached their highest point in public esteem that their naughtiness creeps back into the stories, but now as an adorable trait. The notion that even the child's badness is not reprehensible first appeared in Catherine Sinclair's *Holiday House* in 1839 and reached its height as a literary theme by the 1880s. It was the final stage of the wish for a guiltless childhood. The countless stories of madcap adventures, with much soiling and tearing of clothes and some back talk to servants, seem unspontaneous and even dreary today. One can hardly believe that children ever found them fun. But the flood of such books shows that adults could not get enough of this "delicious childish mischief."

Apparently, it was precisely as these children were being "naughty" that they seemed most precious to adults. Of course, it was exactly at that point in their own childhood activities that the adults had always been stopped. Authors were almost too eager to assure their readers that this mischief does not really show a bad heart. Quite the contrary, it demonstrates the child's innocence by showing the child to be unconscious of the effects of his or her actions. These actions may be quite destructive and may even endanger others, but the child's remorse sets everything right. Honorable little hearts are hurt by the suspicion that they might have been motivated by cruelty. It is always a poignant moment when these little ones become aware that their actions may seriously affect others. For that is the beginning of growth, and the idea that the child will grow up is a melancholy one for the writer.

As children were seen as more perfect symbols of innocence, evil had to be projected onto other figures, sometimes nonhuman monsters. The growing taste for fairy tales allowed authors and readers to indulge their sadism, since it was only at the expense of grotesque figures. This tendency, too, reached something of a high point around 1900. Writers found it possible to assign some evil to children, so long as they were the vulgar offspring of the poor or the newly rich. For devotion to "the child" did not entirely overcome the snobbishness that separated the different worlds of childhood. Stories directed to poor children still sounded preachy and moralistic long after upper-class characters were allowed their mischief. There was also something of a division between boys and girls as they appeared in the imagination of these authors. The liberation of boys, as naughty characters, was accepted by mid-century, whereas girls of the same class had to wait until the end of the century for similar freedoms.

Even the greatest children's classics confirm our sense that Victorian attitudes toward children were dominated by unconscious conflicts, *Alice's Adventures in Wonderland* (1865) and *Peter Pan* (1904) are marvelously inventive and did much to sweep away the remains of the old moralizing tendency. We are now able to enjoy them simply for their sparkling originality. But to their authors and to the public that accorded them such stunning popularity, the stories resonated more deeply than they do today. Lewis Carroll (or Charles Dodgson) was a Victorian bachelor whose life makes painful reading. Shy and stammering, he had the mannerisms of a little girl. He was devoted to girls, and his letters and diaries reveal his fantasies of turning into one. His children's books show an uncommon gift for reproducing the preverbal stage of infant development; space and time have no regular order, animate objects are transformed into inanimate ones and back again, and there are constant threats of death, extinction, and being eaten. Moralizing is lampooned by being kept at the level of sing-song maxims or parody verses. Carroll was, in effect, expressing the child's awareness before the painful stage of moralistic repression. Similarly, his hobby of photographing little girls, sometimes in the nude, may be seen as a way of freezing them before they could grow up. In the history of children's literature, these works are remembered for having abandoned the effort to improve children and for indulging their delight in nonsense. But all this was not just nonsense to children. The conflicts which Carroll so skillfully worked around were troublesome for children then and for the adults who bought the books.

Peter Pan is likewise a record of conflicts and fears, as any good children's story must be. The theme of the play is the loss of the mother, and the tragic figure is the boy who can never go home. Having once been locked out of his home, Peter can never bring himself to trust his mother's love. Late in life, James Barrie realized that this work and almost everything else that he wrote had grown out of his relation to a neurotically possessive and demanding mother. So dreadful was the fear of losing her that it was extended into the fear of being born at all. The very idea of birth raised his separation anxiety. In *The Little White Bird,* the story which formed the basis for *Peter Pan,* the child is told that he was a bird before his birth and he begins to wish that he had stayed that way. "To be born is to be wrecked on an island," Barrie once wrote. This was nostalgia not simply for childhood but for the fetal union itself. Childhood had become that painful for many sensitive spirits. For Barrie was obviously not alone. The opening night audience for *Peter Pan* was almost entirely adult and responded thunderously to Peter's appeal to save Tinker Bell by affirming its belief in fairies. Those adults made him one of the richest authors of his time, a reputation which is hard for readers now to imagine.

Sometime around the turn of this century children, or at least "childhood," reached the highest point it has ever occupied in Western culture. But the definition of childhood that was growing in acceptance was so exalted and so narrow that real children had trouble meeting it. For example, Englishmen who visited America in the early 1800s frequently declared that there were no children there! It just did not seem that the precocious and insubordinate youngsters they met in America were the same kind of beings that were being raised in respectable society in England. Some have thought that this shows that America had already moved further toward a child-centered society by that time. It might be, though, that America lagged behind, representing a simpler society and economy in which children were more capable and more noticeable. Children had once played many roles in the real world. In the nineteenth century they were asked to play just one role, in an unreal world. It was their task to symbolize the innocence which a severely repressed society felt it had lost.

No doubt children benefited from the new status they enjoyed in certain respects. Toys became more elaborate than ever and reflected the most advanced technology of the age. But the very complexity of the toy steamboats, trains, and mills (some of them really steam-powered) almost mocked children's efforts to understand even their play world. The piano and orchestral suites written to amuse children or describe childhood (beginning with Schumann's *Kinderscenen* and Mendelssohn's *Kinderstücke* and extending through the most prominent French composers) likewise make no real concessions to the very young. Like so much of what the nineteenth century tried to do for children, this music seems self-conscious and self-admiring. And like the stories being produced in this Golden Age of children's literature, the music did not nourish children's imagination as the older folklore had.

For all their obvious goodwill, Victorians had little to offer their children that the children needed. They may have sensed this themselves; it could be one reason that those who could afford to do so were eager to give their children over to nannies even after their weaning, and to boarding schools later. The parents had problems of their own. It may even have been better to leave these children to the care of classes which had suffered less from the mounting repressiveness. For it was necessary that other changes come about—changes in the economy and the relations between classes, a closer knowledge of child development, and a greater appreciation of the range of individual differences—before the Victorians' obvious sympathy and desire to do the best for children could bear fruit.

Sixteen

Growing
Pains
and
Revolution

At the same time that small children were receiving more respectful attention in Western society than ever before, the teen years were becoming a matter of concern. Youth was increasingly seen as a problem, especially among the favored classes, which were prolonging the years of childhood irresponsibility. Before 1800 youth was a time of preparation for adult life, when young people took on increasing rights and duties. The transition to adulthood was very long, but it was organized so that children could see that they were making progress. During the nineteenth century childhood was extended into something called adolescence, when teenagers were left to concentrate on the tensions and stresses of those years of growth. These youngsters were excused from participation in the larger society while they concentrated on personal growth. But almost from the beginning of this change, some of them could see that their new status involved a loss of rights as well. It is no accident, then, that the first clashes between the generations merged with the social revolutions of the nineteenth century.

The primary cause of the change in the social position of the young was economic. Before industrialization, parents had to make occupational choices for their children, since training for handicraft skills would take many years. Children often had their first introduction to the wide world at age 10 or 12, as boys left for apprenticeship and girls for domestic service. Some, no doubt, never adjusted to their parents' choice. But we need not imagine that parents were insensitive to their children's wishes in the matter. Benjamin Franklin remembered being 12 when his brother left home (in the 1710s):

> There was all appearance that I was destined to supply his place and be a tallow-chandler. But my dislike to the trade continuing, my father was under apprehensions that if he did not find one for me more agreeable, I should break away and get to sea, as his son Josiah had done to his great vexation. He therefore sometimes took me to walk with him, and see joiners, bricklayers, turners, braziers, etc., at their work, that he might observe my inclination and endeavor to fix it on some trade or other on land.

However, it was Ben's love of reading which "at length determined my father to make me a printer, though he had already one son of that profession." Having entered upon their calling, children were playing parts in the adult world and had a recognized status there, even though they were not yet considered adults. Rights and responsibilities came gradually, with a number of milestones on the way to maturity. In some respects they were still considered children for years afterward. But the adult world was not a foreign and unknown territory to them.

Also, children in preindustrial Europe were not all thought of as alike. There were important class differences, for example. Gentlemen's sons were sent to school, often away from home. These boys recognized that they were destined to be leaders, and they learned how to take orders and how to give them, as appropriate in a hierarchical society. They would already be lording it over many adults, especially the servants at school and at home. Those headed for the church or politics or law would soon be in university and very conscious of the status that would be theirs shortly. Other middle- and upper-class boys were destined for the army, business, medicine, or government office, and would already be training on the job by their late teens. Among the working classes, also, there were gradations of status. Boys apprenticed in the better trades or crafts were assured of higher prestige and income than others. For girls, service in a richer household gave the right to look down on servants in more ordinary homes. Even in the same family there was an important difference between the eldest child and younger ones, especially where there was an inheritance to pass along. The biggest difference of all, of course, was that between boys and girls. The two sexes hardly seemed to belong to the same world.

These distinctions gave children very specific identities. They could not have thought of themselves as forming one big group with common interests or a common grievance. It is true that the roles toward which they were heading were not of their choosing. But their parents' choice had been made so early that they had gotten used to the idea. There was no possibility of mounting a general rebellion against the adult world. For, beyond the fact that they were divided among themselves, they were already launched into society and making progress toward full membership in that adult world.

Besides this, young people were allowed groups of their own, which gave them a sense of belonging and even of power. These were not organizations *for* youth, designed and run by well-meaning adults. Rather, they were truly controlled by the young people themselves. English boarding schools, for example, were virtually self-governing institutions outside the hours of instruction. The boys were expected to govern themselves by their own rules of fair play. Late in the eighteenth century, when masters attempted to establish adult domination, there was a rash of mutinies at Harrow, Rugby, Winchester, and Eton. The last was at Marlborough in 1851, marking the final assertion of independence before the schools successfully imposed the new standards of adolescence. Elsewhere officer candidates, clerks, and even apprentices had their own fraternities, which served as families for boys far from home. Many of them retained the kind of degrading initiation ceremonies that had once bound young warriors to the tribe. Their prime function was friendship—keeping their members from being bullied or from contracting unwise marriages or debts, and providing company while carousing. In this way, too, the young had an assured place within society.

Even in rural villages, where young people were closest to their families, they acted together for certain purposes and on certain occasions. Festivals like May Day and Midsummer Day allowed them the freedom to ridicule their elders with impunity, as the tradition of chosing Lords of Misrule for these holidays gave them an outlet for social satire. Their elders tried to smile at themselves at least once a year, if that was what it took to keep young people happy the rest of the time. But the greatest concern of the youth groups was in regulating courtship within the villages. If promiscuity began to interfere with normal courtship habits, the offending party might find a gorse bush hung over her door. Or if a widower from another village should threaten to compete with local boys, the boys would find ways to discourage or humiliate him. If all efforts failed, they could be counted upon to make the couple's wedding night a memorable one by raising a ruckus outside their window. This charivari, or "shivaree," in which the newlyweds were embarrassed with dirty songs and ribald effigies, was celebrated in some French villages well into the nineteenth century.

But like all community traditions, these faded as Europe became industrialized. Villages grew into towns, and adults became too grownup and inhibited to take part in the songs, games, and dancing that had once bound the various age groups together. They even began to frown on the children for maintaining their separate customs. When the community lost the ability to entertain itself, the young people suffered most. For as the festivals declined, they were robbed of their one area of full participation with adults.

In urban society, also, the young were losing their status in the world of work. Apprenticeship and training programs were done away with as the old crafts declined. After 1800 England and France repealed laws requiring apprenticeship, thereby allowing employers to hire children without helping them toward a marketable skill. Naturally, the groups that had formed around these training programs died away. Young people were more likely to live at home while working. However much they might be earning, they remained mere children as long as they lived with their parents. And however hard they might work, they were not becoming more skilled as they got older.

Higher on the social scale, it was becoming more difficult to enter the professions. The population of Europe was growing faster than the professions. In Germany and France the problem was particularly acute, since the rich would actually lose their class position by having to go into business. Those governments felt a responsibility to expand the army and the bureaucracy just to give employment to aristocratic children. Elsewhere, students were simply kept in school for longer than ever before. Whereas in the sixteenth century they had come to the English universities at about 17, by the nineteenth century the age on entering was closer to 20.

In short, youth was being extended and trivialized. Just as small children were being given a nursery world of their own, so adolescents were being segregated from adult society. They were no longer gaining independence throughout their teen years, so that the transition to adulthood was becoming more abrupt and frightening. In addition, the young were being treated more nearly alike. Rich and poor, girl and boy, first child and youngest, none of them enjoyed any real status.

As young people were driven together in this way and kept down, a few of them rebelled. The early nineteenth century witnessed the first youthful demands for social change. Of course, we are speaking here of students who were on the verge of adulthood. But they still bore the primary mark of childhood—dependence. And they were, in effect, asserting that the young have as great an understanding of fundamental values as the old.

The most influential of all revolutions, the French Revolution of the 1790s, was not a conflict between generations. The French were careful to reconcile the age groups by festivals honoring old and young. But something of a generational revolt did arise in Germany immediately after the wars against Napoleon. Before his final defeat in 1815, Napoleon humiliated the scores of tiny states that made up Germany. The collapse of those petty authoritarian governments had seemed to discredit the entire older generation. Even the autocratic German family suddenly seemed to lack legitimacy. As the veterans of those wars came back to the German universities, they brought with them an experience of the world that powerfully impressed the younger students there. Suddenly, the universities were engaged with the great questions of society. These veterans had no patience with the juvenile traditions of the old student fraternities and dueling societies. They scorned the fagging system, by which older students had traditionally used the younger ones as servants and had helped themselves to their belongings. Such practices now seemed to serve no purpose but to teach docility and conformity, at a time when these radicals were talking about abolishing all institutions and living in perfect freedom. They dramatized their revolt by breaking with fashion and wearing their hair loose, rather than powdered and pigtailed.

Such a revolt required a new kind of student organization, so the student unions, or *burschenschaften,* were formed. Administrators were quite right in seeing these as a direct threat to their authority in university affairs. Their first reaction was to suppress them. As a result, representatives from half of the German universities met at Wartburg Castle in 1817 to discuss their common grievances. There were speeches, singing, gymnastics, toasts, torchlight parades, and the burning of conservative books as the delegates discussed more far-reaching demands. One of them, Karl Sand, was inspired by the festivities to assassinate an older writer who was guilty of influencing the young with a cynical conservatism. Of course, the government then took the universities in hand, dismissing sympathetic professors and abolishing the unions. Sand himself was executed, having bungled his attempt to protest by suicide. He did serve as an example, but not the kind that the government had intended. Rather, he was the first cult hero among the youth of Europe. Girls sighed over prints of his portrait. Songs celebrated his exploit, and pieces of his scaffold were saved as relics. As far away as Italy, Poland, and Ireland, the news of Sand's martyrdom and of the Wartburg Festival inspired nationalistic movements among the young of those captive peoples. Although they were not immediately successful, they did popularize the notion that only a youthful radicalism could rejuvenate a nation.

A very different kind of youth revolt emerged in France in 1830. The political revolution in Paris during that year had achieved its very limited aims. But some of the students of Paris continued to press for something far more radical. In effect, they produced the first youth "counterculture." Of course, there had always been students driven to a bohemian life by sheer poverty. But now a larger number were choosing that life for the pleasure of shocking their elders. They lived in squalor, dressed like gypsies, minstrels, pirates, or walked about naked. Some went in for Satanism, the occult, and Eastern religions. If asked to explain themselves, they professed to be complete hedonists— living only for pleasure. Their parents had no right to condemn them, they insisted, for the parents themselves had no real convictions in politics or religion. The older generation was motivated by materialism, greed, and snobbery. Surely the simple enjoyment of life was a nobler ambition than that.

The revolution, they imagined, would be carried out by aesthetic means. For they would change the whole sensibility of the public by acting out its unacknowledged fantasies and thereby undermining its defenses. And sure enough, the tourists flocked to the Latin Quarter to be shocked and excited. Some of those in the movement seriously hoped a breaking down of barriers and a more positive acceptance of life would solve the problems of bourgeois society. Others were more self-indulgent and made the whole affair seem silly. They even said that the point of their rebellion was that people should remain more childlike. The ultimate expression of this commitment was a Suicide Club, whose members promised to die rather than allow themselves to grow up. One member was reported to have kept his oath, but most of the Bohemians had gone back to straight society within five years. A few became active socialists. The memory of this youth rebellion continued to resonate through French culture for many years after the fad had passed. Playwrights and artists who lived through these years, such as Dumas, Hugo, and Delacroix, commonly featured young rebels in their work.

When revolution swept over all of Europe in 1848, its leaders did not expect much help from the young. Marx and Engels were still in their twenties at the time. But as they wrote their inflammatory tracts it did not occur to them to make any particular appeal to the young. They may well have expected them to be reactionary. After all, the burschenschaften had been fiercely nationalistic, anti-Semitic, and against all notions of class consciousness. They had divided humankind along generational lines.

But there was one country in which students did help to organize rebellion in that year. The huge empire of Austria was ruled from Vienna, and the university of that city was riddled by burschenschaft cells. German students coming there to study medicine and engineering had brought the student unions with them, and the reactionary rule of Metternich had turned these into secretive and subversive organizations. As soon as the students heard of the momentary success of revolts elsewhere in Europe, they began organizing workers in the city and turning the university itself into a fortress. They demanded the political reforms now standard among liberals—a constitution, democracy, and a free press. Most of all, they insisted on the dismissal of Metternich, who had been the prime mover in outlawing the burschenschaften 30 years earlier.

In the end, the young people helped ensure the failure of the revolution. Some of their nonnegotiable demands seemed impractical and needlessly provocative. Their impatience undermined the efforts of older liberals to compromise for the sake of securing at least part of the program. In fact, the students seemed to enjoy confronting them almost as much as they liked fighting the Emperor's supporters. Sometimes it seemed that they were not so much interested in their political goals as in quarreling with the older generation. Eventually, the army put a bloody end to the rebellion. And it did not soften the Emperor's heart when he was told that the rebels were scarcely more than children.

The one country of Europe that was too backward for revolution in 1848 was Russia. When the young were radicalized there in the 1860s it was with a peculiar ferocity and determination. Many of the earliest student radicals in Russia were the children of liberal-minded parents, but they despised the romantic idealism of their parents almost as much as the autocracy of the Czarist regime. The soft-minded liberalism of their fathers had not kept the latter from serving that regime as bureaucrats. But the younger generation was determined to avoid such compromise. They prided themselves on their realism and materialism and declared themselves atheists and "nihilists." By this they meant that they believed in nothing but what they could see and what had force. Accordingly, they were enthusiastic about science, Darwinism, and literary realism. All this was going to make them tougher than their parents, they hoped.

To these young radicals, the only institution of Russian life which seemed worth saving was the peasant commune. After the revolution, when the rest of the social and political framework had been destroyed, they thought that life could revert to that kind of natural community. Some of them could not wait, and dropped out of their universities to join the peasants, hoping to gain their allegiance to the revolution by sharing their simple existence. For all their vaunted realism, these heirs of the middle class worked up a romantic admiration for the peasants' traditional wisdom and their ageless way of life. But the peasants never figured them out. They looked askance at the girls' bobbed hair and wondered if they practiced free love. When the Czar's police came after the radicals, sending even minors into Siberian exile, the peasants did nothing to save them.

So it was up to those young radicals who were left to bring

Russia to its knees, without any help from the workers. Mainly, their revolution took the form of trying to assassinate the Czar, the focus of Russian nationalism and something of a father figure for the benighted peasantry. Alexander II, who had earned a reputation as a liberal by expanding the universities and allowing women to attend, became their target. He escaped death several times, until in 1881 four students caught him driving through a narrow street and succeeded in blowing him up. The peasants mourned the Czar rather than the executed assassins. And liberal reform ended. One of those executed for the deed was Lenin's idolized older brother. It was that event that gave the 17-year-old Lenin his lifetime's vocation and his intransigence.

When successful revolution did come, it owed little to the young. Their efforts, in these and later nationalistic revolts, tended to show a self-defeating quality. Suicide was one of the defiant gestures to which young radicals were particularly drawn. Their terrorism, too, seems to have been an end in itself, meeting their need to lash out at society but doing little to change it. Attracted by the most irrational means available, they often discredited the movements they joined. They did, however, make an undeniable contribution to radical change by acting out the emotional rejection of injustice and oppression. As young people dramatized the inhumanity of so many traditional institutions, change may have begun to seem inevitable. Had there been more genuine respect for adolescence at that time, the changes might have come sooner.

Youthful radicalism was, to some extent, a reaction against an adolescence that seemed increasingly confining. As we shall see, the schools, welfare agencies, and juvenile detention facilities that were growing so enormously were designed to contain the growing restlessness of youth. But the deeper cause of this restlessness was industrialization. Technology was changing life so rapidly that the different generations hardly lived in the same world. Social inertia seemed more of a grievance to the young than it did to their parents. They had reason to resent the older generation's failure to train them for the challenges of the future. As it turned out, the well-meaning attempts to protect the young from a more complex and demanding world only made some of them more impatient.

Seventeen

The
Standardizing
of
Childhood

If the nineteenth century had a lofty view of childhood, that view was also rather narrow. It soon appeared that many children, especially the numerous children of the poor, did not fit the stereotype. So determined efforts were made to provide such a childhood for everyone, even if it meant squeezing some of them into the mold. By the turn of this century the major institutions designed to help in this effort had been firmly established. Compulsory schools, official youth groups, welfare agencies, and correctional institutions for the

young were the source of some pride among the more enlightened elements of society. But there were also critics—from
those who resented the expense involved to those who complained of the insensitivity of this effort to standardize children.

The idea that all children should be made to go to school was
not a new one in the nineteenth century. Although many people
still thought of schooling as a family investment or a mark of
privilege, several Protestant states had long hoped to make
education universal. Catholic educators had suggested another
kind of comprehensiveness, in the notion that schools should
dominate the child's moral and social, as well as mental, development. The contribution of the nineteenth century was a democratic idealism which would embrace and regulate all children.
And by the end of that century a developing economy made such
a system feasible.

We have already seen how, in the sixteenth century, moralists
had lamented the lack of supervision of student life in schools
and universities. Education itself became only one of the
schools' goals, as masters tried to gain control over students'
lives. In France first, and then in the rest of Europe, the Church
had provided boarding schools and residential colleges in place
of the traditional boarding arrangements. These stricter schools
were more popular with parents, who were glad to think that
their children were under some form of care and discipline. By
implication, they were agreeing that their children should be
kept away from the influence of the town. At one time the
community had been thought of as an aid in socializing the child,
but now it was viewed as a danger to proper development. The
beginnings of social fragmentation had made parents more conscious of the question of what constituted an ideal childhood.
Imagine the parents' surprise when schoolmasters began to
treat the home itself as a threat to their influence. For already
in the seventeenth century teachers sometimes objected to al-

lowing school holidays because of the relaxation of moral standards when pupils got home.

Social isolation was only one of the ways in which schools were becoming a restrictive influence. They even began to lose contact with the intellectual development of Europe. Whereas medieval schools had prepared students for current professions, the new Humanist curriculum tended toward pure scholarship. Schools continued to concentrate on ancient literature to the exclusion of the growing interest in science, politics, and modern literature. There was a further narrowing as teachers gave more thought to rationalizing their methods. For grading the curriculum so that it proceeded from the simple to the complex led naturally to the age grading of students. By the end of the seventeenth century, some schools had segregated each year of age into its own class. Then each class was given its own room, and finally its own teacher. More and more, children were expected to conform to the teachers' expectations of their particular age group. The tendency then was to teach this more homogeneous group by the class lesson, to the neglect of a more individualized instruction.

Whether or not these changes were educationally sound, they did mean less flexibility in the training and treatment of children. Masters decided that they had a duty to keep parents from pushing children along too fast. Some children resented this treatment; Descartes, the philosopher, complained that his education had been held back on account of age alone. But the schools thought that it was in the best interests of children to keep them from a premature responsibility, from the immorality around them, and even from puberty if they could have managed it.

There were some who had hopes for a more diverse education, but their ideas were successfully kept out of the mainstream. Statesmen would have liked military training for officer candidates. By 1600 a number of new "academies" in Italy and France were teaching horsemanship, military engineering, math, history and geography, heraldry, modern languages, and the courtly graces to the children of the upper class. This curriculum institutionalized what had been done more informally with the pages and squires who had accompanied medieval knights. Some businessmen were calling for training in accounting, languages, navigation, and engineering. So schools were organized around such business courses. But these institutions never caught on with the public, for parents wanted a Humanist education for their children—one that would be associated with the social elite and not with business or technology. Some schools could not have broadened their curriculum even if they had been so inclined, since their original endowments had prescribed the course of study. But other schools remained traditional even without this constraint. For the public seemed to want education to stay the same, and all the more so as other things began to change.

This same resistance to change may have kept girls out of the growing educational establishment. Women have always had the job of conserving social values and customs while men are testing the limits. And even though the education itself was conservative, society did not trust girls with more than the rudiments of learning. Some girls were allowed in elementary schools with boys to learn to read in the vernacular. The richest might have tutors or governesses, and even learn Latin. But the goal of the few girls' schools (outside of convents) was to make their students marriageable. Music and needlework were therefore a more vital part of the curriculum than academic subjects. In fact, now that parents no longer arranged marriages, the only really important skill for a girl was learning how to attract a husband. Intellectual equality might threaten his authority.

In the eighteenth century the major innovation in education had the purpose of fixing still another group of children into place. The hundreds of charity schools founded in France by Jean-Baptiste de la Salle and the Brothers of the Christian Schools (founded in 1684), in England by the Society for Promoting Christian Knowledge (1698), and in Germany by August Hermann Francke and his associates (1695) attempted to socialize the poor child. The burgeoning cities of Paris and London were producing a new kind of poor—rootless masses beyond the reach of prevailing social standards or religious institutions. So these charity schools were meant to counteract the effect of homes which were training children up to crime. They presented an ideal of hard work, regularity, and submission to authority. This was a very different ideal from that held up before upper-class pupils, who were expected to be spirited and self-confident. But it set a standard for a much larger and previously neglected group. No doubt the founders really believed that these values were in the best interests of the children, given the society in which they would live.

These private efforts to extend literacy, industry, and humility throughout the lower classes continued for generations with no help from the state. In England, the Sunday School movement of the 1780s attempted to offer the three R's to children who had to work during the week. In the 1840s there was still work for the "Ragged Schools," designed for children who were too filthy and neglected to be accepted in any of the existing schools. But a large percentage of poor children either did not live close enough to any of these schools or chose not to attend.

By 1800 it seemed that private philanthropy had done all it could. For those who believed that without formal schooling one had missed a proper childhood, there appeared to be only one answer: Only the state could afford to offer a universal education and enforce attendance. There were many who objected to the idea of compulsory education, however. Taxpayers resisted, of course. And economists argued that cheap labor was necessary to their nations' competitive position in world trade. But even philosophers were afraid to see the government enter education. They assumed that the state would use the schools for political indoctrination, and that the established churches would be allowed to enslave children's minds. The greatest political issue of the day was individual liberty and freedom of conscience. If state education was to include religion, as it always had before, people could only assume that the state planned to dictate beliefs to those who had no powers of resistance. English philosopher John Stuart Mill summed up this objection best, in *On Liberty* (1859):

If the government would make up its mind to *require* for every child a good education, it might save itself the trouble of *providing* one. It might leave to parents to obtain the education where and how they pleased, and content itself with helping to pay the school fees of the poorer classes of children, and defraying the entire school expenses of those who have no one else to pay for them. The objections which are urged with reason against State education, do not apply to the enforcement of education by the State, but to the State's taking upon itself to direct that education: which is a totally different thing. That the whole or any large part of the education of the people should be in State hands, I go as far as any one in deprecating. All that has been said of the importance of individuality of character, and diversity in opinions and modes of conduct, involves, as of the same unspeakable importance, diversity of education. A general State education is a mere contrivance for moulding people to be exactly like one another: and as the mould in which it casts them is that which pleases the predominant power in the government, whether this be a monarch, a priesthood, an aristocracy, or the majority of the existing generation in proportion as it is efficient and successful, it establishes a despotism over the body. An education established and controlled by the State should only exist, if it exist at all, as one among many competing experiments, carried on for the purpose of example and stimulus, to keep the others up to a certain standard of excellence.

In the course of the nineteenth century these objections were overborne by the states' desire to provide a proper childhood for every citizen. The beliefs that were imposed through the state schools were reduced to those no one had yet doubted. And even liberals began to see merit in eliminating certain prejudices and habits through a standardized education.

Some of the German states were the first to achieve universal education. Prussia had been committed to the goal of compulsory education since 1717, even though the nation could not afford it then. By 1763 there was state regulation of all schools in the country, and a little later the state began to supervise all schools directly. More and more children were brought into this system until, by 1850, attendance was virtually universal. The religious issue was handled by providing separate state schools for Protestants, Catholics, and Jews. The Prussian government, in line with its ambition to become a great power, distinguished itself by an interest in educational innovation as early as the 1810s, when some of Pestalozzi's ideas were introduced into its schools.

France solved the problem of religious indoctrination by providing only secular instruction at the compulsory, elementary level. Even these schools still included moral instruction and patriotism; no one could yet conceive of an education entirely devoid of these. But religious instruction was allowed in state schools only at the secondary level, which non-Catholics need not attend. In part, the state's willingness to include religion at that level was a result of its desire to lure students away from private Catholic schools, which were considered a divisive influence. For in the nineteenth century the bureaucratic mind was offended by diversity. This was only too evident when a French educator told an English visitor that at that very hour every child in France in a particular grade was having the same geography lesson. When American administrators read this boast they made it their goal as well.

Progress toward the goal of free education for all French children was slow, despite government promises dating back to the Revolution of 1789. It was not until France lost a war to Prussia in 1870 that leaders decided that national power and even survival depended on extending education to all citizens. During the 1880s France found it could afford its goal of free, compulsory, and universal education.

The United States had an advantage with regard to the ideological objection to state education, for all the states had broken their former connections with established churches by 1833. In a sense, the public schools themselves took the place of an established church, with democratic ideology becoming a sort of civil religion. Schools were used to absorb the wide variety of immigrants by giving their children a common introduction to American values. Public education was popular with voters for that reason, although only two-thirds of the states had achieved compulsory education by 1900. The United States has the distinction of being the first nation to treat boys and girls almost equally in its schools—an outgrowth of the nation's early commitment to democratic values. As one French visitor observed,

If we Europeans are astonished by the little boys brought up on the other side of the Atlantic, we must be still more surprised at the little girls. . . . The first impression of the stranger is that there are no sexes in the United States. Girls and boys walk to school side by side, they sit on the same benches, they have the same lessons, and go about the streets alone.

In Britain the struggle for compulsory education lasted longest. Suspicion of the state and the Church of England was widespread even within Parliament. So state control began in a small way, by meager grants to existing schools. But by the 1840s inspectors were being sent out to monitor the use of these grants, and it was inevitable that these inspectors would become increasingly involved in the curriculum. The real breakthrough, however, came in 1867 when the vote was extended to working-class people, many of whom were barely literate. Politicians had surprised themselves with this rather sudden extension of the franchise and hurriedly took up the problem of "educating our masters." An Education Act of 1870 implied the goal of compulsory education, free for all who could not already afford it. By 1880 that goal had been reached for those up to 13 years of age.

Sympathy for children had not accomplished all this. Political, military, and social necessity had spurred a public commitment to children. But whatever the motive, these societies were now in a position to shape all children more closely to their ideal of childhood. Most people assumed that education would continue to be divided according to class and sex. Upper-class children would still attend private (Latin grammar) schools, while the state schools would offer the poor an education in the vernacular. But those devoted to children were already thinking in terms of eradicating all distinctions. Before the end of the century, such changes as the introduction of examinations for bureaucratic offices and for university admissions had begun to break down class divisions among students. The many and subtle ways in which upper-class children had been taught to dominate their social inferiors had become questionable, although the elitist character of some schooling is still an issue, in France and Britain especially.

This ideal of a common educational experience for all children was utterly unprecedented. Previously, schools had fostered differences among children. Only a few had gone to school, and the type of schooling they received had prepared them for different jobs or positions in society. For in a hierarchical society almost no two boys would have occupied exactly the same position. But by 1900 there were deliberate efforts to eliminate such differences. One can see them in the team sports which were encouraged in place of individual competition. Headmasters thought of organized sports as training for adult cooperation and for the impending struggle over national empires. In England games spread from boarding schools to the common schools and even to reform schools. France and Germany fostered the same values of courage and solidarity more directly by introducing universal military training. Whether in sports or at military drill, the boys were encouraged to think of themselves as a team by the uniforms which were coming into fashion. The petty snobbishness which had always spoiled school life was now becoming invisible.

The drill and rugby uniforms which became common in the late nineteenth century symbolized adolescence for that period. Boys were most fondly thought of as team members. These uniforms seemed to stand for submission to rules, patriotism or team spirit, alertness, and hygiene. More important, they emphasized the similarities between children and masked the differences. If adults did not understand each other, at least they hoped that children would initiate a new era of social harmony. After the experience of World War I there was even hope that the children of the world might transcend national distinctions, as symbolized in the World Scout Jamborees.

This brings to mind another of the efforts to homogenize childhood—the adult-led youth group or boys' club. There had been clubs for poor boys in Germany as early as the 1830s which fit this description of an organization designed and run by adults in an effort to shape its young members. Those clubs had been religious in character and might be considered the descendants of the older Catholic confraternities. But by 1900 Germany saw socialist and anti-socialist youths groups organized for the impending political struggle. Their programs included the drill and sports boys were thought to like. But their motive was far more serious, like that of the government-sponsored youth groups of later totalitarian societies.

Even the Boy Scouts, the most notable of these organizations, had this sense of social purpose. Colonel Robert Baden-Powell had been appalled at the boys he saw in the industrial towns of England in the first years of this century. They were pale and unhealthy, with dirty habits (the government was about to prohibit the sale of alcohol and tobacco to minors) and without initiative. He doubted that they could even exist outside cities. Upper-class boys were in worse condition, if possible, affecting a kind of freakish sophistication, à la Oscar Wilde, which was simply eerie in an adolescent. The model Baden-Powell held up for their emulation was that of the self-reliant military scout who had been so important in his campaigns in South Africa. *Scouting for Boys; a Handbook for Instruction in Good Citizenship Through Woodcraft* (1908) was, in effect, a test of one's readiness for war. Could you survive cut off from your headquarters? Can you notice details or cope with injuries? Could you recognize edible plants or build a bridge? Only by some such training could the rising generation arrest domestic decadence, stand up to foreign threats, and ensure race survival. The empire and Britain itself would be in danger if they ever lost these pioneer skills.

In a memorable example, Baden-Powell contrasted the children of his England with those of past or primitive societies:

In South Africa the finest of the tribes were the Zulus. Every man was a good warrior and a good scout, because he had learned scouting as a boy. When a boy was old enough to become a warrior, he was stripped of his clothing and painted white all over. He was given a shield with which to protect himself and an assegai or small spear for killing animals or enemies. He was then turned loose in the "bush." If anyone saw him while he was still white he would hunt him and kill him. And that white paint took about a month to wear off—it would not wash off. . . . It is a cruel test, but it shows that these savages understand how necessary it is that boys should be trained to manliness and not be allowed to drift into being poor-spirited wasters who can only look on a man's work. The ancient British boys received similar training before they were considered men.

Even in that racist age it was thought that European boys could learn something from their "savage" counterparts, given the underlying belief in the similarities between children.

Baden-Powell clearly expected that boys would prefer his program of activities to the peer pressure to grow up too soon. Girls, too, were expected to respond to similar enthusiasms when the Girl Guides were founded in 1909. And the clubs were popular, at least with the middle classes. But the idea that Scouting prepared children for adulthood now seems incongruous. There was an exotic quality to a troop of boys hiking through London parks in South African khaki. Perhaps if they had all emigrated to the empire, as Baden-Powell suggested in the first editions of *Scouting for Boys,* their training would have been more functional. As it was, Scouting simply encouraged the idea that adolescence was slightly unreal. It turned out to be one more form of escapism, part of the wider movement to separate adolescence from the real world.

More impressive minds than Baden-Powell puzzled over the problem of bringing all adolescents up to a good average. American philosopher and psychologist William James offered what he hoped would be a more far-ranging and realistic solution in "The Moral Equivalent of War" (1910):

If now—and this is my idea—there were, instead of military conscription a conscription of the whole youthful population to form for a certain number of years a part of the army enlisted against *Nature,* the injustice would tend to be evened out, and numerous other goods to the commonwealth would follow. The military ideals of hardihood and discipline would be wrought into the growing fibre of the people; no one would remain blind as the luxurious classes now are blind, to man's relations to the globe he lives on, and to the permanently sour and hard foundations of his higher life. To coal and iron mines, to freight trains, to fishing fleets in December, to dish-washing, clothes-washing, and window-washing, to road-building and tunnel-making, to foundries and stoke-holes, and to the frames of sky-scrapers, would our gilded youths be drafted off, according to their choice, to get the childishness knocked out of them, and to come back into society with healthier sympathies and soberer ideas. They would have paid their blood-tax, done their own part in the immemorial human warfare against nature; they would tread the earth more proudly, the women would value them more highly, they would be better fathers and teachers of the following generation.

An interest in the normal development of the child, as we have seen it expressed in educational plans, soon raised a concern over abnormal development and juvenile delinquency. The institutions which the nineteenth century created to handle these problems of delinquency and child welfare give us further insight into the effort to impose a uniform childhood. For here there were few traditions to work against. Rousseau and Pestalozzi had inspired the establishment of schools for the reform of young offenders. But in the early years of the century these were private ventures, like other schools. Governments were slow to respond to the idea of separate treatment of young offenders, and their first efforts showed little imagination. Britain, which used disabled ships ("hulks") as prisons, set one aside for juvenile prisoners in 1823. Older boys bullied the others so viciously that some of the smaller ones tried to break their own bones in order to be transferred to prison hospitals. The first institution which went beyond merely housing young offenders and attempted to rehabilitate them was the New York House of Refuge, founded in 1825. Even it was initially a private philanthropy, to which the courts might send hopeful cases. It immediately inspired similar ventures in the United States and elsewhere.

One of the features of the House of Refuge which received the most notice was its principle of the "indeterminate sentence." This was, of course, an incentive to speedy reform. The institution also tried to avoid identifying its inmates as criminals by bringing in other vagrant children whom they judged to be potential delinquents. The indefinite sentence and inclusion of "potential delinquents" would become standard in all the major European states by 1900. There were even countries (Germany and Italy, for example) which followed the logic of this approach to the extent of trying to ignore the distinction between neglected children and young offenders in their welfare institutions.

This seemed like a humane approach to the problems of these children, and no doubt many of them benefited from the more sympathetic treatment. But the best of intentions led to unforeseen difficulties. Indefinite sentences might lengthen imprisonment as well as shorten it. They also implied that the offender had no definite rights against supervisors and lacked the legal recourse of adult prisoners. Lumping neglected children with actual offenders had the unfortunate effect of stigmatizing the former unfairly. When it came to that, almost any young person might be considered a potential delinquent.

Taken together, these reforms would mean that there was no logical limit to government supervision of children. The state would have the resources to extend such a system indefinitely. Zealous child welfare workers would encourage this extension by widening their definition of real or potential delinquency. Eventually, the public would begin to think of adolescence per se as a problem, as the definition of acceptable behavior became narrower.

The potential for abuse increased with each new reform. In the 1840s British and American magistrates began to experiment with probation for young offenders to keep from sending them to jail. Since probation hardly seemed like punishment, judges and juries were not as restrained in finding the young guilty. In practice this meant that children who might have gotten off scot free were now placed under supervision. With this trend was coupled a change in British law which allowed young defendants to request a summary judgment, instead of a public trial, for lesser charges. Punishments tended to be lighter since the rules of evidence were somewhat relaxed. But ironically these efforts to separate juvenile offenders from the ordinary courts and to lighten their punishment probably contributed to the rising statistics on delinquency which were now making headlines.

With the news of a general increase in crime, the motive for the juvenile justice system changed. Originally, it had arisen out of a simple humanitarianism; now it came from a desire to bring the crime rate down. What better way to fight crime than by nipping criminal behavior in the bud? The new science of criminology was finding, not surprisingly, that most criminal careers began in childhood. Unfortunately, this made the potential offender as interesting to the authorities as the convicted juvenile. But once the goal became prevention, all the young might become objects of suspicion.

No one was so consistent as to suppose that the children of the rich were as likely to turn to crime as the children of the poor. Some believed that the poor inherited their criminal traits. But they had also heard that poor parents bred their children up to crime, sending them out in the morning with instructions to bring back a certain sum of money, no matter how they got it. These were the children who were often found sleeping in the streets and preying on each other. Governments became alarmed at the immensity of the task of regulating the neglected children of their cities. The British Parliament heard testimony that there were 200 "flash houses" in London, serving as headquarters for 6000 young criminals.

The most attractive solution to the problem was to spread it out. If cities bred this crime, the answer was surely to send the children away. With this in mind, legislators made it possible to remove children from unwholesome homes. They were often put in the care of philanthropies like the New York Children's Aid Society. This organization placed some 60,000 children in foster homes in the western states in the 30 years after its founding in 1853. In Britain, Dr. Thomas Barnardo's homes for neglected children sent 24,000 to the colonies between 1876 and 1914. These areas were glad to take in these often unkempt children. But many administrators echoed the words of one: "I find that the greater number of applicants for children have no other aim in view than to secure cheap labor."

With so many children to place, such agencies had to advertise, which meant creating an image of the kind of children they had to offer. The general sentiment in favor of children was enlisted in this effort. When possible, the Children's Aid Society simply let the children speak for themselves, by printing letters like the following from "A Fourth Ward Child":

Dear Mr. Macy: I thank you for your kind letter. I have a good home and many kind friends to care for me. I think the country is a beautiful place. I wish little children would go in the country; there are many things they can get here without stealing or begging, for we have got a nice orchard full of nice fruit. I go out some days nutting. Mrs. F. says she is going to dress me warm this winter and take me a sleigh-riding. Mrs. F. took me in the carriage about two weeks ago to hear Mr.

F., a Missionary, address the Sabbath School at W.; he told us some pretty stories; I hope I shall profit by it.

Mr. Macy, I want to tell you what Mrs. F. has taught me to do. I can make coffee, and milk the cow, and make buckwheat cakes. I think it is better for little children to be in the country, and learn all these pretty things, than to be in that wicked city. I love the country, and think I am a good girl. Mrs. F. tells me I am sometimes. The young ladies teach me, and hear me my lessons; and teach me to sew. Please give my love to Mr. Gerry, and the ladies, and my teachers, and the children, with much respect. A.F.

These agencies could not pretend that their children had fine manners, but the ads did suggest that they possessed noble souls. It was not the impossibly exalted image then current in some fiction, which made all real children suffer by comparison. It came closer to the heroes of Horatio Alger's many novels of lower-class youth, like *Ragged Dick* (1866):

Washing the face and hands is usually considered proper in commencing the day, but Dick was above such refinement. He had no particular dislike to dirt, and did not think it necessary to remove several dark streaks on his face and hands. But in spite of his dirt and rags there was something about Dick that was attractive. It was easy to see that if he had been clean and well dressed he would have been decidedly good-looking. Some of his companions were sly, and their faces inspired distrust; but Dick had a frank, straightforward manner that made him a favorite.

Even this model put many poor children in the shade. When the standard image was even this appealing it became harder for the reform schools to generate any sympathy for their admittedly unlovely inmates. They felt that they were being criticized by implication and attacked the resettlement agencies for misrepresenting their charges, citing cases of delinquency among them even after relocation.

For the first time in history, the child's image became a matter of professional concern. Those who worked with wayward or neglected children had to keep them before the public's attention. Only thus could they guarantee the funding needed to continue their work and their jobs. Naturally, they wanted to create sympathy for these children. This would ensure that the public's help was given in a good spirit and would tend to raise their own status as well. But they could not give the impression that children were too noble, for fear that their job would seem too easy. Above all, they could not claim to be solving the problem, for then there would be a question whether they would be needed much longer. Their agencies would be threatened with closure and their staff with dismissal. If they could not claim some success, however, people would wonder if all their efforts had been wasted.

There was one argument that avoided all these pitfalls: They could claim that the problem of juvenile misbehavior was growing. In other words, despite some success, the public would need to make an even greater commitment to this worthwhile effort. This is the iron law of bureaucratization, and child welfare agencies proved no different from others. Whether or not it was justified, the agencies encouraged the message that children were a growing problem. Perhaps they were convinced it was true, as they collected more statistics on the problem than ever before. At any rate, the rising figures on juvenile delinquency became a major concern at the turn of this century. The news that the problem was increasing was at variance with the image of childhood innocence which was so prevalent. Perhaps many people kept both of these conceptions in their heads—that children were the closest thing to human perfection but that many were being sadly corrupted. Thus it was that the child experts themselves were often responsible for growing suspicions.

The great study of adolescence which American psychologist G. Stanley Hall published in 1904 popularized the view that children were a problem even to themselves in those turbulent years of life. The two large volumes of *Adolescence* gave ample evidence that all children had temptations to anti-social behavior. It was a wonder that more of them were not causing trouble.

> The child from nine to twelve is well adjusted to his environment and proportionately developed; he represents probably an old and relatively perfected stage of race-maturity, still in some sense and degree feasible in warm climates, which, as we have previously urged, stands for a long-continued one, a terminal stage of human development at some post-simian point. At dawning adolescence this old unity and harmony with nature is broken up; the child is driven from his paradise and must enter upon a long viaticum of ascent, must conquer a higher kingdom of man for himself, break out a new sphere and evolve a more modern story to his psycho-physical nature. Because his environment is to be far more complex, the combinations are less stable, the ascent less easy and secure; there is more danger that the youth in his upward progress, under the influence of this "excelsior" motive, will backslide in one or several of the many ways possible. New dangers threaten all sides. It is the most critical stage of life, because failure to mount almost always means retrogression, degeneracy, or fall.

Hall saw females as having a different evolutionary history and function, that of consolidating genetic advances. Biologically, then, he expected them to exhibit less of the stress that was now associated with adolescence. But socially, he could "not help sharing in the growing fear that modern woman, at least in more ways and places than one, is in danger of declining from her orbit; that she is coming to lack just confidence and pride in her sex as such."

To maintain the ideal of childhood innocence in this atmosphere could only result in a constant disappointment with real children. And thus the institutionalization of childhood betrayed the vision of childhood which had inspired it. The effort to bring all children up to the nineteenth-century ideal simply demonstrated the lack of realism in that ideal. Those who clung to the ideal could only be embittered by the stubborn deviance of so many youngsters. Indeed, the institutions themselves were tempted to disparage some children—the children of the streets—by way of demonstrating the need for boys' clubs, welfare services, and education.

Adolescence in general came to be perceived as a "problem." In an earlier age the Puritans had considered youth a problem. But they thought it was a spiritual or moral problem which might be resolved for any individual at any moment. In the changed culture of the late nineteenth century, adolescence was seen as a biological and psychological problem. As such, it seemed more intractable.

In short, adolescence was a disease. Girls were not so commonly afflicted as boys and had milder attacks. Many of them were quarantined sufficiently that there was less anxiety on their account. At first, it was thought that the poor were most subject to infection, as they resisted the new schools and the standards of respectable society. They showed little interest in the clubs which had been designed to head off potential delinquency. But the closer the social pathologists looked, the more it appeared that even the sons of good families were infected.

For many, this medical metaphor became real in a growing concern over masturbation. Before the nineteenth century the subject was rarely mentioned or was referred to only obliquely in the moralistic literature on childhood. In the Victorian period the subject became more prominent, just as a general sexual repressiveness was growing. The older moral objections were now disguised as medical advice to give them greater urgency. Masturbation was blamed for a lengthening list of ailments, from baldness to epilepsy and even insanity. Theories were devised to show how it dissipated one's vital energies and mental powers. And whereas older books had only recommended dietary measures and cold baths, after 1850 some were suggesting surgery to discourage it. The greatest concern was evident in Britain and America, from 1850 to about 1880. But German and French medical texts show a similar anxiety, which fell markedly only in the 1920s.

This fear gets to the heart of the problem of adolescence in Victorian culture. One of the underlying reasons for the isolation and institutionalization of teenagers was adult anxiety over their sexual awakening. It was the one feature of childhood with which Victorians were least equipped to deal. The creation of adolescence was a kind of compromise. Adults would try not to consider teenagers as children (despite their continuing dependence) if they would concentrate on their intellectual tasks and emotional problems and not try to act too grownup. In the meantime, adolescents would be given their own clubs, magazines, books, fashions, and hobbies to keep them happy. These restrictions fit well with the obvious need for more education in an increasingly complex world and the need to reduce the child labor force in a mature economy. It also kept teenagers from developing a political awareness, which could only be a disruptive element in the emerging democracies.

Thus, the concept of adolescence made good sense in the social circumstances of that time. But it was adopted for emotional reasons. Victorians began to criticize earlier periods which had expected children to take on larger rights and responsibilities in those years. So there was some surprise when anthropologists began to report that the tensions that justified a special concern for teenagers were not present in some societies. Bronislaw Malinowski, in *Sex and Repression in Savage Society* (1927), claimed that Oedipal conflicts were not apparent where the repressiveness of the Victorian family did not exist. From that time on, the prison of adolescence has been crumbling. That understanding of the teen years has begun to seem quaint and even damaging, even though it has not been replaced by any other concept as definite or unified.

Despite criticism the twentieth century has maintained the institutions which embodied the concept of adolescence. For we are still convinced that they brought real improvement to many young lives. The "cottage-type" home for delinquents, with its family atmosphere and farm setting, is as much the ideal now as it was when Johann Wichern first introduced it in Germany in 1833. The juvenile prison at Elmira, New York, was the first prison to call itself a reformatory (1889). And if the goal of moral reformation rather than simple punishment has not fulfilled its promise as applied to adult offenders, we are reluctant to stop trying with the young. We still model our courts after the Juvenile Court of Cook County (Chicago), which in 1899 reached the final stage in the humanitarian treatment of deviant children. Psychologists had a more important role than lawyers in this agency. They tried to get past the question of guilt in order to address the more pressing problem of restoring each child to a "good family home"—the best way they could think of ensuring that the offender would not come to the notice of the state again. Perhaps there were dangers even here. The change from punishment to treatment or therapy encouraged the authorities to become ever more intrusive.

The nineteenth century's effort to standardize childhood was far from successful. Books, magazines, and other artifacts give an impression of greater uniformity than ever existed. Even today, English schoolteachers report something like "culture shock" at meeting village children who have grown up hardly 50 miles from London but who seem to belong to a different age.

They despair of awakening the restlessness and curiosity which they think will be good for these children. As one put it,

> The village children . . . are convinced that they have something which none of the newcomers can ever have, some kind of mysterious life which is so perfect that it is a waste of time to search for anything else. . . . They are never imaginative because, again, they don't need to be. They find it impossible to want anything which they can't actually see in the village or which isn't theirs already.

This sense of frustration is a legacy of the effort to mold children to a more acceptable pattern. The youngsters this modern-minded teacher met did not "seem to want their childhood."

She is part of a long tradition. Her Victorian predecessor in East Suffolk could count on an average attendance of 31 out of over 60 children in her care. Illness was then a common excuse for keeping children away from this imported culture. And some parents still needed the pittance that children could earn by rock picking and weeding. Farmers could raid the school for harvest workers, and parsons virtually dictated whether a girl's need for further schooling overrode some parish widow's need for a domestic servant. Some of the children resented the school's culture: "I looked forward to leaving school so that I could get educated. . . . I was a child when I left but I already knew that our 'learning' was rubbish." There is, to be sure, a difference between education, as the awakening of the child's mind, and schooling, as the standardizing of children.

Even the most basic desire to end the economic exploitation of children was not fully successful. There were still occasions for philanthropists to badger the authorities on behalf of children, as in the exotic cases of those sold by their parents to circuses or other attractions as child performers. Even Josef Hofmann, the celebrated piano prodigy, had to be stopped by the authorities in the middle of an American trip in 1887. His tour was cut short after 42 concerts because of protests that the 11-year-old was being overworked. The Society for the Prevention of Cruelty to Children found so much to do that it became a positive terror to some poor parents. They saw the society's activities in terms of spying on and kidnapping children, where the society could only see the growing magnitude of parental cruelty.

It is always easy to deflate the reputations of reformers. Only those who are seeking to help are ever criticized for not succeeding or for having mixed motives. The educators, social workers, and scoutmasters who sought to meet children's needs in a changing world were simply aware of their humanitarian concern. Only in retrospect do we see that the institutionalization of childhood made growing up more difficult. With hindsight it is obvious that the rise of experts on children would lead to excessive regulation, and that there would eventually be a noisy revolt against professional meddling. But it would be a shame if we did not also recognize the goodwill of the specialists and bureaucrats who tried to ensure more humane treatment of children and the benefits which their reforms produced for many.

Eighteen

The
Demythologizing
of
Childhood

Since the early eighteenth century Europeans had been congratulating themselves on their growing concern for children. They knew there were still negligent parents, but there was a widespread feeling that new methods of handling children and a new sympathy were helping to ensure the progress of the human race. Right-thinking people supported child labor laws, universal education, and a more flexible approach to problem children, in hopes of brightening the children's lives. They were stimulated in these efforts by their view of the child as a precious, almost angelic being. And they were even willing to extend this regard to the ragamuffin children of the streets by trying to see through appearances.

Then along came science, like the wolf in some tale, bringing a new view of humanity and of the child. This picture was not as flattering; it found little to say of humans' spiritual qualities, emphasizing our animal characteristics instead. Naturally, the child's image suffered the most from this new emphasis, since it had been the most exalted.

All this did not start with Charles Darwin, but he was the first writer who could not be ignored by the public at large. His works erased the line between humankind and the animals. Children especially had to be seen in a new light. After all, they had not even begun the humanizing process. This fact is what had endeared them to Rousseau when he called them natural beings, but it seemed very different when Darwin pointed out the child's closest relatives in nature. The shock was such that children were taken down from their pedestal and, for the first time, were studied with real care. Scientists soon realized that they knew almost nothing of how children grew. Speculation on the subject had been based on introspection like Rousseau's or on certain philosophical assumptions. But scientists, of course, make it a practice to assume as little as possible and face the bald facts. What, then, were the facts?

In 1840 Darwin kept a diary on one of his children by way of beginning the systematic study of human development. He published it in 1877, stimulating other scientists to do the same. They asked when certain responses began in the child, when various motor skills developed, when moral considerations entered the child's mind.

He did not spontaneously exhibit affection by overt acts until a little above a year old, namely, by kissing several times his nurse who had been absent for a short time. With respect to the allied feeling of sympathy, this was clearly shown at 6 months and 11 days by his melancholy face, with the corners of his mouth well depressed, when his nurse pretended to cry. Jealousy was plainly exhibited when I fondled a large doll, and when I weighed his infant sister, he being then 15½ months old. Seeing how strong a feeling jealousy is in dogs, it would probably be exhibited by infants at an earlier age than that just specified, if they were tried in a fitting manner.

Sometimes Darwin admitted surprise and even amusement:

A little later (2 years and 7½ months old) I met him coming out of the dining room with his eyes unnaturally bright, and an odd unnatural or affected manner, so that I went into the room to see who was there, and found that he had been taking pounded sugar, which he had been told not to do. As he had never been in any way punished, his odd manner certainly was not due to fear, and I suppose it was pleasurable excitement struggling with conscience.

It was not easy for these baby biographers to get away from their preconceptions. They often realized, too late, that they were ignoring some behavior because they knew it would not lead to later accomplishment. But the child could not have known that. To the child, false leads were as important as the rest of his or her actions. Following all of those threads was proving harder than the scientists had expected.

One thing they did notice was that children were not simply developing in response to their environment, as Locke had led them to expect. Children seemed to have a developmental timetable of their own, more as Rousseau had imagined. The timetable proved more interesting to the scientists than the learned behavior, because it was less suspected. Also, they thought that it retraced the evolutionary history of the human race and told them much about the "primitive mentality"—which was a subject of growing interest just then.

Many other things intrigued these scientists, and by 1900 child study was splitting along several lines. Some studies concentrated on the differences between children. The importance of this approach can hardly be overestimated. Before this, writers had assumed a single standard for child development, with the result that an ever-increasing number of children seemed out of step. Scientists now recognized that they were studying not *the* child but a normal range of abilities. Where taken seriously, this meant that children were freed from the necessity of living up to rigid expectations of "childhood," flattering as these might be. It even made it possible to think of children with physical and mental handicaps as real children, although we still cannot be said to have fully absorbed this lesson.

Darwin's cousin Francis Galton was one of the first to try to raise the measurement of differences to a really scientific level. Having been struck by the amount of genius among his own relatives, he pioneered the study of hereditary influence on intelligence. But he hoped that his findings would stimulate a commitment to eugenics, bringing all children closer to one end of his scale. In 1905 Alfred Binet and Theophile Simon, working for the French Ministry of Education, created the classic IQ test. This was meant to identify mentally deficient children and the degree of their retardation so that they could be put into special classes more appropriate to their needs. It was immediately translated into other languages. One particularly fruitful study was begun in 1911, when the American Arnold Gesell started recording the timetable of normal development through mass observation at the Yale Clinic for Child Development. He, like Binet, wanted to use his measurements to recognize the range of what could be considered normal in order to help the truly abnormal.

The first two decades of the century saw the development of many other measures—of the child's aptitude, achievement, and physical growth. Frequently, these tests were commissioned by governments that wanted to create the mass armies needed for twentieth-century warfare. As before, concern over child development was not limited to those who had only the child's welfare at heart.

Others were beginning the difficult study of intellectual development. James M. Baldwin, another American, tried to explain how the child could even learn to perceive, much less learn to think, for Locke's old associationalist psychology now seemed very deficient. In its place Baldwin offered a rather speculative view of the genetic or developmental nature of logic. For it was clear that the child's mental apparatus was not ready to begin observing or discriminating among impressions without a considerable creative effort. The infant did not respond to a specific stimulus, or only with its intellectual faculties. Rather, the whole body responded, and to a whole situation. When perceptions did come, they were not simply added to previous knowledge, but the two were assimilated to each other. Suddenly, the child's accomplishment in inventing the idea of an object seemed more remarkable than anyone had dreamed, quite aside from the personal creation of a logic which would allow thought. This approach led to Jean Piaget's classic research in the 1920s in Switzerland, which showed that the structure as well as the content of our minds must be developed by time and experience.

Another approach to child study ran counter to these two. This was behaviorism, which viewed the child's actions solely as the product of environmental influences and attempted to apply its discoveries to child-rearing practice. The United States and the Soviet Union found behaviorism particularly congenial, for both countries were committed to ideologies which asserted the fundamental equality of all and the importance of environment over heredity. American John B. Watson applied Ivan Pavlov's conditioning techniques to children, in the hope of creating the kind of character that Americans had traditionally valued—independent, self-reliant, and objective. Actually, that type was more at home on the vanishing frontier than it would be in the increasingly bureaucratized and urbanized society of the twentieth century. But the new experts did not ask parents what they thought the goals of child rearing should be; they simply told them. They assumed that parents would not want children who cried or were dependent or emotional. To that end, they taught parents how to condition their children in such a way as to avoid conflict or tension.

Behaviorism was a break with all notions of the child's inner nature. Whatever was going on inside the child was of no concern to these investigators. They saw no hope of discovering what went on inside if it never manifested itself in action, and they thought it would be unscientific to speculate on the matter. But the impatience with which they waved this question aside suggested that they were dismissing the notion of human norms altogether. Their techniques could be applied in the interest of fitting the child into any kind of social environment, real or imaginary, following what we might call the Lockean tradition.

Always before, notions of the child's nature had had implications for society. For Rousseau and his followers, the child's supposed needs had offered a basis for judging that child's social environment, but the child's innocence could no longer be a rebuke to elders. If the child was infinitely malleable, society could not be making unreasonable demands. Having reduced character to behavior and behavior to conditioned responses, scientists were not bound by moral standards. Theoretically, parents might even be encouraged to start spanking again, so long as it was understood that spanking was not punishment (which would have implied the obsolete concept of guilt) but only conditioning.

Watson's advice was bound to cool the relations between

parents and children. For one thing, he was concerned about the common practice of showing too much affection toward children. To hear him tell it, children were being kissed to death in the early years of this century. He recalled a two-hour car ride in which one child had received no fewer than 32 kisses from mother, nurse, and grandmother. It nauseated Watson. He feared that this kind of conditioning led to sentimentality, dependency, and an invalid complex. It obviously was not satisfying, for look at the women who were carrying on so. They were so hungry for the child's affection that they were kissing the child on the lips. The same thing had probably happened to them as babies. Watson suggested:

> There is a sensible way of treating children. Treat them as though they were young adults. . . . Let your behavior always be objective and kindly firm. Never hug and kiss them, never let them sit in your lap. . . . In a week's time you will find how easy it is to be perfectly objective with your child and at the same time kindly. You will be utterly ashamed of the mawkish, sentimental way you have been handling them.

Watson felt that he was fighting against a century or more of such coddling.

Between 1925 and 1945 the books of child-rearing advice, especially in America, were along these lines. Watson's *Psychological Care of Infant and Child* (1928) replaced L. E. Holt's *The Care and Feeding of Children* (1894) as the authoritative work on parenting and changed the emphasis from nutrition to conditioning. Whereas the books of the last several decades had recommended loose scheduling, up-to-date parents now did their best to follow the strict feeding schedules and early toilet training that scientists were recommending. They began to feel guilty over their lapses and over the emotional problems which seemed to result from these methods. For although children were not to experience guilt in the new era of scientific relativity, the behaviorists encouraged guilt among parents who could not be entirely consistent in following their advice. Eventually, the strain became too much for many parents, who began to bring their problems to pediatricians like Benjamin Spock.

As we shall see in the next chapter, Spock's reaction against behaviorism relied on a fourth line of research, the study of the child's emotional development. Perhaps Sigmund Freud would have agreed with Watson that there was something peculiar in the kind of obsessive devotion some adults lavished on children in the years around the turn of this century. But he was far from thinking that changing outward behavior would make the problems disappear. Childhood was not, in his view, simply a convenient time for establishing "good" behavior patterns; rather, it was the most fateful part of life. The neuroses that troubled his patients in Austria seemed always to go back to their earliest years.

An understanding of child development was central to psychoanalytic theory, unlike the other psychologies of that day, which started from the mind of the normative adult. And Freud presented the only theory that would have explained the child's emotional development, as opposed to simply describing it. The theory explained very surprising, even bizarre, behavior almost as easily as more normal development. Some complained that it explained things too easily and that there was no hope of checking its explanations under controlled conditions. But though it could not be demonstrated with the objectivity behaviorists sought, the theory won increasing acceptance because of the subjective assurance of those who found their own behavior laid bare. The main block to acceptance was Freud's view of the child's nature. In 1905 his essay on "Infant Sexuality" appeared, pointing out how much of the child's activity ran on the same kind of energy that would eventually be devoted to sex. Indeed, he thought there was already a sexual dimension in the child's interests, deriving from the experience of family life. For family life involved a certain rivalry for the love of its members.

The outcry was tremendous. To a society which had valued children as symbols of sexual innocence, Freud's views seemed the height of perversion. Freud said that he himself had resisted these ideas for almost five years. Of course, he had defined sex very widely, to include pleasures that are not usually associated with that concept. But he had shown how they could be related to adult genital sexuality. So he was shunned as a moral degenerate. Freud had not meant that children are depraved, because he accepted sexual inclinations as perfectly natural. But his contemporaries assumed that he was degrading childhood, for they could only think of sex as shameful, if not positively nasty. Obsessed with their own repressed sexuality, they had looked to children for a vision of purity. To have to see them in the same light as adults now seemed to demean children.

Darwin and Freud have worn us down. Whatever we may think of their theories in detail, it is no longer possible to view children as angelic beings. The mythology of the perfect child had added to the repression children suffered, so that losing these illusions may represent a gain. It will be too bad if we find that we cannot take children seriously without such illusions. But clearly, "the child" has passed the peak of its reputation.

This development did not, however, mean a decline of professional commitment to children. Child study became a field in its own right, drawing on various scientific disciplines, and was institutionalized in the 1920s. Starting in 1923, the Laura Spelman Rockefeller Memorial Fund supported child study institutes at a number of American universities, and state governments soon followed that lead. The main resistance came from women's colleges, which were afraid that sponsoring studies of children and nursery care would be typed as women's work. Their efforts to give female education more academic respectability was always threatened by association with women's immemorial role. So the lead was taken by men and by women at coeducational institutions.

It has taken the public some time to learn how to translate science into practical wisdom. The most unfortunate result of the rising scientific knowledge was that when it was reported, the journalists and their public generalized far beyond what the scientists were finding. The public still thought they were talking about "the child." For writers did not have the space nor readers the patience to consider the scientists' qualifying statements. All studies were looked upon as conclusive. All correlations were assumed to be perfect. All dangers lay on one side of the issue. Thus it was too easy to translate highly specific findings into much more general conclusions and from there into simple commands. Readers could not have known how small or atypical the sample may have been, how things like "intelligence" or "creativity" were being defined or measured, or how great the probability of the correlations. Scientists themselves had a hard time remembering that their new field was as yet in its infancy. The public was impatient to learn the one best way to raise a child. And while educated people were suspicious of traditional advice, they did not know that even science must be read with some sophistication.

Freudian ideas were particularly open to this kind of application. If certain tensions are known to cause psychological problems, it is tempting to assume that they invariably do so. Actually, it may be that what is found in the sick could be found in us all, to varying degrees. But the first reaction was to suppose that where there is a problem there must be a solution. If tension can lead to neurosis, then we must ensure tension-free lives for our children. If an unrepressed life sounds desirable, then it must be possible. To this end, the popular mind has turned Freudianism into preventive medicine. Freud himself held out no hope for this kind of perfectionism and would have dismissed the ideal of an entirely unrepressed and uninhibited life as a fantasy. He felt more drawn to the pessimism of the Greeks than to the optimism which has become more characteristic of Western civilization.

Myths die hard. Darwin and Freud have not entirely succeeded in ridding us of the idea that children represent some form of perfection. When it appeared that children were not perfectly "pure" and "good" by nature, we reacted by redefining perfection. Whatever children are by nature is defined as goodness. Their natural instincts, whatever they may be, must not be thwarted. Science often inhibits us from deciding what we want for our children, so far as that choice must be ours. We recognize that the child has natural propensities which we cannot ignore. We are very conscious of the fact that nature may take its revenge on our methods, since we have such imperfect knowledge even of normal development. In short, we often seem to be submitting to nature rather than coming to terms with it. The most characteristic approach of our century has been to liberate or even abandon children to follow their own "nature." But that is a topic that deserves a chapter of its own.

Nineteen

The
Liberation
of
Children

The great issue in politics over the last several centuries has been liberalism. The "liberty" involved is the right of each person to pursue happiness in his or her own way, so far as that is consistent with our living together. Before liberalism, the prevailing view was that people were happier working toward common goals and that their personal worth derived from their service to others. Unfortunately, those who had exercised leadership toward those common goals often proved to be self-serving and were justly resented. So their powers were curtailed in the interest of greater rights for their subjects. This individualistic premise is still at the basis of our prevailing political philosophies.

In the nineteenth century liberalism was applied to political and economic life. In the twentieth century it has been applied to the family and education. The family is increasingly seen not as a unit but as a collection of individuals. It is coming to be assumed that those individuals will stay together only as long as they are getting something out of the arrangement. The idea that the essence of legal marriage is to provide security for the children to be born has given way to the assumption that marriage is for the purpose of legitimating sexual relations. In practice, this may mean that the children involved are neglected. Or, more positively, it may mean a liberation of children from unnecessary demands and pressures which they always faced before.

Several justifications have been offered for modern "permissiveness." At first it was an ethical matter: We all have a right to be free, so parents should not dominate their children any more than is necessary. Later, a psychological argument arose: We must all be free from family pressures if we are to develop healthy personalities. There is even an economic element in this liberalism: Whereas a developing economy needs entrepreneurs and compulsive workers, a mature economy needs consumers and a work force concentrated in the service occupations. Permissiveness seems the right way to produce people who can work with people and who will indulge themselves as consumers. Finally, parents now worry more over whether their children will like them, whereas their earlier fear was lack of respect. As society has become fragmented there are fewer people to whom we can turn for the love we need. So parents are now afraid to risk losing the goodwill of their children. The hope is that love will be the best discipline toward all these goals.

Two works in particular stand as symbols of this new and

more liberal attitude: A. S. Neill's *Summerhill: A Radical Approach to Child Rearing* (1960) and Benjamin Spock's *Baby and Child Care* (1946). As popular as these works have been, they obviously express a feeling our society finds compelling, whether or not the books have been a major cause of the new attitude.

Neill's work describes the school he founded in England in 1921. He had been distressed to see how the traditional boarding school twisted children's nature, making them hypocritical, docile, uncreative, and mean—at best. At worst it produced neurotics. Neill could think of no problem the schools did not help create, much less solve. Traditional education produced a society marked by hatred, timidity, failure, and unhappiness. He was not interested in preparing children to fit into such a society or into a consumer economy. His brand of liberalism owes more to Freud's emphasis on psychic health. But at its basis Neill's liberalism is ethical: Children have a right to happiness, just as adults do.

In Summerhill children are free to be themselves. They run the school, making decisions by majority vote and imposing fines on those who break the students' own rules. Neill steps in only when a student threatens the safety of another and must be expelled. Classes are optional and some pupils never attend. We should note that most of Neill's first pupils were problem children. He claims it usually takes about three months of idleness to undo the damage other schools have done, at which point the child begins to show up in class again.

Classes are quite ordinary, taught by conventional methods. In fact, state inspectors have reported that the instruction is old-fashioned and rather poor. But like Rousseau, Neill believes the method does not matter if children are properly motivated. And the key to motivation is freedom. He even dislikes methods like those used in Montessori schools, where teachers manipulate the child's environment and thereby guide the child's choice of tasks. For this kind of unobtrusive direction is authoritarian and deceitful, and he thinks the child can see through such methods.

Neill admits that his students do not score very well on standardized tests, although some reach the best universities. But he does not think that this is a very telling criticism, for his measure of success is personal happiness, not academic development. The point of childhood is not to prepare for adulthood; it is to enjoy being a child. He boldly states that he would rather produce a happy street sweeper than a neurotic scholar. On the other hand, he suspects that his students would do better than most at tasks requiring some originality or creativity because they are more self-motivated and sure of themselves than the typical English schoolchild.

By this point the reader of *Summerhill* is wondering what the school contributes, if it does not insist on classes or adult discipline. Neill's answer is that it offers the approval that is so important to the child's self-image. The main thing about the school is that it is positive about children, accepting them as they really are. There is no moral instruction and no moralizing criticism of actions. Neill is under no illusions about children. He expects no gratitude from them. He and his pupils sometimes fuss at each other. But he thinks that they work out their problems better by treating one another as equals than others do who have had morality imposed on them. For this only teaches them to manipulate the rules of morality for their own advantage. But in Summerhill's school assembly the children judge one another and learn to think through the rights of others as against their own. Thus, morality is their own creative discovery and their own free choice.

The school has had remarkable success with a rather difficult group of children. Neill's pupils seem to learn to respect one another and the property of others. Neill thinks they are more friendly, active, and tolerant than their counterparts in other schools. Indeed, he feels justified in extending his pedagogical principles to society at large. If all children could be raised along these lines, he says, it would solve all the world's problems. The need for politics and religion would vanish. Or, to put it another way, society would have attained a higher religious outlook. The book ends with the affirmation that "only love can save the world."

Just as Rousseau's writing on childhood led him into a statement of his basic beliefs, so Neill ends by revealing his religious sense. Even his implied criticisms of religion are on the basis of Christian values—"love and hope and charity." It is here that Neill parts company with Freud and his pessimistic "realism." Freud believed there was no final cure to the problem of repression; neither did he believe that it would end when society eased up. He was drawn to Greek tragedies in choosing the psychological terms to describe the forces dominating a person's life. Neill is like most liberal educators in being optimistic. Having begun by stating his "complete belief in the child as a good, not an evil, being," he is not satisfied in patching children up to send them back into a corrupt society. Rather, he would like to exhibit them as models for society.

The public is divided over Neill's book, as one can see in the scribblings in any library copy. Readers argue with each other in his margins. For he has shown our ambivalence over whether children's accomplishments or their happiness are our main concern. Naturally, we would rather not sacrifice either. But Neill has presented our dilemma more sharply, perhaps, than we would like.

When a group of psychologists was asked to comment on Neill's enterprise, they agreed that he was succeeding. But they did not think he understood the reasons for his success. He is an old-fashioned Freudian who believes that a decline of repressiveness is what is helping his pupils. In the view of neo-

Freudian ego-psychologists, the main problem children have in Western societies is that of forming a personal identity. They believe Neill is successful because he is such a good model and offers pupils a feeling of acceptance. In other words, his school succeeds for the same reason that some strict schools do, because the child identifies with strong and sympathetic adults. They also wonder whether Neill appreciates the value of a certain level of anxiety. Demanding teachers will create tension in their students by way of stimulating creative responses. And who is to say that we must all be underachievers for fear of crossing nature? Might not a sense of accomplishment be a part of one's happiness?

As for Neill's former students, they have reported a general approval of their experience at Summerhill. Some advised against staying at the school too long, being critical of the level of instruction there. Most reported having adjusted well to regular schools again, which may not have been welcome news to Neill. But most reported that they were using his techniques to raise their own, more self-directed, children. Obviously, they considered his methods successful.

The most exceptional feature of Summerhill is that it has been operating for such a long time. The typical life span of the thousands of "free schools" which have been opened in the United States is about one year. They have failed for a variety of reasons. Some are ambivalent in the matter of happiness as against achievement and hope to maximize both. Thus, they may become confused and discouraged. Most teachers are not as secure as Neill and become disappointed when their liberated children do not seem as grateful or cooperative as expected. In fact, such schools often attract teachers who are still working through their own rejection as children and are therefore especially vulnerable. They are unlikely to be very positive models and sometimes openly reject the role. Worst of all, they ignore naughtiness. Neill recognized that his students' antics were often distress signals, and he could always be counted on to make some unlikely response to show that he cared.

It does not appear that free schools will ever become the rule. Such gifted teachers as Neill will always be rare. The very concept of liberation works against institutionalization. An institution designed to free children from institutionalization is a contradiction, after all. One wonders, too, whether the battle for liberation is not already over in many areas, without further campaigns of this kind. Are schools still the "little hells of intrigue, hate, and jealousy" Neill remembered from his own Victorian boyhood? Summerhill's function was to provide breathing space from an impossible family situation. The problem now is to provide *any* kind of family situation.

One reason free schools have had a difficult time in the United States is that they must define themselves against public schools which already are rather "free" in certain respects. "Progressive education" dates back to the turn of the century, when John Dewey was forcing his colleagues to think what democracy implied in terms of education. Democratic education could not be the same as elite education, he observed. For an elite, education meant the mastery of a traditional culture which reflected their static worldview and added to their status. Mass education should mean practical training for citizens of a more open and progressive society. It would take place in a social and cooperative setting, not in an intensely individualistic and competitive one. It must allow scope for creativity in problem solving. And it should add dignity to labor by taking an active rather than a contemplative view of learning.

What Dewey called "progressive education" got its impetus from the "progressive movement," a political campaign that reasserted the rights of the individual against the growing power of big business and unresponsive government. His attack on elitism and tradition suited the nation's ideology and its mood, so that there was considerable enthusiasm for his slogans—"the child-centered school," "educating the whole child," "creative self-expression," and "teaching children, not subjects." The experiment worked, as all educational experiments do—so long as they run on the enthusiasm of their first proponents. The impact of the ideas on the American school can hardly be imagined by those who have grown up on this side of these changes.

But as the public began to forget what earlier schools had been like, it came to think of progressivism as a failure. Indeed the liberation of the child and the school from bondage to tradition was carried so far as to dismay even Dewey. It proved easier to criticize the older curriculum and methods than to decide what was needed to replace them. In the absence of firm goals, many progressive teachers emphasized social adjustment, letting peer authority substitute for adult guidance. Worst of all, the public complained, Dewey's focus on meeting the moral and technical challenges of the future had turned education into a means of subversion. For students were encouraged to think in terms of social change before they learned to make sense of the existing system. Before, schools were intended to conserve cultural and social standards. Now educators assumed that they had a duty to encourage social change.

Opposition to progressive education built up in the Cold War period as part of a generally conservative trend. It peaked in 1953 with the publication of several reasoned but bitter attacks. In 1955 the Progressive Education Association disbanded, declaring that it had accomplished its goals. Its critics might have agreed to that assessment more readily than its friends.

Since that time the issue of liberating the child has gone further than the debate over strict or permissive schools. It has invaded the family itself. The book which is most often identified with this trend, and blamed for it, is Spock's *Baby and Child Care,* which first appeared in 1946. For some time doctors had been hearing from parents about the difficulty—or downright impossibility—of keeping children on the strict schedules advocated in behaviorist child-rearing manuals. The goal of "efficient" management of the child's needs had been adopted to reduce friction between parents and children, but in fact it was leaving them both badly frayed. Spock was a pediatrician and not a psychologist; he at first called his book *The Common Sense Book of Baby and Child Care.* Thus, he avoided the appearance of scientific dogmatism. But there was a scientific basis to his libertarianism. It was, in fact, the first extended presentation of Freudian advice in the popular literature on child rearing.

Spock was careful not to use Freud's technical terms. Doing so would only have alarmed parents, to whom Freud was still a bogeyman. But when Freud's ideas were extended to such matters as demand feeding, toilet training, thumb-sucking, or bed-wetting, and put in ordinary language, they seemed quite sensible. Where Spock differed from Freud was in his tone. He exuded confidence, expecting the child to turn out well. He thought that parents worried too much about what the experts might be thinking and that they should trust their instincts more. He soft-pedaled Freud's ideas about conflict within the family and within personality. Spock suggested that the normal condition was a harmony of instincts and concord within the family.

The American public had been prepared for this view of the natural harmony within nature by such works as Margaret Mead's *Coming of Age in Samoa* (1928). That study indicated that many childhood conflicts are avoided in societies that take a more relaxed approach to the child's activities and demands. There is now considerable suspicion that Mead was the victim of a hoax by her Samoan informants. But her message matched the mood of many intellectuals at that time. Spock's most famous example of the wisdom of nature was his report of Clara Davis's experiment on the food preferences of children. She had shown that children who had never eaten anything but milk were able to choose a balanced diet without any guidance. Some readers generalized this discovery into the doctrine that nature will never lead us astray. They ignored the small print, in which it appears that the experimenter had only let children choose from among a few "wholesome, unrefined foods." So the experts had already been at work controlling nature for the child. What if parents were to give children a much freer choice, including junk food? Could the wholesome, unrefined foods compete? This experiment is being carried out on a massive scale in the United States today, and some may think that they have Dr. Spock's blessing on it.

There is a further risk in asserting the advantages of liberating children and their impulses. What if leniency does not result in establishing family harmony, as Spock implies that it will? If it is not nature's fault, then it might be assumed to be the parents' fault. Thus, Spock's kindly advice could inadvertently raise parents' sense of failure. For those who lacked confidence to begin with—those for whom the book was written—*Baby and Child Care* could actually increase anxieties. The author's confidence in the normal child might be no help to those who imagined that they had already irreparably damaged their own.

In the end, there was a limit to the liberation Spock offered children. For although they were to be freed from many of the demands parents formerly made, it was sometimes so they could meet their peers' demands instead. For example, parents read that their children should be allowed to dress, talk, and play like and "have the same allowance and privileges as the other average children in the neighborhood." In short, they should not be made to feel different. Liberation, then, has often meant simply a new choice of authorities. At a time when children need adults against whom to measure themselves, they are being delivered over to their peers. Psychologists now frequently claim that the lack of involvement with role models is leading to the identity problems so characteristic of today's adolescent. Young people cannot convince themselves that they can make the transition to adulthood, because they have had so little contact with adults. Always before, contending with one's parents had been a part of finding oneself.

Thus, the liberation of children has made the search for a personal identity and continuity of character more difficult. Children in certain classes in the West now have more freedom than they can handle. Spock himself has taken notice of the danger in freeing children too soon, only to see them fall into peer group dependence. Each new edition of his work has encouraged a greater measure of parental guidance. On the other hand, Spock is right to remind us of what child-rearing advice was like when his book first appeared. He now admits that he consciously overreacted, but to advice which no one would wish to bring back. For instance, since 1914 the U.S. Children's Bureau has produced a booklet entitled *Infant Care.* In its first edition the underlying assumption was that the child's biological impulses were bad. Such a view had scientific sanction then, which concealed the Victorians' fear of the body. Experts warned that rocking horses, swings, and teeter-totters might encourage masturbation. In general, they put forward the view that the child needs rest, not stimulation or excitement. Mothers were therefore warned to resist the desire to play with their children. As for infants who sucked their thumbs or touched their genitals or cried just to be held, it was feared that they would become self-indulgent. So the experts told how to thwart them, with stiff cardboard sleeves made so that children could not bend their arms, or by pinning a child's sleeves to the sheet.

Infant Care was still being printed in the 1950s. But by that time it was giving virtually the reverse of its original advice. Now it was assumed that what the child wanted must be good for him or her, showing a wholehearted acceptance of the naturalism of Darwin and Freud. Parents were to discourage unwanted behavior by diverting the child's attention, not by thwarting it. Affection and play were important, and parents as well as children were expected to enjoy this play. In fact, it had become a duty to have fun with one's child. Parents were left with the impression that there was something wrong with them if they did not think of child care as a joy rather than a chore. Liberalism seemed adept at raising guilt among parents, if not among children.

Since Spock first wrote, the sciences which tended to justify his liberalism have changed their emphasis somewhat. Psychology and sociology were then concerned with harmony within the personality and the social system. Societies were analyzed functionally, to show how all the parts supported the structure. Psychologists were concerned with adjustment to society and to one's biological drives. The utopias described at that time—from the kibbutz to "Walden Two"—were designed to eliminate conflict between society and the individual. Eliminating friction seemed the way to follow nature. But more recently, scientists have begun to wonder whether nature is really teaching that. Perhaps the normal state of society is not balance. Perhaps the organism needs a certain level of tension for growth and well-being. Even if it were shown that families are never entirely free of conflict, this would not necessarily discredit them. For again, some tension may be necessary to personal development. What might cause trauma in certain cases might more typically be an occasion for positive growth. So even scientists might now agree that learning to cope with conflict is a better approach than trying to eliminate it.

This new mood is apparent among those who have a professional responsibility for children. One psychiatrist has expressed it by saying that with children

unlimited gratification without frustration leads to deep anxiety, primitive behavior, and regressive manifestations. Limit-setting, i.e., frustrations imposed by less-than-perfectly-gratifying people, is absolutely essential to the development of necessary ego functions such as reality testing and impulse control. In this regard, Anna Freud is quoted as questioning whether one could love a really free child.

One never knows how such statements will affect the parents to whom they are directed. As with the liberalizing trend, this swing may justify and rationalize another, opposite set of compulsions.

There is still a future for a liberal approach to child rearing. But it will recognize that children need to liberate themselves, not to have it done for them. Children are tough, and as long as they are given a good start they can grow by interaction with adult authority. Indeed, it would seem that this is the only way for them to mature. We have been all too conscious of the fact that families can be so oppressive that they break the child's spirit. But a hasty liberation has often meant damaging neglect. Perhaps as parents we need only consider how to time our retreats strategically, so that children will feel a sense of accomplishment as they make their own way in the world.

Twenty

The
Identity
Crisis
of
Our
Civilization

ometime around a century ago the image of the child reached its highest point in Western civilization. The exaltation of "childhood" to such heights directed attention to the needs of children as never before in history. But it also raised expectations to unrealistic levels, so that something of a reaction was inevitable. The closer study of "the child" which resulted from this rising interest has, ironically, taken the luster off that image. We have become all too conscious of the problems of rearing children. Partly, this is because we know more about the problems children face in growing up. Partly, it is because we have not given up our hopes of raising ideal children. But mostly, our problem in helping our children is in knowing what we want for them. When challenged, we do not seem at all sure what that ideal childhood would be, or which values are of most importance to us.

In other words, our children are having a hard time growing up because our civilization itself is experiencing an identity crisis. The difficulties of parents and children are part of a more general difficulty in our civilization—a crisis of confidence and moral direction. Neither parents nor the wider society offers children the guidance they need, want, and deserve. Adolescents especially are looking for ideals around which they can build worthwhile lives. But many adults do not trust themselves to give this guidance or are erratic in the model they present. Teachers, too, may be overwhelmed by our present confusion of values. They represent a culture that has ceased to believe in itself, whether by their unremitting criticism of that heritage or by defensiveness and timidity. The question now seems to be whether there are any values left in Western civilization that could inspire us to give our children more direction in life and that could offer them some pride in their heritage.

The collapse of Western culture first became obvious in the 1920s. Europe had just fought a war so ferocious that it filled people with horror and disgust. For years Europeans had been exporting their civilization to the rest of the world's peoples while it colonized them. But now they began to wonder whether that civilization was even worth preserving, seeing what destruction it could produce. Progress had been an illusion if it only made warfare more hideous. For it appeared that, just below the surface, we are still brutal and primitive.

Sensitive adults could hardly believe in themselves after that or explain to children why they should uphold existing institutions or cultural traditions. Art, literature, and historical scholarship reflected a revulsion against old standards. This was most evident in the Dada movement, which glorified the primitive and instinctual elements in humanity. The writers and artists who adopted that name (French for hobby horse) tried to remain utterly open to experience, like children who follow impulse wherever it may lead. They had too much fun shocking the public with their nonsense to convince anyone that they had lost all self-consciousness. But they did popularize the notion that remaining infantile was the way to stay true to oneself. This was a revolt not just against the older generation and its culture but against age and culture themselves.

When adults act like children, children will not be in a hurry to become adult. And while most adults thought the modern trends in art and literature were foolish, their faith in the future of their culture was shaken. Likewise, they began to wonder whether the past was any guide, as, for example, in the matter of child rearing. Parents felt adrift while they waited for authoritative word from the scientists. One midwestern mother in the 1920s complained to a sociologist:

> Life was simpler for my mother. In those days one did not realize that there was so much to be known about the care of children. I realize that I ought to be half a dozen experts, but I am afraid of making mistakes and usually do not know where to go for advice.

The world depression of the 1930s made adults wonder even more seriously about the world they had made. Universities were expanding in those years and helped spread doubts, particularly about religion and capitalism. All of this was reflected in stories about youth. Whereas authors in the first years of the century had treated the problems of youth with an amused condescension, in the 1920s adolescent characters became symbols of genuine bewilderment, even in self-confident America.

Growing numbers of adolescent characters were having a harder time adjusting to social conventions or even seeing the point in them. Writers now clearly sided with these characters and endorsed their judgment on society. Even in the works of French authors, who had never promoted an ideal image of the adolescent like that in German or English literature, literary prestige began to pass from age to youth. There were as many novels about adolescence published in the period 1920–1925 as in all of previous French literature. And whereas before the war adolescent restlessness was pictured as biological in nature, after that upheaval it was seen as social and cultural.

With the rise of Nazi aggression, Western civilization once again seemed worth fighting for. But afterwards, in the 1950s, the cultural depression deepened. America, for example, was within sight of achieving its goals of prosperity, security, and the pursuit of fun. But fulfilling one's goals has a way of raising questions about those goals. Parents looked to their children for some appreciation of the easy life that they had secured. The children tried dutifully to enjoy what they were offered, but they were sometimes not thankful enough to satisfy their elders. They were, after all, being asked to live out someone else's dream. Worse still, many of them sensed the deficiencies in that largely materialistic dream. There was nothing more that parents could do to add to their children's happiness. Some of them became resentful toward a generation that questioned their goals and achievements; others were disappointed in themselves. The link between the generations was thus broken, sometimes with bitterness and sometimes with regret. Very little of an age-old heritage in philosophy, literature, religion, the arts, manners, or mores passed over the gulf between these generations, whatever their feelings for each other.

The children's loss was the greater. The generation born after World War II has no unifying goals or values which could hold a culture together. As a society, we no longer affirm ultimate values that could guide us in arranging our other values in a scale, so we have no way of deciding issues involving these values logically, by reference to agreed principles. We now allow such questions to be settled simply by counting heads in votes and polls which command less and less respect.

The youth revolt of the 1960s is best understood as a reaction to this cultural decay. Novelists of the 1950s introduced us to adolescent characters who were too alienated from society to think of making an impact on it. Those characters were not even sure that they were rising above the evil or stupidity around them. They were losing even the sense of the moral superiority of youth, which had once provided a fundamental belief. So it was almost a relief in 1960 when young people again found social evils that so obviously cried out for action. That was the year in which the U.S. civil rights movement began, with six black students at a lunch counter. It coincided with student-led riots around the world—in Algeria, Turkey, Korea, and Japan. Once again, moral issues had become simple and goals were clear. A youthful revolt against injustice, corruption, and neo-colonialism grew throughout the decade. The New Left movement of 1965 identified this revolt with the younger generation by protesting the concept of adolescence. For the idea that society should indulge adolescents in their irresponsibility seemed to these students an excuse for keeping them in political ignorance.

Along with this young radicalism came a revival of juvenile romanticism in the identification with (or worship of) rock stars. This sent a shock wave through the last pockets of adult authority and assurance. Rock 'n' roll, as it was called in 1955, was music that particularly belonged to the young. Elvis Presley's insouciance and blatant fleshliness earned him the hostility of adults and the delighted devotion of teenagers. For a generation past, children had either behaved or been effectively shunned. Now masses of them looked to rock stars for the heightened experience religion and the arts were not providing. It showed a yearning for an ecstatic or spiritual fulfillment that was largely lacking in modern society. Pop singers acquired a charismatic aura involving their dress, manner, movement, and artistic style. From there, publicity agents could puff their "image" into cultic dimensions.

In 1963 the Beatles, Britain's contribution to this struggle for spiritual independence, added a dimension of good-spirited impudence which even succeeded in winning over many adults. But other groups, such as the Rolling Stones, continued an intransigent attack on received aesthetic and moral standards for the more hard-bitten among the young. Some stars expressed a hostility not just to the Establishment but to their audiences and even themselves. There was a kind of self-revulsion shown in splintering their instruments and electrical equipment as part of their performances. As Dr. Spock observed in 1970, such antics "represent emotional regression all the way back to the one- to two-year-old level, when a child in a spell of anger wants to antagonize and mess and destroy on a titanic scale." To him, it showed that even the young shared this century's "unprecedented loss of belief in man's worthiness." In earlier ages such a feeling would have been resolved in a larger religious perspective. But in the 1960s there were no adults who could say this convincingly or who had the ear of the younger generation. Spock himself threw his support behind the political efforts of the New Left.

Up to this point, the New Left had not attacked the values that the West professed. Quite the contrary: They criticized their elders' failure to live up to the values they had preached to the rest of the world. Outright rejection of those ideals appeared in 1967 with the hippie phenomenon. Like the Dadaists, hippies rejected civilization and all its works. The detailed political programs of the Left for participatory democracy and creative labor seemed beside the point. Hippies saw no need for a violent revolution but simply declared that the New Age had arrived and that they were living in it. "The Revolution" would not substitute new institutions, for all such things go bad in time. Rather, it was a matter of a new consciousness. A free and unrepressive society would allow universal rejuvenation. Once others had seen that personal and national defenses could be dropped, they would flock over to join. There was an infectious silliness in these Flower Children that appealed to Americans especially, and even the leaders of the New Left often deferred to them, thinking that there must be something profound in their commitment to self-realization. But the public always suspected that someday they would have to "pay the piper."

The collapse of this "Woodstock nation" was sobering. Political repression had weighed heavily on the New Left in 1968, in France, Czechoslovakia, Mexico City, and Chicago. But the hippies destroyed themselves. They had imagined that they were living out the most basic and universal of human values—peace, love, and freedom. But for many, that life turned horribly sour. Some of the stars of their "happenings"—Jimi Hendrix and Janis Joplin—took their own lives, whether intentionally or not. And the crowd of runaways that were attracted to the movement sank in a morass of drugs, violence, and prostitution. They had not found the family love they were looking for.

The search for family was obviously at the root of the matter, as was clear from hippies' major topic of conversation—"relating." Relationships had become desperately problematical, and all kinds of attempts were made to break down the interpersonal barriers which they felt. Hundreds of thousands "blissed out" together at rock festivals. Rural and urban communes tried living together like extended families, and polygamous groups enslaved themselves to cult leaders. Others just tried living together without any bonds of commitment. The problem, apparently, was the failure of so many American families and the collapse of the culture that had once encouraged and even enforced family life. Hippies offered to be as accepting and faithful as their families should have been. But in their effort to be utterly open to others they found they lacked the self-discipline even to live together. That was something only the family could have taught. Many hard-working parents just hadn't had the time to build such families.

When journalists pressed hippies for some statement of their values, they talked of being open to "nature" and to the "real self" they believed was trapped inside them. It was the logical culmination of the liberal and naturalistic creed which had come to dominate Western civilization since the time of Rousseau. They had been taught to look to nature for direction and to assert the importance of their desires against all the world, if necessary. And from that perspective, it did not seem that their families had contributed anything of value to their self-realization. Family life only constrained their natures, as far as they could see.

The deficiencies of this naturalism are now clear in practice as well as in theory. For it can justify virtually anything, including the nightmare of drugs. The question now is whether there is an alternative to the naturalistic ethic which might inspire a greater sense of responsibility toward one another and especially toward our children. For this postwar generation will experience problems as parents beyond any their own parents confronted. They are acutely aware that all questions of personal and social goals are up in the air. They will receive less prompting from any official culture than their parents did, in deciding these questions of purpose and value. What, for example, is the proper goal of behavior modification, as psychologists refine our techniques of conditioning children's behavior? How should we use our new power to control heredity? How far must we obey the "dictates" of our animal nature? Is the happiness of the individual or of society or of future generations our first concern? Until we have decided some of these matters, our culture will lack assurance. It will fail to offer the needed conviction to challenged parents. Simply getting tough with children will not avail if those children are not convinced that their parents and the wider society are serving some higher purpose than selfish desires.

Where can we look for guidance as we attempt to rank our values? Some social prophets simply try to peer into the future to guess what is coming in order to welcome it. To them, the rising rates of divorce, abandonment, or abuse prove that the family has no future, at least if it persists in demanding sacrifices. They hold out little hope of shaping that future, except perhaps by science. Scientists have often found alternative paths to our goals when we have met with some obstacle. But insofar as the goal is to produce resilient personalities, social scientists and psychologists have not yet discovered an alternative to the stable, role-differentiated family.

Scientists themselves are quick to point out that they cannot tell us what we should want, only how best to achieve what we have decided on. They have never wanted the job of deciding our ultimate goals. Of course, they can describe the condition of existing societies and can say what kind of personality traits prevail in each and why. They can describe existing families, enlarging the terminology to fit our changing situation (sociologists now speak of the "partial family" as a common type). But it is a matter of indifference to "science" whether human society continues to exist at all. Scientists cannot even tell us whether it is better to focus our attention on actual families as they exist today or on certain ideal family types we might like to reproduce. Until recently, our civilization concentrated its attention on what it took to be the ideal, in the hope of bringing reality into line. Lately we have concentrated on the norm and on describing the most common patterns. For there is no moral judgment involved in simple description and therefore no guilt over the failure to attain some ideal.

But the description of what exists is becoming unbearably

depressing. We have been offered the example of the Ik people of Uganda. In the 30 years since the government forced them off their hunting grounds, they have been driven to the edge of starvation. As a result, they have turned against each other and are now so hostile that all family structure has collapsed. Children are tolerated for three years or so but are then thrust out of the house to fend for themselves. The young do not experience social life; even conversation has virtually ceased in the tribe. Only children attempt any form of social cooperation, in the gangs they form to secure food. But the trust they build up together is eventually destroyed by their own brutal betrayals, as they learn the ways of their people. The anthropologist who lived with this nightmare sensed some "humanity" only in one possibly insane girl, who demanded love from her parents and was consequently killed as a nuisance. Apparently the only joy left in the lives of the Ik is seeing others suffer more than they do. They cannot see that love or care have any value to themselves as individuals. Whether the Ik will last long in this condition is not clear. But it is frightening to think that simple survival does not necessarily imply society or any human values.

Of what use is this description, except to serve as an awful warning? We could never be convinced that such a system had as great a right to our consideration as our other models of human society. And yet we are so desperate for guidance that the public even turns to studies of animal behavior for direction in human relations. The discovery of infanticide in certain animal groups, or aggression and oppression, or friendship and self-sacrifice, is often given front-page treatment. The implication is that this behavior must be natural to humankind as well and therefore should be tolerated in our children. It is, in effect, the culmination of our naturalism. Some react violently to such discoveries if they seem by analogy to justify elitism, sexism, or racism. They assume that we have no choice but to follow wherever the animals' instincts may lead. We are so used to looking to nature for guidance that we forget that we do exercise choice—if only in where to follow "nature." Of course, there are limits to how far humankind can stray from the laws of our world and of our own being. Civilization has ignored the demands of nature too long, perhaps. But we seem to be at the low point of a cycle now, in our mood of helpless acceptance.

What humanity becomes is a matter for decision, even political decision. And the world already has some examples of confidence in the task of child rearing. The Soviet Union is committed to producing more cooperative, productive, and happy citizens and has given child development considerable attention. They do not imagine that the whole burden must rest with the family. The work of A. S. Makarenko in the 1920s suggested that children can take responsibility for each other. Schools are now organized along these lines, with children being rewarded and punished by groups. They thereby acquire a group solidarity that is not at odds with adult society. All this does not preclude competition, which is also handled in groups. Older students are given responsibilities with regard to the younger children in their schools and in turn are entertained by adult occupational or professional groups.

The care the Soviet state shows toward these children is meant to complement family authority rather than to challenge it. At one point the government hoped to enroll all preschool children in state-operated day care. But only 20 percent of all children under age three are currently cared for in those centers (with an enviable ratio of one helper per four children) because the family, once weakened by the loss of some 16 million men in World War II, is making a comeback. The state has seen the wisdom in encouraging family, school, and official youth groups to support one another. And the result is far less anti-social behavior than in Western Europe or the United States.

The West is suspicious of any system in which the pressures for conformity are so great and the possibilities for creativity so small. Still, one cannot assume that the population is restive. Children doubtless feel more secure where the adults seem more sure of their goals. A danger would arise if the purity of the government's motives were suspected. And oddly enough, that may be exactly what makes childhood seem so precious to the Soviets. Their remarkable devotion to children may be precisely a result of their cynicism toward a regime which often stifles spontaneity. Children are symbols of a freedom that is otherwise lacking in the nation's life.

The Israeli kibbutz offers an example of a community which believes in itself and is therefore able to be both kindly and firm with its children. No elaborate plans were made with regard to child rearing on these cooperative farms at first. Communal techniques simply evolved. They are now successfully producing children who are self-respecting, industrious, and content. There have been some surprises, however. Children raised by the community turn out to be rather unemotional, uncreative, and uninteresting to outsiders. They do not have a strong sense of individual identity or make strong attachments to other individuals if doing so seems to mean disloyalty to the group. In other words, they tend to resemble children raised in the close-knit agricultural communities of the past. The older generation is surprised that these children do not share the intellectual interests or the idealistic vision which inspired the pioneers. But the very fact that the children take kibbutz life for granted is evidence of the older generation's success in socializing them.

Some youngsters leave the kibbutz, of course, and without that safety valve this static society might have been blown apart by disagreement. It has also been necessary for these communities to compromise with the desire of families to have more time together and more privacy. As in the Soviet Union, the family in Israel was once considered an oppressive institution and was positively discouraged in the interests of a wider community. In both countries the demand for family life has reasserted itself.

It is interesting that families seem healthier where government encourages other kinds of social bonds, taking some of the burden off the family. Where the job of raising children can be shared more widely, by institutions which genuinely support one another, it becomes less erratic.

At present, both of these systems are reaching for a balance of family care and community aid. But both systems are made possible only by ideological commitments which are incompatible with Western liberalism. For this reason, the kibbutz is not growing beyond 4 percent of Israel's population, and the Soviet example in child care is only being held up to us in the way Sparta was presented to the ancient Greeks, as a corrective but not a pattern to be followed slavishly.

Even beyond the problem of finding the right direction for our child-rearing efforts, we seem to be searching for a new motive for doing the right thing by our children. It is obvious that warm feelings alone will not assure commitment to the child's development. At one time we might have been told that we owed it to our own parents to pass on the care they gave us, but the more usual appeal these days is to our selfishness. Economist Robert Heilbroner has pointed out that not only the distant future but our own lives may be affected if we do not do better by our children. If the relative wealth of the West begins to decline, only one thing could maintain present social bonds. That one thing, he says, is the sense of human identification which is fostered in the family. Of course, concern for our children will be the only real encouragement toward a more provident use of resources for the distant future. But even in the near prospect, some willingness to sacrifice will be necessary if we are not to scramble wildly for what is left in a contracting economy. The motive of self-interest served us well in stimulating us to expand our economy. But the one form selfishness can safely take now is devotion to our descendants, to our flesh and blood.

The search for a motive for caring for our children is itself an indication of our present difficulty. For the very notion of motive suggests that the child's welfare is not sufficient reason in itself. Why must there by anything more basic, some ulterior benefit which will accrue to us personally? Duty may strike us as a weak motive in comparison with selfishness, yet some sense of duty is still buried within us. We know that comforting the dying, for example, is of no value as we usually calculate value. But we are inwardly convinced that it is a good thing. Even if we were told that other societies scorned the idea, we would not be shaken in this conviction. So it might be with our service to children.

The Judeo-Christian tradition introduced a value unknown to the world of its day—the ideal of service, not just to the state but to one's neighbor. Service replaced dominance as the mark of one's worth. We have seen that Jesus, in his many expressions of this ideal, used children as the most obvious recipients of our service. Those European barbarians who adopted Christianity had their own values, which did not mix easily with this view of things. Few could accept or even understand such an inversion of their aristocratic code. Therefore, European societies tended to single out certain groups as specialists in service. Women were the last to be left with this duty. Searching for some distinction even in that humble sphere, women sometimes made themselves martyrs to good works. Often their service was given so officiously and with such self-advertisement that it was a burden to its recipients. But one cannot blame women for resenting their position. The ideal of service, freely given, had already been subverted by the fact that it was extorted instead.

The abuses of this ideal, however, do not discredit it. The notion of a society founded on an ideal of service is, after all, only realistic. We all serve each other. Doctors serve their patients and lawyers their clients. Businesspeople serve their customers, politicians their constituents, and presidents their public. Our economy is more and more concentrated in the "service industries." We can, if we like, imagine that we do our work only for the rewards—in position, salary, or esteem. Or we may, in another mood, think of our society in terms of mutual service and solidarity. It is up to us to decide which of these views is more likely to lead to the kind of society we would want to be part of, and which would give us more personal satisfaction.

Historically it was necessary to go through a phase in which we thought in individualistic and selfish terms. For at one time the bulk of the population was identified as servants just by virtue of their unfortunate birth. They had to assert their freedom before we, their descendants, could recognize that service can be given freely. Housewives were the last group that needed to revolt against their status as a "servant class." But now we can see that a social order based on individualism is failing to meet some of our most basic human needs. Now, since we may think of others as serving us too—however they may think of themselves—it need not cost us our self-respect to see ourselves in the same role. And children will be the major beneficiaries of a charitable impulse.

For the past 200 years we have been encouraged to think of the pursuit of happiness as an individual thing. The government panels and commissions that have researched the problems of youth and of the family tend to avoid certain recommendations, knowing that they would go against this ingrained individualism. Since they take the rights of adults as axiomatic, it is children that have to adjust. And we pretend that government can somehow meet children's needs if the rest of us refuse our responsibilities. Actually, there is little that a change in the laws could accomplish in many areas, for people cannot be forced to be caring parents. Some of the greatest changes in the legal status of the family have come not from a revision of the laws themselves but from changes in the meaning of such terms as "cruelty." Similarly, a great deal of the desertion and indifference which is so noticeable today is caused by changing attitudes. More can be changed by the pressure of public opinion than by laws. We are slow to criticize each other, openly at least. But we might stop accepting the suggestion that more personal freedom is needed to ensure the good life. The plight of a generation of neglected children has already shown that we all suffer from the effects of that idea. In 20 years the incidence of suicide among those aged 15–24 tripled, and that group reported increasing depression and self-doubt.

To preach incessantly on this subject of service would be wearing and might become intolerably pious. It would sound like the Victorian cliché of "living for others." But we need to establish the habit of inquiring first about the needs of children. Politicians cannot be expected to raise such questions, since children cannot vote. But there is nothing to keep the rest of us from considering the welfare of children to be axiomatic, since they are the most truly helpless. What if we stopped asking what children can put up with and started asking what is best for them? What if we were to remind ourselves periodically that the first few years are more decisive in children's development than any comparable period in parents' lives? Doing so might establish a climate of opinion which would give the proper dignity to our service.

Not only would children be the major beneficiaries but our attitude would also give them a sense of direction for their own lives. Adolescents especially are searching for worthwhile causes. That is the age when they could best learn that they will have duties toward others and that these duties will be part of a happy and worthwhile life. One of the most frequent suggestions of experts on youth is that teenagers need some responsibilities so that they can feel they are being integrated into society. Such duties would give them the self-respect which many of them now lack. A hundred years ago, as life was rapidly becoming more complicated, the reaction was to give children a world of their own. There they were encouraged to indulge themselves before they had to face an uncertain and sometimes ugly adult world. Adults meant well in all this, but it was a mistake. They should have been thinking of ways to prepare children for the duties they would have as adults. Without an ideal of service, it was inevitable that that generation and later ones would become more self-centered. Now the need is to help our children learn to accept responsibilities. There will be no shame in this if adults themselves have recognized service as a fundamental part of life.

There may be some danger in this advice. The people who most need it are not those who are likely to have picked up this book. There may be a greater number of concerned parents now than ever before in history, who are being ignored because they are not part of the problem. They should not feel driven to martyr themselves or to smother their children with attention. Kids need some room in order to grow. Anxious attention can be almost as bad as neglect. Nor should we feel it necessary to provide a tension-free existence for the child. Some conflict seems to be necessary for full development. We should try not to be discouraged by their disagreement or even ingratitude. For we still have a duty to teach our children what we know, just as we owe them the right to quarrel with it.

Generally, however, excessive care for children is not our characteristic failing. What we have trouble remembering is that, in a sense, all human children are born prematurely. They do not have the instincts that would determine their mature character or guarantee that they will grow into truly human beings. Humanness is not natural but cultural. By neglect, we can deprive children of a secure personal identity. "Secure identity" should not be thought of as some new form of salvation. It is not the end of one's development. In fact, it is only the beginning—the precondition of adult growth and happiness. But we cannot be sure that children will make even this beginning without a greater commitment of time and interest on the part of parents and society.

The
Lesson
of
This
History

As we look back over hundreds of years of the history of attitudes toward children, the one inescapable lesson must be the ambivalence that adults have always shown toward children. It gets in the way of understanding children, and it spoils even our well-meant efforts in their behalf. Coming from so deep within us, this ambivalence does not seem likely ever to change.

Most of us cannot really think about children. When we try, we end up thinking about *ourselves* as children. That is what "childhood" turns out to be—our confused and troubled memories of the most important time of our life. After all, our deepest memories are of that period, and the greater number of them are unconscious. These half-remembered feelings have a great poignancy for us and inspire devotion to the children in our care, but mainly they remind us of the need to work through *our* old problems. Children may give us hope that this will be easy to do, for at first glance they may seem innocent, happy, ready to be helped. But the longer we watch, the more they may disappoint us and the more intractable those problems may become. So there is no contradiction between being sentimental about "childhood" and being bored with our own kids, especially if we were hoping that they could live out some fantasy of ours.

We would have preferred the lesson of this history to be that children have risen gradually in the esteem of a progressive civilization. But obviously such improvement as there has been has been very uneven. For example, one would think that those "permissive" parents of the baby-boom generation in America, who invested time in the home and created huge industries to satisfy a youth market, should be able to look back with pride on their record. But it is that "child-centered" generation that is now voting itself government benefit raises at the expense of those very children. While Social Security is politically untouchable, the number of children falling into poverty increases alarmingly (54 percent in ten years).

Progress is spotty. One might also suppose that because governments have passed laws against child labor it must have disappeared by now in all self-respecting nations. But it turns out that our homes are full of the products of child labor. Certainly child actors are a mainstay of our TV and magazine advertising (and how much distress would the outtakes reveal?). Children we don't see produce our carpets in Morocco and India, polish gems in Thailand, make glassware in Mexico, mosquito coils in Indonesia, toys in China, textiles in the Philippines, are posed for child pornography in Denmark and the Netherlands—all for export. This does not include children working in agricultural production in the United States and USSR, as construction workers, peddlers, ragpickers, prostitutes, and house servants in numerous countries, as soldiers in the Near East. This is the sort of knowledge we would rather be sheltered from.

Even the sexual abuse of children shows the kind of ambivalence we are discussing. Pedophiles are in love with childhood, and their difference from others of us may be more a matter of degree than we imagine. We are becoming more aware of this abuse, perhaps because it is actually increasing. There is, after all, greater opportunity for it given the disarray of many households, our careless day care arrangements, and a general relaxation of inhibitions. We have expressed some doubt about the assumption that it is primarily *unwanted* children who are abused, since we are so likely to want children for the wrong reasons. Certainly some forms of abuse have come into the open to a remarkable degree, with groups like the North American Man-Boy Love Association and the British Pedophile Information Exchange lobbying for the decriminalization of child molestation. They are hoping that using our new jargon of sexual freedom and individual (children's) rights may succeed in legalizing child molestation—and in our secular culture legalization is tantamount to normalization.

The case against pedophilia or child labor is emotional and therefore easy. Trusting our reactions in such areas, we tend not to think through the issues of child welfare. Suggestion of the advantages that some children would derive from work will be frowned away as disloyal while we thoughtlessly pass laws to punish school dropouts. But school is the greatest humiliation and drudgery that many persons will ever face, as it often was for their parents before them. Charity might suggest that children be allowed to give it up if they have landed some job that is teaching them more. Laws to lengthen the school day, the school year, the school career are not necessarily in children's interests. They are for society's convenience—keeping kids off the streets—and for the nation's competitive advantage. And they give voters a good conscience.

If we were entirely faithful to our recent political rhetoric, our schools would be producing industrial robots. Fortunately, this is where a brighter side of our ambivalence may save the day. For in a confused way we realize that we should be training our children not only to contribute to the economy and *make* money but to *spend* that money. And that is what they learn in the humanities, where we think about what life is all about—what all our work is leading to, and what is worthwhile in and of itself. We may hope that the punitive sound of our new educational rhetoric will not destroy a traditional commitment in this area.

Child care politics often reveals our worst side. Right now, it centers on institutionalized child care, which of course is for the convenience of parents and not the child's choice. It allows adults to indulge their freedom—freedom to abandon families, to work, or just to shop. We have decided that those adult freedoms, rather than the needs of the most helpless among us, are axiomatic and absolute. As religion has declined in the life of our society, we are now free to make absolute any values we please, and we have made absolute our individualism and self-fulfillment. Everything else must adjust to that valuation, so other arrangements will be made for the children. Although we may be horrified at the idea of spanking, we debate whether there should be a nationally guaranteed right to child care—to soften our neglect. We could do with another Charles Dickens to give us a child's-eye view of that world.

Our ambivalence comes out very clearly in this politicizing of childhood. Characteristically, we show that something has become important by asking government to address it, as we are now doing with the needs of children. We imagine that we are showing our seriousness by doing so. But politicization is the triumph of power over love. Love means doing the right thing for people, whereas power means forcing other people to do their (or our) duty. Love makes demands on us; through politics we make demands on others. So more and more we will be taxing society to meet our children's needs. We have enough conscience about the matter to protest that other institutions can be just as good for children as our homes, and in small doses they may be. In the end, though, we will not be guided by what is *best* for children but by what they can stand. They are the ones who have to be tough. Meanwhile we will fight for the high ground by arguing over funding levels; those who are willing to go another cent on the sales tax to ensure happy childhoods will feel justified, while opponents will be open to attack as anti-children.

Unfortunately, government can't love a child, or create human bonds. This is not to say that it shouldn't try to help, given the wreck of so many families. But power is addictive, and the state cannot avoid pressing further on the authority of families. Even welfare legislation which tries to strengthen the family to do its job can hardly be written without making the family accountable to the state and therefore, in effect, a government agency. This is a dilemma, and it is fortunate that legislators are beginning to show uncharacteristic restraint in this area.

It is the curse of government that it can destroy more easily than it can create in this area of human relations. As an example, lowering the age for required parental consent for a child's marriage was one small triumph of state-sponsored individual rights over family authority. The damage caused by this change has been linked to increasing welfare costs—which are government's way of learning when it has made a mistake. So my state is now discussing instituting a waiting period before marriages—which is, of course, a belated attempt to accomplish what families once tried to do. The state will find, however, that these powers are not symmetrical; it could *destroy* the moral authority of the family but it is powerless to *establish* a similar authority.

The real solutions to the sensitive problems of family and child nurture lie in our attitudes, commitments, priorities—changes we must make in ourselves rather than in our circumstances—and these are elements that might respond to sermons more readily than to laws. No one should use this awareness as an excuse to *decrease* our government's fiscal commitments toward child welfare and education, which are pitifully, ridiculously small in relation to other programs and to human need. But no one should imagine that his or her responsibility ends with taking the "right" line on the latest legislative proposal.

Those who rear children must have the authority to guide them. The state cannot keep from destroying rival authorities because it is (rightly) suspicious of any exercise of authority—except its own. Families have often misused their powers, so there is a strong temptation to curtail those powers. But if parents or guardians are prevented from dealing with children in their own way, as wrong as they may seem to some observers, they will be unable to take their responsibilities seriously and will add neglect to their other failings. The *burden* of child rearing may be shared, but the *responsibility* for it cannot be. Politicians will need to realize that the critical factor will be not their program for the family but a family's *response* to that program. Governments cannot do what families or institutions of a more natural growth refuse to do. Attitudes and personal commitments are crucial, and this is the reason that programs which have worked in one community may not work in others. Some will use the state's help to help themselves, and some will not.

Things are becoming very difficult for legislators, given the complexity of politicizing these issues and our uneasy consciences. How are we to affirm the value of life while allowing abortions for those with a true need? What responsibility does government have to *children* who are having children, often alone? Or to children who are having abortions, alone? Does the ability to conceive make one an adult, and does that status mean parents need not be informed or involved in their children's misadventure or its resolution? It is surprising to find people who not only have answers to these unprecedented questions but are strident about them.

The violence of our opinions hides our confusion. The question of abortion, only barely removed from our feelings for children, is deeply troubling. Many who do not think that abortion is invariably immoral may yet feel that the current vast number of abortions is obscene. We cannot wish that 1.5 million mothers each year bear children if some of those children will be blamed as mistakes. But it is morally numbing to think of fetuses being disposed of in ways that we wouldn't treat *once-*human remains. We wonder whether even the children who survive a private and agonized decision over their right to life will increasingly become the focus of second thoughts. The vehemence of the debate and the lack of reasoned argument shows that this is the most distressing issue facing our society.

Children are supposed to represent hope, and even a book which is about experience might be expected to end on an upbeat. But history has not given us reason to expect steady progress in the treatment of children, however our attitudes may shift. Rather, it suggests that our conflicts about childhood and children are a part of the human condition. It appears that childhood will continue to be an individual matter, and that human beings will share very unequally in the enjoyment of it. But, taking a broad view, are there reasons to be hopeful? Will women, who suffer disproportionately—at least in economic terms—from our obsession with freedom, make a natural constituency for more responsible values? Will children who have lived with broken promises be determined not to burden their kids with the same? Will greater sexual freedom paradoxically bring back a realization that marriage itself was originally for the security of children rather than the legitimation of sex? Could economic decline actually bring families together, as some thought it did in the Great Depression? Will we ever be satiated with our own toys and acquire a greater appreciation for life, pure and simple, which children represent so beautifully?

Time will tell. In the meantime we may consider another source of our ambivalence toward childhood, coming not from the beginning of our lives but from the prospect of their end. In the words of Leon Kass (in *American Scholar,* Spring 1983):

> It is probably no accident that it is a generation whose intelligentsia proclaim the meaninglessness of life that embarks on its indefinite prolongation and that seeks to cure the emptiness of life by extending it. For the desire to prolong youthfulness is not only a childish desire to eat one's life and keep it; it is also an expression of a childish and narcissistic wish incompatible with devotion to posterity. It seeks an endless present, isolated from anything truly eternal, and severed from any true continuity with past and future. It is in principle hostile to children, because children, those who come after, are those who will take one's place; they are life's answer to mortality. . . . One cannot pursue youthfulness for oneself and remain faithful to the spirit and meaning of perpetuation.

In short, are we becoming more childish as we can no longer make sense of death? Kass goes on to suggest a way to overcome this terminal selfishness:

> In the young, aspiration, hope, freshness, boldness, openness spring anew—even if and when it takes the form of overturning our monuments. Immortality for oneself through children may be a delusion, but participating in the natural and eternal renewal of human possibility through children is not.

To transcend oneself in the young is to overcome one's ambivalence, since self-transcendence removes us from competition with our children. Finding a measure of immortality in fostering the young is not just a selfish act. It can enrich the generation which will remember us.

Notes

The works cited first in each section are those which serve as authorities for specific facts, or sources for the quotations, in the respective chapters. In most sections I have added other titles (after "see also," etc.) as suggestions for further reading.

Chapter 1

Alice Payne Hackett, *70 Years of Best-Sellers, 1895–1965* (New York: R. R. Bowker, 1967); Urie Bronfenbrenner, *Two Worlds of Childhood: U.S. and U.S.S.R.* (New York: Simon and Schuster, 1972); Ray Helfer and Henry Kempe, eds., *The Battered Child* (Chicago: University of Chicago, 1974); Jay Mechling, "Advice to Historians on Advice to Mothers," *Journal of Social History,* 9 (1975), 44–63; Freda Rebelsky and Cheryl Hanks, "Fathers' Verbal Interaction with Infants in the First Three Months of Life," *Child Development,* 42 (1971), 63–68; Sarane Spence Boocock, "The Social Context of Childhood," *Proceedings of the American Philosophical Society,* 119 (1975), 419–429; Margaret Mead, *Culture and Commitment: The New Relationship Between the Generations in the 1970's* (New York: Columbia University, 1978); J. Walters and N. Stinnett, "Parent-Child Relationships: A Decade Review of Research," *Journal of Marriage and the Family,* 33 (1971), 70–111; William F. Kenkel, "Marriage and the Family in Modern Science Fiction," *Journal of Marriage and the Family,* 31 (1969), 6–14; Mary Jo Bane, *Here to Stay: American Families in the Twentieth Century* (New York: Basic

Books, 1975). See also Valerie Suransky, *The Erosion of Childhood* (Chicago: University of Chicago, 1982).

Chapter 2

Samuel Noah Kramer, *History Begins at Sumer* (Garden City, NY: Doubleday, 1959); Antonia Fraser, *A History of Toys* (London: Delacorte, 1966); Ruth Benedict, "Child-rearing in Certain European Countries," *American Journal of Orthopsychiatry,* 19 (1949), 342–350; Oscar Chrisman, *The Historical Child* (Boston: Richard G. Badger, 1920); H. Blümner, *Home Life of the Ancient Greeks* (New York: Cooper Square, 1966, orig. 1893); William Barclay, *Train Up a Child* (Philadelphia: Westminster, 1959); Mircea Eliade, *Rites and Symbols of Initiation* (New York: Harper and Row, 1975); Fielding Garrison and Arthur F. Abt, *Abt-Garrison History of Pediatrics* (Philadelphia: W. B. Saunders, 1965); Garrett Hardin, "The History and Future of Birth Control," in *What a Piece of Work Is Man,* eds. James D. Ray and Gideon Nelson (Boston: Little, Brown, 1971). See also John Boswell, *The Kindness of Strangers: The Abandonment of Children in Western Europe from Late Antiquity to the Renaissance* (New York: Pantheon, a division of Random House, 1988).

Chapter 3

W. K. Lacey, *The Family in Classical Greece* (Ithaca, NY: Cornell University, 1968); H. I. Marrou, *A History of Education in Antiquity* (New York: New American Library, 1956); Philip Slater, "The Greek Family in History and Myth," *Arethusa,* 7 (1974), 9–44, further substantiated in his *The Glory of Hera* (Boston: Beacon, 1968); and Barclay and Blümner. References to redeeming the first-born are found in Exodus, chapters 13, 22, and 34; to the mother's responsibility in education in Deuteronomy 4, 6, and 11; and to child sacrifice in II Kings 16, 21, and 23. See also David Bakan, *Slaughter of the Innocents: A Study of the Battered Child Phenomenon* (San Francisco: Jossey-Bass, 1971).

Chapter 4

Carle Zimmerman, *Family and Civilization* (New York: Harper, 1947); Chester Starr, *Civilization and the Caesars: The Intellectual Revolution in the Roman Empire* (New York: Norton, 1965); Plutarch, *The Lives of the Noble Grecians and Romans* (New York: Modern Library, 1932); Aubrey Gwynn, *Roman Education from Cicero to Quintilian* (Oxford: Clarendon, 1926); *Quintilian's Institutes of Oratory: Or, Education of an Orator,* trans. John Selby Watson (London: Henry G. Bohn, 1856); George Frederic Still, *The History of Pediatrics* (London: Dawsons, 1965); Nathaniel Weld, "Some Possible Genetic Implications of Carthaginian Child Sacrifice," *Perspectives in Biology and Medicine,* 12 (1968), 69–78; Mortimer Chambers, ed., *The Fall of Rome: Can It Be Explained?,* second edition (New York: Holt, Rinehart and Winston, 1970); and Barclay.

Chapter 5

William L. Langer, "Infanticide: A Historical Survey," *History of Childhood Quarterly,* 1 (1974), 353–365; the chapters by Lloyd deMause and Richard B. Lyman, Jr., in deMause, ed., *The History of Childhood* (New York: Psychohistory, 1974); George Boas, *The Cult of Childhood* (London: Warburg, 1966); Charles N. Cochrane, *Christianity and Classical Culture* (New York: Oxford University, 1957); Norman Powell Williams, *The Ideas of the Fall and of Original Sin* (London: Longmans, 1927); Henri Rondet, *Original Sin: The Patristic and Theological Background* (Shannon: Ecclesia, 1972); Joachim Jeremias, *Infant Baptism in the First Four Centuries* (London: SCM, 1960), and *The Origins of Infant Baptism* (Napierville, IL: Alec Allenson, 1963); *The Golden Legend of Jacobus de Voragine* (London: Longmans, 1914); and Barclay.

Chapters 6 and 7

Zimmerman, and deMause et al., especially the chapter by Mary Martin McLaughlin. Marc Bloch, *Feudal Society* (Chicago: University of Chicago, 1964); Norman Kiell, *The Universal Experience of Adolescence* (New York: International Universities, 1964); R. W. Southern, *The Making of the Middle Ages* (New Haven: Yale University, 1953); Ilene H. Forsyth, "Children in Early Medieval Art: Ninth Through Twelfth Centuries," *Journal of Psychohistory,* 4 (1976), 31–70; Luke Demaitre, "The Idea of Childhood and Child Care in Medical Writings of the Middle Ages," *Journal of Psychohistory,* 4 (1977), 461–490; Lotte Burchardt Graeffe, "The Child in Medieval English Literature from 1200 to 1400" (Ph.D. dissertation, University of Florida, 1965); Nicholas Orme, *English Schools in the Middle Ages* (London: Methuen, 1973); Edward Rimbault, ed., *Two Sermons Preached by the Boy Bishops,* in *Camden Miscellany,* n.s., 14 (1875); Peter Raedts, "The Children's Crusade of 1212," *Journal of Medieval History,* 3 (1977), 279–323; James B. Ross and Mary M. McLaughlin, eds., *The Portable Medieval Reader* (New York: Viking, 1949). See also the interesting psychohistorical speculation in William H. Blanchard, "Medieval Morality and Juvenile Delinquency," *American Imago,* 13 (1956), 383–398; Herbert Moller, "The Social Causation of Affective Mysticism," *Journal of Social History,* 4 (1971), 305–338; Herbert Moller, "The Meaning of Courtly Love," *Journal of American Folklore,* 73 (1960), 39–52; and Barbara Hanawalt, *The Ties That Bound: Peasant Families in Medieval England* (New York: Oxford University, 1986).

Chapter 8

David Herlihy, *The Family in Renaissance Italy* (St. Charles, MO: Forum, 1974); articles by Diane Owen Hughes and Lawrence Stone in *The Family in History,* ed. Charles Rosenberg (Philadelphia: University of Pennsylvania, 1975); Richard A. Goldthwaite, "The Florentine Palace as Domestic Architecture," *American Historical Review,* 77 (1972), 977–1012; James Bruce Ross, "The Middle-Class Child in Urban Italy, Fourteenth to Early Sixteenth Century," in deMause; Josef Kunstmann, *The Transformation of Eros* (Edinburgh: Oliver and Boyd, 1964); W. Robertson Davies, *Shakespeare's Boy Actors* (New York: Russell and Russell, 1964); W. J. Ong, "Latin Language Study as a Renaissance Puberty Rite," *Studies in Philology,* 54 (1959), 103–124; John Aubrey, *Aubrey's Brief Lives,* ed. Oliver Lawson Dick (Harmondsworth: Penguin, 1972); Richard Steele, *Spectator,* no. 157 (1711); Karl E. Fritzsch and Manfred Bachmann, *An Illustrated History of Toys* (London: Abbey, 1966); and Fraser. The famous mistakes Sigmund Freud made in his *Leonardo da Vinci and a Memory of His Childhood* (New York: Norton, 1964, orig. 1910) do not affect my argument; see K. R. Eissler, *Leonardo da Vinci: Psychological Notes on the Enigma* (New York: International Universities, 1961). See also Diane Owen Hughes, "From Brideprice to Dowry in Medieval Europe," *Journal of Family History,* 3 (1978), 262–296.

Chapter 9

Roland Bainton, *Here I Stand: A Life of Martin Luther* (New York: New American Library, 1955); articles by Richard Trexler, Gerald Strauss, Lewis Spitz, and Natalie Davis in *The Pursuit of Holiness in Late Medieval and Renaissance Religion* (Leiden: Brill, 1974); Gerald Strauss, "The State of Pedagogical Theory c. 1530: What Protestant Reformers Knew About Education," in *Schooling and Society: Studies in the History of Education,* ed. Lawrence Stone (Baltimore: Johns Hopkins University, 1976); F. V. N. Painter, *Luther on Education* (St. Louis: Concordia, 1889); Philippe Ariès, *Centuries of Childhood* (New York: Random House, 1962); Jacob Burckhardt, *The Civilization of the Renaissance in Italy* (New York: New American Library, 1960, orig. 1860); and Rondet. The reference to John Calvin's *Institutes of the Christian Religion* is to book IV, xv, 20. David Hunt, *Parents and Children in History: The Psychology of Family Life in Early Modern France* (New York: Basic Books, 1970).

Chapter 10

Joel Hurstfield, *The Queen's Wards* (Cambridge, MA: Harvard University, 1958); H. S. Bennett, *The Pastons and Their England* (Cambridge: University Press, 1932); Stone's article in Rosenberg; Ivy Pinchbeck and Margaret Hewitt, *Children in English Society: From Tudor Times to the Eighteenth Century* (London: Routledge and Kegan Paul, 1969); Charles Carlton, *The Court of Orphans* (Leicester: University Press, 1974); and M. G. Jones, *The Charity School Movement* (Cambridge: University Press, 1938). See also Elizabeth Godfrey, *English Children in the Olden Time* (London: Methuen, 1907).

Chapter 11

References to the sources for this chapter may be found in my articles "English Puritans and Children: A Social-Cultural Explanation," *Journal of Psychohistory,* 6 (1978), 113–137, and "Breaking the Icon: The First Real Children in English Books," *History of Education Quarterly,* 21 (1981), 51–75. Alan Macfarlane, *The Family Life of Ralph Josselin: A Seventeenth-Century Clergyman* (Cambridge: University Press, 1970), and (ed.) *The Diary of Ralph Josselin, 1616–1683* (London: Oxford University, 1976); *John Amos Comenius on Education,* ed. Jean Piaget (New York: Teachers College, 1967); Will S. Monroe, *Comenius and the Beginnings of Educational Reform* (New York: Scribners, 1900). On New England Puritans, see Edmund Morgan, *The Puritan Family: Religion and Domestic Relations in Seventeenth-Century New England,* second edition (New York: Harper and Row, 1966); Peter Gregg Slater, *Children in the New England Mind, in Death and in Life* (Hamden, CT: Archon, 1977); and John Demos, *A Little Commonwealth: Family Life in Plymouth* (New York: Oxford University, 1969).

Chapter 12

J. A. Passmore, "The Malleability of Man in Eighteenth-Century Thought," in *Aspects of the Eighteenth Century,* ed. Earl R. Wasserman (Baltimore: Johns Hopkins University, 1965); Boas; Philip Greven, *The Protestant Temperament: Patterns of Child-rearing, Religious Experience, and the Self in Early America* (New York: Knopf, 1977); Philip Greven, ed., *Child-rearing Concepts 1628–1861* (Itasca, IL: F. E. Peacock, 1973); Derek Jarrett, *England in the Age of Hogarth* (New York: Viking, 1974); William H. Blanchard, *Rousseau and the Spirit of Revolt* (Ann Arbor: University of Michigan, 1967); Adolphe Meyer, *An Educational History of the Western World* (New York: McGraw-Hill, 1972); Lucien Malson, *Wolf Children and the Problem of Human Nature* (New

York: Monthly Review, 1972). See also R. Freeman Butts, *A Cultural History of Western Education,* second edition (New York: McGraw-Hill, 1955); Ellwood P. Cubberley, *The History of Education* (Cambridge, MA: Houghton Mifflin, 1920); and Linda A. Pollock, *Forgotten Children: Parent-Child Relations from 1500 to 1900* (New York: Cambridge University, 1983).

Chapter 13

F. J. Harvey Darton, *Children's Books in England,* second edition (Cambridge: University Press, 1966); Bruno Bettelheim, *The Uses of Enchantment: The Meaning and Importance of Fairy Tales* (New York: Random House, 1977); J. H. Plumb, "The World of Children in Eighteenth-Century England," *Past and Present,* 67 (1975), 64–95; Adrian P. L. Kempton, "Education and the Child in Eighteenth-Century French Fiction," *Studies on Voltaire and the Eighteenth Century,* 124 (1974), 299–362; Noel Perrin, *Dr. Bowdler's Legacy: A History of Expurgated Books in England and America* (New York: Atheneum, 1969); *Dictionary of National Biography;* Boas and Fritzsch. On the origin of nursery rhymes, the safest guide is Iona and Peter Opie, eds., *The Oxford Dictionary of Nursery Rhymes* (Oxford: Clarendon, 1952). See Anne Pellowski, *The World of Children's Literature* (New York: R. R. Bowker, 1968), for a bibliography of the many histories of children's literature.

Chapter 14

E. A. Wrigley, *Population and History* (New York: McGraw-Hill, 1969), and "Family Limitation in Pre-industrial England," *Economic History Review,* second series, 19 (1966), 82–109; Jean Fourastié, "Three Comments on the Near Future of Mankind," *Diogenes,* 30 (1960), 1–16; Peter Laslett and Richard Wall, eds., *Household and Family in Past Time* (Cambridge: University Press, 1972); Peter Laslett and Karla Oosterveen, "Long-Term Trends in Bastardy in England," *Population Studies,* 27 (1973), 255–286; Jean-Louis Flandrin, *Families in Former Times: Kinship, Household, and Sexuality* (New York: Cambridge University, 1979); Thomas McKeown, *The Modern Rise of Population* (New York: Academic, 1976); Robert V. Wells, "Family History and Demographic Transition," *Journal of Social History,* 9 (1975), 1–20; John R. Gillis, *Youth and History* (New York: Academic, 1974); Samuel X. Radbill, "Pediatrics," in *Medicine in Seventeenth-Century England,* ed. Allen Debus (Berkeley: University of California, 1974); B. R. Mitchell, *European Historical Statistics, 1750–1970* (New York: Columbia, 1975); and the works by Langer, Garrison, Still, and Hardin. See also Lawrence Stone, *The Family, Sex and Marriage: England 1500–1800* (London: Weidenfeld, 1977); Lutz Berkner, "The Stem Family and the Developmental Cycle of the Peasant Household: An Eighteenth-Century Austrian Example," *American Historical Review,* 77 (1972), 398–418; and Orest and Patricia Ranum, eds., *Popular Attitudes Toward Birth Control in Pre-industrial France and England* (New York: Harper and Row, 1972).

Chapter 15

E. P. Thompson, *The Making of the English Working Class* (New York: Random House, 1963); Robert Wood, ed., *Children 1773–1890* (London: Evans, 1968); excerpts from the testimony of Matthew Crabtree, in the *Report from the Select Committee on the Regulation of the Labour of Children in the Mills and Factories of the United Kingdom* (1832); Andrew Ure, *The Philosophy of Manufactures* (New York: A. M. Kelley, 1967, orig. 1835); Friedrich Engels, *The Condition of the Working Class in England* (Stanford, CA: Stanford University, 1968, orig. 1845); Geoffrey F. A. Best, *Shaftesbury* (New York: Arco, 1964); Peter Coveney, *The Image of Childhood* (Harmondsworth: Penguin, 1967); Angus Wilson, *The World of Charles Dickens* (Harmondsworth: Penguin, 1972); Sylvia Manning, "Families in Dickens," in *Changing Images of the Family,* eds. Virginia Tufte and Barbara Myerhoff (New Haven: Yale University, 1979), 141–153; Phyllis Greenacre, *Swift and Carroll: A Psychological Study of Two Lives* (New York: International Universities, 1955); Alison Lurie, "The Boy Who Couldn't Grow Up," *New York Review of Books* (Feb. 6, 1975), 11–15; Andrew Birkin, *J. M. Barrie and the Lost Boys* (London: Constable, 1979); Erik Erikson, *Childhood and Society,* second edition (New York: Norton, 1963), pp.

237–238; Gillian Avery and Angela Bull, *Nineteenth-Century Children: Heroes and Heroines in English Children's Stories, 1780–1900* (London: Hodder and Stoughton, 1965); Bernard Wishy, *The Child and the Republic: The Dawn of Modern American Child Nurture* (Philadelphia: University of Pennsylvania, 1968); and the works cited by Darton, Fraser, and Slater. See also Clark Nardinelli, "Child Labor and the Factory Acts," *Journal of Economic History,* 40 (1980), 739–755; Howard Wolf, "British Fathers and Sons, 1773–1913: From Filial Submissiveness to Creativity," *Psychoanalytic Review,* 51 (1965), 197–214; Jonathan Gathorne-Hardy, *The Rise and Fall of the British Nanny* (London: Hodder and Stoughton, 1972); Iris Brooke, *English Children's Costume Since 1775* (London: A. and C. Black, 1930); Phillis Cunnington and Anne Buck, *Children's Costume in England, from the Fourteenth to the End of the Nineteenth Century* (New York: Barnes and Noble, 1965); and Ellery Sedgwick, *Thomas Paine* (Boston: Maynard, 1899).

Chapter 16

Earlier work on this subject is conveniently summarized in Gillis, and Anthony Esler, *Bombs, Beards and Barricades: 150 Years of Youth in Revolt* (New York: Stein and Day, 1971). Esler reprinted some of those works in *The Conflict of Generations in Modern History* (Lexington, MA: D. C. Heath, 1974), but special mention should be made of two of the most influential: Lewis S. Feuer, *The Conflict of Generations: The Character and Significance of Student Movements* (New York: Basic Books, 1969), and Peter Loewenberg, "The Psychohistorical Origins of the Nazi Youth Cohort," *American Historical Review,* 76 (1971), 1457–1502.

Chapter 17

The works by Ariès, Meyer, and Gillis; John Lawson and Harold Silver, *A Social History of Education in England* (London: Methuen, 1973); John W. Adamson, *Pioneers of Modern Education in the Seventeenth Century* (Cambridge: University Press, 1905); Foster Watson, *The*

Beginnings of the Teaching of Modern Subjects in England (London: I. Pitman, 1909); Bernard Bailyn, *Education in the Forming of American Society* (New York: Vintage, 1960); Robert Bremner, ed., *Children and Youth in America: A Documentary History* (5 vols., Cambridge, MA: Harvard University, 1970–1974); *Fourth Annual Report of the Children's Aid Society* (New York: John P. Prall, 1857); Ivy Pinchbeck and Margaret Hewitt, *Children in English Society: From the Eighteenth Century to the Children Act, 1948* (London: Routledge and Kegan Paul, 1973); Frank Musgrove, *Youth and the Social Order* (Bloomington: Indiana University, 1964); Joseph Hawes, *Children in Urban Society: Juvenile Delinquency in Nineteenth-Century America* (New York: Oxford University, 1971); George Rosen, *A History of Public Health* (New York: MD Publications, 1958); René Spitz, "Authority and Masturbation," *The Psychoanalytic Quarterly,* 21 (1952), 490–527; Richard Rapson, "The American Child as Seen by British Travellers, 1845–1935," *American Quarterly,* 18 (1965), 520–534; and articles on conscription, education, and juvenile offenders in the eleventh edition of the *Encyclopedia Britannica* (1911). The final quotations are taken from Ronald Blythe, *Akenfield: Portrait of an English Village* (New York: Pantheon Books, a division of Random House, 1969), with permission. See also Thomas Laqueur, *Religion and Respectability: Sunday Schools and Working Class Culture* (New Haven: Yale University, 1976); Jo Manton, *Mary Carpenter and the Children of the Streets* (London: Heinemann, 1976); Gillian Wagner, *Barnardo* (London: Weidenfeld and Nicolson, 1979); Michael B. Katz, *The Irony of Early School Reform: Educational Innovation in Mid–Nineteenth Century Massachusetts* (Cambridge, MA: Harvard University, 1968); David B. Tyack, *The One Best System: A History of American Urban Education* (Cambridge, MA: Harvard University, 1974); R. Freeman Butts, *Public Education in the United States: From Revolution to Reform* (New York: Holt, Rinehart and Winston, 1978); Richard L. Darling, *The Rise of Children's Book Reviewing in America, 1865–1881* (New York: R. R. Bowker, 1968); John Springhall, *Youth, Empire, and Society: A Social History of British Youth Movements, 1883–1940* (Hamden, CT: Archon, 1977); Anthony M. Platt, *The Child Savers: The Invention of Delinquency* (Chicago: University of Chicago, 1969); Steven L. Schlossman, *Love and the American Delinquent: The Theory and Practice of "Progressive" Juvenile Justice, 1825–1920* (Chicago: University of Chicago, 1977); Wiley

B. Sanders, ed., *Juvenile Offenders for a Thousand Years: Selected Readings from Anglo-Saxon Times to 1900* (Chapel Hill: University of North Carolina, 1970); Fred and Grace Hechinger, *Growing Up in America* (New York: McGraw-Hill, 1975); Joseph F. Kett, *Rites of Passage: Adolescence in America, 1790 to the Present* (New York: Basic Books, 1977); and Oscar Handlin, *Facing Life: Youth and the Family in American History* (Boston: Little, Brown, 1971).

Chapter 18

Howard E. Gruber, *Darwin on Man* (New York: Dutton, 1974); William Kessen, *The Child* (New York: John Wiley, 1965); Milton J. E. Senn, *Insights on the Child Development Movement in the United States* (Chicago: Society for Research in Child Development, 1975); J. E. Anderson, "Child Development: A Historical Perspective," *Child Development,* 27 (1956), 181–196; Robert R. Sears, *Your Ancients Revisited: A History of Child Development* (Chicago: University of Chicago, 1975). See also Juliette Louise Despert, *The Emotionally Disturbed Child— Then and Now* (New York: Vantage, 1965); Michael H. Stone, "Child Psychiatry Before the Twentieth Century," *International Journal of Child Psychotherapy,* 2 (1973), 264–308; Stephen Kern, "Freud and the Discovery of Child Sexuality," *History of Childhood Quarterly,* 1 (1973), 117–141.

Chapter 19

Harold H. Hart, ed., *Summerhill: For and Against* (New York: Hart, 1970); Herbert Kohl, "Closing Time for Open Ed?," *New York Review of Books* (Dec. 13, 1973), 48–50; Suzanne Fremon, "Why Free Schools Fail," *Parents Magazine* (Sept. 1972), 50 ff.; A. Michael Sulman, "The Humanization of the American Child: Benjamin Spock as a Popularizer of Psychoanalytic Thought," *Journal of the History of the Behavioral Sciences,* 9 (1973), 258–265; Michael Zuckerman, "Dr. Spock: The Confidence Man," in Rosenberg; Urie Bronfenbrenner, "The Changing American Child—A Speculative Analysis," *Journal of Social Issues,* 17 (1961), 6–18; Martha Wolfenstein, "Fun Morality: An Analysis of Recent American Child-training Literature," in *Childhood in Contemporary Cultures*, eds. Margaret Mead and Wolfenstein (Chicago: University of Chicago, 1955); Lawrence A. Cremin, *The Transformation of the School: Progressivism in American Education, 1876–1957* (New York: Knopf, 1961); and Erikson and Meyer. See also Daniel R. Miller and Guy E. Swanson, *The Changing American Parent* (New York: John Wiley, 1958); Geoffrey H. Steere, "Freudianism and Child-rearing in the Twenties," *American Quarterly*, 20 (1968), 759–767; and Nancy Weiss, "Mother, the Invention of Necessity: Dr. Benjamin Spock's *Baby and Child Care*," *American Quarterly*, 29 (1977), 519–546.

Chapter 20

William J. Goode, *World Revolution and Family Patterns* (New York: Free Press, 1963); Bronfenbrenner, *Two Worlds of Childhood;* Bruno Bettelheim, *The Children of the Dream* (New York: Avon, 1969); W. Tasker Witham, *The Adolescent in the American Novel, 1920–1960* (New York: Ungar, 1964); Justin O'Brien, *The Novel of Adolescence in France* (New York: Columbia University, 1937); Herbert Hendin, *The Age of Sensation* (New York: Norton, 1975); Alexander Mitscherlich, *Society Without the Father* (New York: Schocken, 1970); Benjamin Spock, *Decent and Indecent: Our Personal and Political Behavior* (New York: McCall, 1970); Colin M. Turnbull, *The Mountain People* (New York: Simon and Schuster, 1972); Robert Heilbroner, *An Inquiry into the Human Prospect* (New York: Norton, 1974); Miles F. Shore, "The Child and Historiography," *Journal of Interdisciplinary History*, 6 (1976), 495–505. See also Edgar Friedenberg, *The Vanishing Adolescent* (Boston: Beacon, 1959); Kenneth Keniston, *The Uncommitted: Alienated Youth in American Society* (New York: Harcourt, Brace and World, 1965); Robert Coles, *Children of Crisis* (5 vols., Boston: Little, Brown, 1967–1977); Christopher Lasch, *Haven in a Heartless World: The Family Besieged* (New York: Basic Books, 1977); George Paloczi-Horvath, *Youth Up in Arms: A Political and Social World Survey, 1955–1970* (New York: David McKay, 1971); Caleb Foote, Robert Levy, and Frank Sander, eds., *Cases and Materials on Family Law* (Boston: Little, Brown, 1966); Joseph Goldstein, Anna Freud, and Albert Solnit, *Beyond the Best Interests of the Child* (New York: Free

Press, 1973); Stephen J. Morse, "Family Law in Transition," in Tufte and Myerhohf; Edward Shorter, *The Making of the Modern Family* (New York: Basic Books, 1975); and Barbara Finkelstein, "Uncle Sam and the Children: History of Government Involvement in Child Rearing," *Review Journal of Philosophy and Social Science,* 3 (1978), 139–153.

Index

ABOUT THE AUTHOR

C. John Sommerville is Professor of History at the University of Florida. He received a Ph.D. from the University of Iowa in 1970 and taught there and at Stanford University prior to moving to Florida. Sommerville is the author of the most widely cited bibliography on the history of childhood, "Toward a History of Childhood and Youth," which first appeared in the *Journal of Interdisciplinary History.* He is also author of *Popular Religion in Restoration England* (University Presses of Florida, 1977) as well as articles on the history of childhood and the history of religion.